From School to Work

A Cooperative Education Book

by
J.J. Littrell
Arizona State University
Tempe, Arizona

The Goodheart-Willcox Company, Inc.
South Holland, Illinois

Manufactured in the United States of America
Library of Congress Catalog Card Number 83—25359
International Standard Book Number 0—87006—457—6

23456789—84—98765

Library of Congress Cataloging in Publication Data

Littrell, Joseph J.
  From school to work.

  Includes index.
    1. Education, Cooperative.   2. Students—
Employment.   3. Career education.   I. Title.
LB1029.C6L58 1984   370.11'3   83—25359
ISBN 0—87006—457—6

Introduction

From School to Work is exactly what its title implies. It's a book written to help you and other cooperative education students make smooth transitions from school classrooms to meaningful jobs.

Successful transitions begin with having successful work experiences. This book discusses the responsibilities you will have to your school and employer as a cooperative education student. You will also learn about the skills you will need to succeed at your work experience and at future full-time jobs. These skills include the ability to communicate effectively, solve basic math problems, dress appropriately for work, and work safely on the job.

Once you have your work experience under control, you can start preparing for full-time employment. *From School to Work* guides you step-by-step through the career planning process, the job hunt, and job adjustment. It also explains how to manage the money you earn so that you can build a secure and satisfying life, financially and personally.

Being successful on the job is also influenced by your ability to follow and lead others. By participating in school and community organizations, you have many opportunities to develop good leadership skills. The final chapters of this book can help, too. They examine the qualities of a good leader, describe vocational education organizations, and give guidelines for conducting group meetings.

Contents

Cooperative education

Cooperative education gives a student the opportunity
to work at a real job under real working conditions.

Participating in cooperative education

Cooperative education is a school program designed to prepare students for work. It is called cooperative because an employer and a school join together and cooperate as a team. The program enables students to work with full-time employees in business and industry. It also gives students an opportunity to learn at two places—at school and at work.

Cooperative education is very valuable to those students who want to begin working right after high school and succeed in an occupation. Cooperative education bridges that gap between school and the world of work. It helps students make the adjustment from being full-time students to becoming full-time employees, 1-1.

THE COOPERATIVE WORK EXPERIENCE

A cooperative work experience works like this. A local employer agrees to employ a student (you) part-time. The employer provides on-the-job training to help you prepare for a career goal. This is called work experience education. At school, you take classes for approximately half of the day to meet requirements for graduation. You also take a cooperative education class where you learn how to set career goals, apply for jobs, and manage your finances.

The cooperative education program is usually under the leadership of a special teacher called a cooperative education coordinator. The coordinator is more than a teacher to you. He or she is your contact with the place where you work. The coordinator is the person who helps guide you through a successful work experience by helping you make decisions, solve problems, and expand your knowledge.

One responsibility of the coordinator is to review your application for a work experience and help you match your occupational goals with a suitable part-time job. Both the coordinator and an employer carefully consider your qualifications for a work experience before assigning you to a training station. A *training station* is a school-approved job where you learn skills while you earn income.

Your training station might be at a manufacturing company, hospital, hairdresser, bank, construction site, local garage, or insurance company. The types of training stations available will depend mostly on the area where you live and go to school. You are usu-ally responsible for providing your own transportation from school to work.

When you report for work, you will be assigned to a certain person or supervisor who will help you learn the job. Under this person you will learn as much as you can about the job and the company and develop the skills required for the job.

Remember, the cooperative work experience is a three-way relationship involving you, the employer, and the cooperative education coordinator, 1-2. You have the most to gain from this relationship — skills, knowledge, and work experience.

THE BENEFITS OF COOPERATIVE EDUCATION

Participating in a cooperative work experience has many benefits. Cooperative education can help students in the following ways:

- Acquire marketable skills. Every occupation requires certain skills and knowledge necessary to qualify for a job. Students gain skills by working in a real job under real working conditions.
- Become aware of career goals. Cooperative education gives students a chance to test

BERNIE NOVIA

BERNIE NOVIA

1-1 Cooperative education is designed to help students make smooth transitions from their classrooms to meaningful jobs.

some of their career interests. They find out what they like to do and what they can do. They can also discuss their career goals with others at work and at school.

- Learn to work with others. Students learn to communicate with other people such as supervisors, other employees, and customers. As new employees they learn how to conduct themselves in a work situation.
- Gain on-the-job experience. Actual experience in a work situation helps students get other jobs in the future. It also helps them make the personal transition from school to work.
- Earn money. Cooperative education work experiences provide opportunities for students to earn incomes. The expression "earn while you learn" applies to cooperative work experiences.

Business and industry also benefit from the cooperative education program. As job trainers, employers earn recognition in the community for their willingness to help young people. Employers also receive interested part-time workers who are eager to learn and do a good job. The employer has the opportunity to train a student for a specific job and employ that student for a specific length of time. At the end of that time, the work relationship may end between the employer and student. Or the employer may offer the student full-time employment. Often employers are so pleased with the job performance of students that they offer students full-time employment when they graduate.

A NEW OUTLOOK FOR TONY

At 7:30 in the morning on a February day in northern Texas, it's cold! It seemed even colder to Tony when his car didn't want to start. The engine coughed once, then twice, and finally started. Tony muttered to himself,

BERNIE NOVIA

1-2 For a work experience to be successful, the student, cooperative education coordinator, and the employer need to work together cooperatively.

"Eleven more car payments to make, and it needs a new battery."

As Tony began driving to school, he started thinking about quitting school and looking for a job. Throughout his three years in high school, he'd had nothing but discouragement. Freshman year had been okay, but from then on, school had been a drag. Today wasn't going any better.

Tony had not failed any subjects at school, but he had not studied much either. Three things accounted for Tony's lack of enthusiasm. One, he had no goals for himself. Two, his study habits were very poor. And three, he had burdened himself with several months of car payments.

Tony was about to become a high school dropout when a friend suggested he sign up for the ICT program.

"What's that?" asked Tony.

"It's part of the cooperative education program called Industrial Cooperative Training. You go to school for half of the day and work part-time. You get paid for the work you do, and you get school credit for the job."

"Oh, I've heard about that," Tony said, "but how do I get into the program?"

"Go see Mr. Alexander," his friend said. "He's the ICT coordinator. You've had two courses in auto mechanics and have always been good at working on cars. Maybe you could get a job at an auto repair shop. Then you wouldn't have to quit school."

Tony finally went to see Mr. Alexander and applied to participate in the cooperative education program. The day Tony was accepted, his outlook on life seemed to change. All summer long Tony looked forward to his senior year and his cooperative work experience.

In the fall, Tony began his work experience with an automotive service center. He learned how to tune cars and how to repair brakes, transmissions, and other car parts. He also learned a little about running a business. It was hard work, but Tony enjoyed it. Not only did Tony get his car paid off and learn new skills, he also improved his school grades. He even made the "B" honor roll the second half of the school year.

Questions to discuss

1. Why do you think Tony's outlook on life changed when he was accepted into the cooperative education program?
2. Why do you think Tony's grades improved his senior year?
3. How do you think participating in the cooperative education program benefited Tony?
4. What do you think would have happened to Tony if he had dropped out of school his junior year?

AN ALTERNATIVE FOR JANET

Janet was about to complete her junior year with high honors, just as she had completed her freshman and sophomore years. Janet really enjoyed school. She was a good student, and she liked her teachers. She also knew the career path she planned to follow after high school. But Janet was concerned about her senior year. She decided to talk with a guidance counselor about her concerns.

Janet explained to the counselor that she had carried extra subjects every year in high school. She had also gone to summer school for two summers. She now had so many credits that she only needed one required subject to graduate. If she went to school over the summer, she could graduate in August. Instead of staying in school all of next year just to carry one or two classes, she thought she would finish high school early. "What do you think?" she asked the counselor.

The counselor was familiar with Janet's record. "Yes, Janet, you could graduate in August," the counselor said. "Of course, the school would lose one of its favorite cheerleaders. There is another alternative. You might consider participating in the cooperative education program. The department of business education certainly speaks highly of your ability."

"Thank you," Janet responded. "I have thought about the Co-op program, but I plan to go to college. There is no doubt in my mind that I want a career in business, but I don't want to be a file clerk or a typist. My goal is business management. Sure, I can type and keep books, but what I want is to be a business executive."

"An office education work experience is not just for students who want to be file clerks, typists, and secretaries. It can also be helpful to a student like you. Obtaining office experience and learning to work cooperatively with others could certainly be a plus for a person pursuing a career in business management."

Janet quickly said, "I know my communication and computer skills are lacking. I also feel that I'm not ready to go away to college in the fall. I think my Dad would like me to stay in high school another year because money is tight right now. What do you think I should do?"

"Janet, I can't tell you what to do. That is for you and your parents to decide. I will say this. Cooperative education is a proven method of training students for a career. It can and will contribute to a person's employability."

"Office work is exciting to me, and I know it would be good experience for a career in business. Another thing, I will need money to help pay some of my college expenses. Who should I talk with about enrolling in cooperative education?"

The counselor referred Janet to the office education coordinator. After talking with the coordinator, Janet signed up for a computer class and for cooperative education the next year. During her senior year Janet was a cheerleader, one of the leading actresses in a school play, and president of the Office Education Association at school.

Questions to discuss

1. Do you think Janet made the right decision by not skipping her senior year and by participating in cooperative education instead of going straight to college? Why?
2. How do you think participating in the cooperative education program benefited Janet?
3. What problems might Janet have faced if she had gone straight to college and skipped her senior year in high school?

to Review

1. Explain how a cooperative work experience works.
2. Name one of the responsibilities of the cooperative education coordinator.
3. What is a training station?
4. Who is usually responsible for providing transportation for the student from school to work?
5. What are the benefits of the cooperative education program?
6. How do employers benefit from the cooperative education program?

to Discuss

1. What is cooperative education?
2. How does cooperative education help students make the adjustment from being full-time students to becoming full-time employees?
3. If you were having a problem with your work experience, who should you talk to about it?
4. Why are you in the cooperative education program?
5. How do you think your cooperative work experience will affect your future occupational and career plans?

to Do

1. Divide into groups of four or five. As a group, make a list of the adjustments you as students may have to make from being students to becoming employees. Then, each group share their findings with the class.
2. Write a one-page summary explaining what you expect to gain from your cooperative work experience.

As a cooperative education student, you will have new
school hours and new responsibilities.

What your school expects

After studying this chapter, you will be able to:

☐ Explain what your school and coordinator expect of you as a cooperative education student.
☐ Identify ways you can improve your learning skills.

As a cooperative education student, your daily schedule will be different from those of other students. You will be adjusting to new school hours and work hours. You will be meeting new people and accepting new responsibilities. You will be out on your own more which means you will have more freedom. Your success in the cooperative education program depends a great deal on how well you handle your freedom and responsibilities.

FIND A JOB

What do your school and coordinator expect of you as a cooperative education student? They expect you to get and keep a job that is approved by the school. Although coordinators are able to find job openings for many students, students share in the responsibility of finding jobs. Therefore, if you don't have a job when you begin the cooperative education program, your job is finding a job. That means you need to spend every hour you would spend at a training station hunting for a job. (See *Part Four, The Job Hunt*).

GET A SOCIAL SECURITY NUMBER AND A WORK PERMIT

Before you begin your work experience, you will need to get a social security number. If you

DEPARTMENT OF HEALTH AND HUMAN SERVICES
SOCIAL SECURITY ADMINISTRATION

Form Approved
OMB No. 0960-0066

FORM SS-5 — APPLICATION FOR A SOCIAL SECURITY NUMBER CARD
(Original, Replacement or Correction)

MICROFILM REF. NO. (SSA USE ONLY)

Unless the requested information is provided, we may not be able to issue a Social Security Number (20 CFR 422-103(b))

INSTRUCTIONS TO APPLICANT ▶ Before completing this form, please read the instructions on the opposite page. You can type or print, using pen with dark blue or black ink. Do not use pencil.

		First	Middle	Last
NAA	NAME TO BE SHOWN ON CARD			
NAB	FULL NAME AT BIRTH (IF OTHER THAN ABOVE)	First	Middle	Last
	1			
ONA	OTHER NAME(S) USED			

STT / 2 MAILING ADDRESS — (Street/Apt. No., P.O. Box, Rural Route No.)

CTY	CITY	STE	STATE	ZIP	ZIP CODE

CSP / 3 CITIZENSHIP (Check one only)
- ☐ a. U.S. citizen
- ☐ b. Legal alien allowed to work
- ☐ c. Legal alien not allowed to work
- ☐ d. Other (See instructions on Page 2)

SEX / 4 SEX
- ☐ MALE
- ☐ FEMALE

ETB / 5 RACE/ETHNIC DESCRIPTION (Check one only) (Voluntary)
- ☐ a. Asian, Asian-American or Pacific Islander (Includes persons of Chinese, Filipino, Japanese, Korean, Samoan, etc., ancestry or descent)
- ☐ b. Hispanic (Includes persons of Chicano, Cuban, Mexican or Mexican-American, Puerto Rican, South or Central American, or other Spanish ancestry or descent)
- ☐ c. Negro or Black (not Hispanic)
- ☐ d. Northern American Indian or Alaskan Native
- ☐ e. White (not Hispanic)

DOB / 6	DATE OF BIRTH — MONTH DAY YEAR	AGE / 7	PRESENT AGE	PLB / 8	PLACE OF BIRTH — CITY	STATE OR FOREIGN COUNTRY	FCI ☐

MNA / 9	MOTHER'S NAME AT HER BIRTH	First	Middle	Last (Her maiden name)
FNA	FATHER'S NAME	First	Middle	Last

PNO / 10

a. Has the person listed in Item 1 above or anyone acting on that person's behalf ever applied for a Social Security number card before? ☐ YES(2) ☐ NO(1) ☐ Don't know(1)   If yes, when: ➡ MONTH YEAR

b. Was a card received? ☐ YES(3) ☐ NO(1) ☐ Don't know(1)   If you checked yes to a or b, complete Items c through e; otherwise go to Item 11.

SSN c. Enter Social Security number. ☐☐☐ — ☐☐ — ☐☐☐☐

NLC d. Enter the name shown on the most recent Social Security card.

PDB e. Date of birth correction (See Instruction 10 on page 2) MONTH DAY YEAR

DON / 11	TODAY'S DATE — MONTH DAY YEAR	12	Telephone number where we can reach you during the day. Please include the area code.	HOME	OTHER

ASD **WARNING:** Deliberately furnishing (or causing to be furnished) false information on this application is a crime punishable by fine or imprisonment, or both.

13 YOUR SIGNATURE

14 YOUR RELATIONSHIP TO PERSON IN ITEM 1 ☐ Self ☐ Other (Specify)

WITNESS (Needed only if signed by mark "X")   WITNESS (Needed only if signed by mark "X")

DO NOT WRITE BELOW THIS LINE (FOR SSA USE ONLY)

DTC	SSA RECEIPT DATE

SSN ASSIGNED ☐☐☐ — ☐☐ — ☐☐☐☐

NPN

BIC SIGNATURE AND TITLE OF EMPLOYEE(S) REVIEWING EVIDENCE AND/OR CONDUCTING INTERVIEW

DOC	NTC	CAN

TYPE(S) OF EVIDENCE SUBMITTED

☐ MANDATORY IN PERSON INTERVIEW CONDUCTED   DATE

DATE

IDN	ITV	DCL

FORM **SS-5** (8-83)   3

2-1 To receive a social security number, you must complete this application form and return it to the nearest social security office.

are under age 16, you will also need a work permit. You should obtain a social security number and a work permit before you apply for a work experience.

You need a social security number if your work is covered by social security or if you have certain kinds of taxable income. Your social security number is also used for federal income tax purposes. Your employer needs to know your social security number before you can be paid. To obtain a social security number, you can apply for one at any social security office, 2-1 and 2-2. You may also be able to get a social security application form from your school or post office. You should apply for a number at least two weeks before you will need it. You will need evidence of your age, identity, U.S. citizenship or immigrant status when you apply.

If you have a social security number but have lost your social security card, contact a social security office and ask them to send you another one. You should also contact the social security office if you change your name so you can get a new card showing your new name.

A work permit makes it legal for a student under age 16 (age 18 in some states) to work for an employer. A work permit limits the number of hours a student can work each school day and the types of jobs a student can do. Work permits are issued by schools. Check with your coordinator to see if you will need a permit before you can begin work.

ABIDE BY THE TRAINING AGREEMENT

During your work experience, you will be expected to assume the responsibilities outlined in your cooperative education training agreement, 2-3. A *training agreement* is similar to a contract. It outlines the purposes of the cooperative education program and defines the responsibilities of everyone involved. This includes you (the student), your parents or guardian, the coordinator, and the employer. Although the wording varies from state to state, all training agreements serve the same general purposes:

- To assure the employer that the student is committed to the work experience.
- To assure the student that the employer is committed to training him or her to do the job.
- To assure the parents or guardian that their son or daughter is involved in a well-planned educational experience.
- To assure the coordinator that all parties understand their responsibilities and are committed to the student having a successful work experience.

FOLLOW THE TRAINING PLAN

In addition to the training agreement, there is the training plan. A *training plan* consists of a list of skills, attitudes, and habits that you plan to learn during the work experience, 2-4. The plan is usually developed by you, the

2-2 After your social security application is processed, you will receive a social security card with your name and number on it.

COOPERATIVE VOCATIONAL EDUCATION TRAINING AGREEMENT

The cooperative _____ program in Vocational Education is planned to develop a student academically, economically, and socially. To meet these goals, there are responsibilities the student must realize and agree to carry out to the fullest extent. As a participant in Cooperative Vocational Education, are you willing to assume the following responsibilities?

1. To realize that I am under the jurisdiction of the school throughout the school day, i.e. class, training station, and club activities.

2. To know that the Coordinator is the recognized authority for making adjustments or changes in the training received through employment.

3. To know that it is my responsibility throughout the year to be well dressed and groomed both in school and at the training station.

4. To carry out my training received through employment in such a manner that I will reflect credit upon myself and upon Vocational Education.

5. To perform all my duties in a commendable manner and perform related study assignments with earnestness and sincerity.

6. To work toward the group and individual achievement goals.

7. To be regular in attendance in school and at the training station. (This includes days at the training station when school is not in session such as: teachers' meetings, winter break, etc.)

8. To be on time at the training station.

9. To notify my employer as soon as I know I will be absent from work.

10. To notify the coordinator as early in the day as possible when I know I will be absent from school.

11. To know that on a day I am absent from school, I must also be absent from work unless given special permission by the teacher-coordinator.

12. To know that if I use a car as transportation to and from my work, I will observe all traffic laws and school policies. Any infraction of traffic laws and/or school policies may be sufficient cause to terminate the use of my car in connection with all Vocational Education activities.

13. To conduct myself in a satisfactory manner, both at the training station and in the classroom, or my training may be discontinued and I may be removed from Vocational Education.

14. To know that if I am removed from Vocational Education, I will receive a failing grade for both class instruction and the training station learning experience and will lose all credits.

15. To understand that if I am required to leave school because of disciplinary reasons, I cannot report to my training station as this is the same as any other classroom subject for which I am enrolled.

16. To agree to not quit or change jobs without first talking the situation over with my parents and coordinator.

17. It shall be agreed that parties participating in this program will not discriminate in employment opportunities on the basis of race, color, sex, national origin, or handicap.

18. A student should be released from the training station if necessary to attend local, state, regional, and national club activities.

I fully understand the above statements, and I agree to cooperate in carrying them out.

Date _____   School Year _____ 19____ to _____ 19____

_____   _____
Student's Signature   Coordinator's Signature

_____   _____
Parent's Signature   Employer's Signature

HOMEWOOD-FLOSSMOOR HIGH SCHOOL, FLOSSMOOR, IL

2-3 A training agreement outlines the purposes of the cooperative education program and defines the responsibilities of everyone involved.

STEP-BY-STEP TRAINING PLAN

The step-by-step training plan distinguishes Cooperative Education Programs from unsupervised work experience programs. This plan consists of a list of skills, attitudes, and learnings necessary for reaching a specific job and career goal. The list may be developed by the employer, the student, and the coordinator. The purpose of the plan is to guide the student toward progress on the job and in personal growth toward his or her career objective.

The student compiles a weekly job diary and periodically checks his or her accomplishments on the job as identified in the training plan. The coordinator selects specialized class materials which relate to the student's job and career needs. These are studied on an individual basis in class. Finally, at the quarter grading conference, the employer, the student, and the coordinator review and evaluate the accomplishments, and set up new goals as needed.

The flexible training plan defines the steps for the student, the employer, and the coordinator to follow for maximum growth of the student toward his or her career goals.

The _____ will permit _____
       (training station)   (student)

from _____ to enter their establishment as an employee
        (high school)

under the supervision of _____ for the purpose of gaining
                       (training supervisor)

knowledge and experience in the occupational career area of _____

in the position of _____ for approximately _____
                     (job title)

hours a week/day at a wage of _____.

Coordinator _____ Student _____

Training Supervisor _____

HOMEWOOD-FLOSSMOOR HIGH SCHOOL, FLOSSMOOR, IL

2-4 A training plan outlines the skills, attitudes, and habits you want to learn during the work experience.

Student Learner _____ Birthdate _____ Soc. Sec. No. _____

Job Title _____

Training Station _____

Address _____

Phone _____ Ext. _____ Supervisor's Name _____

Job Definition:

Description of Training Station Duties:

1.	9.
2.	10.
3.	11.
4.	12.
5.	13.
6.	14.
7.	15.
8.	16.

Career Objective:

LEARNING ACTIVITIES & EXPERIENCES	TRAINING STATION	SCHOOL INSTRUCTION GROUP	INDIVIDUAL	REFERENCES AND EVALUATION	TIME SCHEDULE

1. COMPANY ORIENTATION
  A. Learn history of the company
  B. Learn general employee rules and regulations:
    1. Proper dress
    2. Break time
    3. Lunch time
    4. Check-in and check-out time
    5. Sick leave procedure
    6. Sick "call-in" procedure
    7. Time sheet
    8. Location of work schedule
    9. Payroll procedures
    10. Employee benefits
    11. Salary
    12. Other_____
 	
  C. Learn company structure:
    1. Organization chart
    2. Department structure
    3. Chain of command
  D. Learn about advancement possibilities or possible change of work duties
  E. Other _____					

2-4 (continued)

LEARNING ACTIVITIES & EXPERIENCES	TRAINING STATION	SCHOOL INSTRUCTION GROUP	INDIVIDUAL	REFERENCES AND EVALUATION	TIME SCHEDULE
2. HUMAN RELATIONS					
A. Learn to interpret attitudes and personalities of co-workers					
B. Learn to understand or take directions and receive constructive criticism					
C. Be willing to admit lack of understanding and show initiative by asking for assistance					
D. Learn to be tackful in requests or suggestions relative to work					
E. Learn to make new friends with other employees					
F. Exhibit willingness to do any task requested					
G. Learn proper telephone etiquette:					
1. How to make telephone calls					
2. How to answer the telephone					
3. How to take messages					
H. Learn to correct any personal offensive habits					
I. Learn to deal courteously with customers, employees, and employer					
J. Learn to follow established routines and methods					
K. Learn to follow through in a job to its successful completion					
L. Become familiar with names, titles, and location of various company employees					
M. Other _____					
3. WORK ATTITUDES					
A. Learn to be on time for work					
B. Learn to be punctual and dependable					
C. Learn to notify the employer when absences will be necessary					
D. Learn to work during school vacations if needed by employer					
E. Learn to show efficiency and productivity on the job					
F. Learn to be well groomed and appropriately dressed on the job					
G. Learn to show initiative both on the job and at school					
H. Learn to continue on the same job as long as it is deemed feasible by employer and/or coordinator					
I. Learn to notify coordinator and employer if any problems arise that may interfere with quality or quantity of work production					
J. Learn to respect and abide by all rules and regulations connected with the job and company					
K. Learn to show honesty and respect toward all company property, goods, and/or services					
L. Other _____					

2-4 (continued)

LEARNING ACTIVITIES & EXPERIENCES	TRAINING STATION	SCHOOL INSTRUCTION GROUP	INDIVIDUAL	REFERENCES AND EVALUATION	TIME SCHEDULE

4. SAFETY AND HOUSEKEEPING
  A. Safety:
    1. Locate possible danger areas in and around the general work area and correct or report to superiors
    2. Find sharp corners and protrusions that might cause injury and correct or report
    3. Secure heavy objects that might fall on legs and feet
    4. Anchor filing cabinets or other equipment that might tip
    5. Place clothing, hair, or wearing accessories in a secure position when operation of designated equipment takes place
    6. Use proper equipment and procedures if climbing or reaching is necessary
    7. Review general work safety policies
    8. Learn and observe all company safety policies
    9. Other_____
  B. Housekeeping:
    1. Maintain attractiveness of the work area
    2. Learn to keep necessary equipment and materials in neat arrangement
    3. Learn to set up the work area
    4. Learn to clean up work area
    5. Miscellaneous:
      a. Empty waste baskets
      b. Empty ashtrays
      c. Clean desks
      d. Make coffee
      e. Dust
      f. Sharpen pencils
      g. Turn on/off lights and/or machinery (equipment)
    6. Other_____
 	
5. PROPER PENMANSHIP
  A. Learn to write all materials legibly
  B. Learn to form all figures and symbols so as to avoid misreading
  C. Learn to write all information in the proper areas of any form
  D. Other _____					

2-4 (continued)

LEARNING ACTIVITIES & EXPERIENCES	TRAINING STATION	SCHOOL INSTRUCTION GROUP	INDIVIDUAL	REFERENCES AND EVALUATION	TIME SCHEDULE
6. GOOD WORK HABITS A. Learn to plan the work to be done B. Learn to save time and steps by proper routing of papers C. Learn that proper timing is important in getting work completed D. Learn to maintain standards of neatness and accuracy in all work E. Other _____					
7. FILING A. Learn to file by the alphabetic system B. Learn to file by the numeric system C. Learn to check for proper authorization D. Other _____					

8. OFFICE MACHINES
A. Learn to operate:
  1. Liquid Duplicator
  2. Mimeograph
  3. Offset
  4. Photocopy
  5. Ten-Key Calculator
  6.
  7.
  8.					

9. TYPEWRITING A. Learn to properly arrange unarranged manuscript material in form for printing B. Learn to use proper publishers' proofreading marks C. Learn to plan and to type text materials around pictures, charts, and illustrations D. Learn to develop speed with accuracy in all typewritten work E. Learn to type materials on special forms to adjust line spacing to fit form F. Learn to set up and type statistical forms and reports G. Learn to use proper erasing technique for what is being typed H. Other _____					
10. CLEAN WORK AREA A. Learn proper methods for storing supplies B. Learn to clean and maintain office equipment C. Other _____					

2-4 (continued)

employer, and the coordinator. The purpose of the plan is to help you progress on the job toward your career goals. Like training agreements, training plans vary in form. Some are detailed plans, while others consist of a few general statements describing what the student will learn.

Another purpose of the training plan is to identify in writing your training supervisor. The supervisor is the person who helps teach and guide you on the job. This is the person the coordinator contacts about your progress.

To help you, the coordinator, and the employer evaluate your progress, most schools require students to keep a weekly or monthly job record. Sometimes this record is called a *training station report*. Each week or month you write down the duties you performed and the skills and attitudes you learned at work. Periodically you and your coordinator check your accomplishments to see if you are progressing toward the goals in your training plan. During these evaluation checks, you learn how much you have accomplished and what job skills you still want to achieve, 2-5.

STUDY AND LEARN

Cooperative education students sometimes say, "I want to work, not study." You will need to do both to be successful in your cooperative education work experience and your future career. Learning to study is not difficult. You probably have heard the saying, "There are tricks to every trade." There are tricks to studying too. To develop good study habits, practice the following tricks:

Trick #1: Make sure you clearly understand the assignment. When you don't understand what to do, ask the teacher.

JOE WALTERBACH

2-5 Periodically you and your coordinator will meet to evaluate the progress you are making in your work experience.

Trick #2: Set aside a time and a place to study. If possible, study at the same time every day. Make this your quiet time with no TV, radio, or stereo to interfere with studying.

Trick #3: When it is time to study, go to your study place and get started at once. Go there with the attitude that studying is the one and only thing you want to accomplish. Don't waste time daydreaming or thinking of other things you need or want to do.

Improve your reading skills

The skill that is basic to all studying and schoolwork is reading. The better you read, the more effective your studying will be and the more you will learn. Poor readers are usually slower learners because they take a longer amount of time to read and complete their assignments. However, a person's reading skills can be improved. The more a person reads, the easier reading becomes and the faster the person can read. Therefore, poor readers can improve their reading skills by setting aside more time for studying and reading. Or they can seek special help by getting involved in a reading improvement program at their school.

To learn more from what you read, look at the chapter title, the subheads, and the illustrations. What are the main ideas the writer is trying to tell you? When you know the main ideas, reading is easier. Don't just read words by themselves; read sentences and paragraphs to get the meaning. Very seldom will one word give meaning to an idea. It takes many words together to express a thought, idea, or fact.

Participate in class

In your cooperative education class and your other courses, give your full attention to the teacher. Be a good listener. Focus your full attention on the teacher or speaker and think about what is being said. Also, be sure to sit where you can see and hear well.

If you do your assignments, you will find it easier to be a contributor in class. State facts as you know them. Ask questions about ideas or facts that you don't understand in the assignment. Even lessons that seem uninteresting take on a new meaning when you become involved in the discussion and participate in class, 2-6.

2-6 Participating in class can help you learn more and enjoy the time you spend in the classroom.

Take notes

Many students improve their learning skills by taking notes after they read an assignment. They go back to each page or paragraph and write down the main ideas in a study notebook. This is called summarizing. Summarizing helps you remember what you have read. It also helps you review the information for a test.

When you take notes, organize them by chapter, assignments, or dates, whichever is best for you. Write the notes in your own words. Be brief. Read each paragraph, but don't try to copy the entire paragraph from the book. Just summarize the main idea and write it in your notebook.

Taking notes in class also helps reinforce learning and helps you identify the most important points in the material you are studying. The better organized you are as you take notes, the more helpful your notes will be to you when you are studying. When you begin taking notes, write the lesson title or topic and the date at the top of the page. During the lecture, write down the main headings and leave space to write comments under each heading. Don't try to write entire sentences. Just write down a few words or phrases to help you remember the main ideas. After class or during study time, check over your notes. Make sure you wrote down all the ideas and facts you want to remember.

To be successful in your cooperative education work experience, you need to be a good student as well as a good worker.

to Review

1. What do you do if you don't have a job when you begin the cooperative education program?
2. What are the purposes of a training agreement?
3. What are the purposes of a training plan?
4. How do you and your coordinator determine if you are progressing toward the goals in your training plan?
5. What can you do to develop good study habits?
6. What is summarizing? How can it help you improve your learning skills?

to Discuss

1. As a cooperative education student, what will your school and coordinator expect of you?

2. Why is it so important for students, employers, parents, and coordinators to read and follow a training agreement?
3. Why are training plans an important part of the cooperative education program?
4. How can you improve your reading skills?
5. What can you do to be a better class participant?

to Do

1. As a cooperative education student, you will be adjusting to new school and work hours. What will be your weekly schedule? Make out a daily time schedule for each day of the week beginning with when you get up and when you go to bed.

Include the time you spend going to school, going to work, eating, recreating, studying, and relaxing. Then evaluate your schedule. Do you have any free time to spend as you please? Are you allowing yourself enough time for study? Are you getting enough rest? What changes, if any, would you make in your weekly schedule?

2. Take a close look at the training agreement you will sign or have already signed to participate in a cooperative work experience. Make a list of the responsibilities you have as a cooperative education student as outlined in the agreement. Then rank the responsibilities in the order of their importance. Which responsibility do you think is the most important? Why? How important are the other responsibilities you have? Share your thoughts with the class.

GARRETT TURBINE ENGINE CO.

Your employer will expect you to be
at work every day and to be on time.

3

What your employer expects

After studying this chapter, you will be able to:

☐ Explain what your employer expects of you as a cooperative education student worker.
☐ Identify things you can do to promote good working relationships with your supervisor and co-workers.

As an employee, there are certain guidelines you will be expected to follow. Your employer will expect you to attend work regularly, be on time for work, and perform well on the job. Your company or business will also expect you to be honest, loyal, and cooperative. Your ability to meet these expectations will depend partly on your health and fitness.

You may be thinking you have many responsibilities to meet as an employee. You're right. When you work for someone else, you will need to work by your employer's rules. Employers expect the people they hire to use their skills and abilities to help the business operate and make a profit. Your employer will expect the same from you: to use your skills and training to the best of your ability.

GOOD ATTENDANCE

Both the employer and the school will expect you to be at work (the training station) every working day. When a person is absent, it causes extra work for others. Poor attendance also reduces the effectiveness of the work experience.

Since absenteeism is a major concern of employers and vocational coordinators, many schools often require students and their parents to read and sign an absenteeism policy. This type of policy stresses the importance of regular attendance at school and at work. By signing the policy, students are saying they will attend school and work regularly and will notify their employers and coordinators if they must be absent. Violating this policy may cause the student to be dismissed from work and from the work experience program.

Students with good attendance records avoid asking for time off from work to do personal errands. It is best to schedule doctor appointments, car repairs, and other personal needs outside of working hours. In case of illness, death in the family, or an emergency, you should contact your employer and your school coordinator to explain your absence from work. This is the courteous action to take. Reporting your absence also shows your employer that you are a dependable and responsible employee. A dependable worker most likely will be given more responsibility, advancements, and pay raises.

PUNCTUALITY

One of the most irritating things to an employer is a worker who is constantly late. Being late may make your employer think that you are not interested in your job and that you have an "I don't care" attitude. Being late is inconsiderate, and it is not tolerated in the working world. You can't make up being late one day by going in early the next day. You must be on time every day.

Do not make the mistake of thinking that being three minutes late once in a while will make little difference. It does make a difference. You are hired to be at work at a specific time. It is your responsibility to be there at that time or before, not later. Plan your schedule so you will always be on time. If you take a bus to work, you may have to take one that gets you there early. If you drive, bicycle, or walk, allow plenty of time for any delays such as rain, snow, and traffic lights. In other words, you should try for five minutes early not five minutes late.

Some companies require workers to check in and out by punching a time clock, 3-1. This method clearly shows when you are late. If you are late, the company may withhold or dock a percentage of your pay. Being late is a bad habit, and it can be costly. Develop the good habit of being on time.

PERFORMANCE

Although you will be learning new skills on the job, your employer will expect you to have some basic knowledge and skills in your area of employment. For example, if you are going to be employed in a welding shop, you should have some prior training in welding. If you

BERNIE NOVIA

3-1 Checking in and out of work by a time clock clearly shows your employer when you are on time and when you are late.

will be employed as a typist, you will need to know how to type. You can't expect your employer to teach you the basics of welding or to teach you how to type on the job.

Your employer also will expect you to put forth your best effort while on the job. As a beginner, you probably will not be expected to do as much as an experienced worker. But you will be expected to have the same work standards. For example, if you are a typist, you may not be expected to type a letter as fast as someone who has had five years of typing experience. But you will be expected to type the letter correctly and accurately. As you gain more experience, you will be expected to increase your speed. Working fast and efficiently should be one of your goals at work.

COOPERATION

To be effective at your job, it is important for you to get along with your supervisor and co-workers. To show you want to be cooperative, accept your share of the work and perform your job to the best of your ability.

Make sure you follow directions carefully. Always ask questions when you do not understand how to do a certain task.

Be friendly, respectful, and considerate of other workers' feelings. A smile and a few minutes of friendly conversation are good ways to promote good working relationships. Also be enthusiastic about your job. Expressing enthusiasm will help you become a part of the working team, 3-2.

Working with your supervisor

Your supervisor has the role of seeing that work gets completed. The supervisor is also responsible for the quantity and quality of the product or service. When one or both is lacking, the supervisor must take the necessary steps to correct the problem. The supervisor may suggest a new way for getting the job done. Or the supervisor may encourage employees to work faster. You need to realize that your supervisor probably has a supervisor to whom he or she must report. Therefore, your performance on the job directly influences your supervisor's job performance.

JEAN SWEENEY

3-2 Being cooperative and enthusiastic will help you get along well with your co-workers.

This, in turn, affects the progress of your company or employer.

At times you may be assigned tasks that you would rather not do. Very few workers enjoy sweeping the floor or washing windows, but these are jobs that must be done. You must remember that you are a beginner. Beginners start at the bottom and must work themselves up. Accept the tasks you are given with a pleasant face and perform these jobs as well as you would any others.

Sometimes you may not mind the tasks you are assigned but dislike the way you are told to do them. Different supervisors will have different ways of supervising. You may have the type of supervisor that shouts out orders with no explanations. These types of bosses appear to be very impersonal and to operate strictly on a business level. They avoid working with employees on a personal basis. This type of boss might say, "Bob, clean up the storeroom before you leave work today. And you better do a good job."

Then there are other types of bosses who make requests rather than give orders. They usually explain why decisions are made and why certain tasks must be done. This type of boss might say, "Bob, there's going to be an inspection at the plant tomorrow, and everything needs to look as nice and clean as possible. I'd like you to be in charge of cleaning the storeroom today. I'm sure you can do a good job."

No matter what type of boss you have, work with your supervisor not against your supervisor, 3-3. Try to adapt to his or her style of management. You will find there are all types of people in the working world. You will have to prepare yourself to get along with all kinds of people and all kinds of supervisors.

Accepting criticism

Another responsibility of your supervisor is to give constructive criticism. The only way you will know how to do something better is to be told or shown a better way to do it. The only way you will know you are not working as fast as you should is to be told you need to work at a faster pace. Without constructive criticism, workers would never improve their skills or learn to work more efficiently.

That's the purpose of job evaluations. During your cooperative work experience, your supervisor will be asked to evaluate your job performance—to give constructive criticism. A sample job evaluation is shown in 3-4. Your supervisor's evaluation should help you and your coordinator identify your strengths and weaknesses at work.

As an employee, it is your responsibility to accept criticism with a good attitude. Listen to what your supervisor has to say and follow through on his or her suggestions. Be glad and thankful your supervisor takes an interest in your work and wants to help you do your best on the job.

HONESTY

Your employer expects you to do an honest day's work for an honest day's pay. That means doing the job you are assigned and not wasting time. An employee who loafs on the job is actually stealing time away from his or her employer. Employers can not afford to pay employees for services not performed.

Being honest on the job also includes not taking or using your employer's supplies for personal use. Although you may work in a grocery store, this doesn't mean you can take a few groceries without paying for them. Although you may work in an office, this doesn't mean you are entitled to take home typing paper, pens, tape, and other supplies. Businesses have been known to go out of business due to the dishonesty of their employees.

Anyone caught stealing from an employer or other workers can expect to be fired. Once a person gets a reputation for being dishonest, it will be difficult for that person to get hired for other jobs.

LOYALTY

Loyalty means being faithful to your co-workers and to your employer. Workers who are loyal to their employers are proud of their companies and the products or services they provide. These workers speak well of their companies at work and outside of work. Therefore, you need to have a positive attitude about your work and your employer.

If at times you find there are policies or decisions your employer or supervisor makes with which you disagree, talk with your coordinator about them. Do not gossip with other students or workers at your work station. Most likely your coordinator will be able to help you understand why such policies and decisions were made. Or the coordinator can help you decide how to deal with problem situations.

GOOD HEALTH AND FITNESS

Your employer expects you to be alert when you arrive on the job and to remain alert during the work day. Your alertness and job performance will depend on your health and fit-

ness. To stay healthy and physically fit you need to follow three basic guidelines:
- Eat well-balanced, nutritious meals.
- Get adequate sleep and rest.
- Get regular exercise and physical activity. See 3-5.

It is next to impossible to look and feel your best if you only get five hours of sleep each night, skip breakfast and have a cola and potato chips for lunch, or only exercise once a month.

In addition to good physical health, you need to stay healthy and fit mentally. You may be in perfect physical health but appear pale and ill if you are unhappy. To keep mentally fit remember to make time for play as well as work. Set aside time to spend with friends and to participate in new activities. Exercising your brain is just as important as exercising your body.

BERNIE NOVIA

3-3 Make a special effort to work with your supervisor and to respect his or her decisions.

JOB EVALUATION

INSTRUCTIONS: Read carefully the descriptions given for each of the qualifications listed below. Then place a check mark (✓) in the column which, in your opinion, most accurately describes the student's standing. Evaluate each qualification without regard to the student's rating on any other qualification. Please return by _____ in the stamped, self-addressed envelope provided.

Thanks,

NAME OF STUDENT _____

FIRM _____

Rating for 1st quarter _____ 3rd quarter _____

2nd quarter _____ 4th quarter _____

Supervisor's Signature _____

Date _____

	0 1	2 3	4 5	6 7	8 9
1. COOPERATION—ability to get along with others	Is antagonistic, pulls against rather than works with others	Is difficult to handle	Usually gets along with others	Cooperates willingly, gets along with others	Gets along well with others, is friendly and helpful
2. INITIATIVE—tendency to go ahead	Takes no initiative, has to be instructed repeatedly	Takes very little initiative, requires urging	Does routine work acceptably	Is fairly resourceful, does well by himself or herself	Is resourceful, looks for things to learn and do
3. COURTESY	Has been discourteous to the public and staff	Is not particularly courteous in action or speech	Usually is polite and is considerate of others	Is considerate and courteous	Is very courteous and very considerate of others
4. ATTITUDE TOWARD CONSTRUCTIVE CRITICISM	Doesn't profit by criticism, resents it	Doesn't pay much attention to criticism	Accepts criticism and tries to do better	Accepts criticism and improvement noted	Accepts criticism and improves greatly
5. KNOWLEDGE OF JOB	Has not tried to learn	Pays little attention to learning job	Has learned necessary routine but needs supervision	Understands work, needs little supervision	Knows job well and shows desire to learn more
6. ACCURACY OF WORK	Is extremely careless	Is frequently inaccurate and careless	Makes errors; shows average care, thoroughness, and neatness	Makes few errors; is careful, thorough, and neat	Very seldom makes errors, does work of very good quality

	0	1	2	3	4	5	6	7	8	9
7. WORK ACCOMPLISHED	Is very slow; output is unsatisfactory		Is slower than average		Works with ordinary speed; work is generally satisfactory		Works rapidly; output is above average		Is fast and efficient; production is well above average	
8. WORK HABITS	Habitually wastes time, has to be watched and prodded along		Frequently wastes time, needs close supervision		Wastes time occasionally, is usually reliable		Seldom wastes time, is reliable		Is industrious, concentrates very well	
9. ADAPTABILITY	Can't adjust to changing situations		Is slow in grasping ideas, has difficulty adapting to new situations		Makes necessary adjustments after considerable instruction		Adjusts readily		Learns quickly, is adept at meeting changing conditions	
10. PERSONAL APPEARANCE— neatness and personal care	Is extremely careless		Often neglects appearance		Is passable in appearance, but should make effort to improve		Is very good in appearance; looks neat most of the time		Is excellent in appearance; looks very well all of the time	
11. ATTENDANCE	Too frequently absent for continued employment		Not regular enough in attendance		Usually dependable		Dependable		Never absent except for an unavoidable emergency	
12. PUNCTUALITY	Too frequently tardy for continued employment		Very often tardy		Punctuality could be improved		Seldom tardy		Never tardy except for an unavoidable emergency	

MATURITY LEVEL: _____ Below Average _____ Average _____ Above Average
(Please check one)

3-4 Several factors are considered when you are evaluated on the job.

HOMEWOOD-FLOSSMOOR HIGH SCHOOL, FLOSSMOOR, IL

INGALLS MEMORIAL HOSPITAL

3-5 Jogging regularly is one
exercise that will help you stay
healthy and physically fit.

to Review

1. Why is it important for you to be at work every working day?

2. What should you do if you are unable to attend school and work?

3. What can you do to make sure you will get to work on time?

4. Although a beginning worker probably will not be expected to do as much as an experienced worker, the new worker will be expected to have the same work_____.

5. Why is loafing on the job a form of dishonesty?

6. How do workers express their loyalty to their employers?

7. If you find it difficult to be loyal to your employer because you disagree with policies and decisions he or she has made, what should you do?

8. What can you do at work to show your supervisor and co-workers that you want to cooperate with them?

9. What three basic guidelines do you need to follow to stay healthy and physically fit?

to Discuss

1. Does your school have a cooperative education absenteeism policy? Why do you think some schools require students to sign this type of policy?

2. What should you do if your supervisor assigns you to do a task you'd rather not do?

3. Describe the perfect type of supervisor.

4. What is the purpose of job evaluations?

5. When your supervisor tells you that you did something wrong on the job and shows you the correct way to do it in the future, how should you react?

6. If you were an employer, what would you do if you caught one of your employees loafing on the job? Stealing company supplies?

to Do

1. A cooperative education student decided to leave his work station early one Friday although the supervisor had not given the student permission to do so. Discuss in class what, if anything, the employer and the school coordinator should do about this student's behavior.

2. Make a list of things for which a student could be fired from his or her work experience. Discuss in class why each behavior might cause the student to be fired.

Skills for work

Good communication skills have helped this young
salesman sell many bicycles.

Communicating on the job

To work well with other people, you have to be able to communicate. Communication is the process of conveying a message, a thought, or an idea in such a way that the message is received and understood. Through communication, people share ideas, facts, opinions, and feelings.

Good communication is very important in the working world, because poor communication can be costly to you and your employer. It's important to ask your supervisor how to perform a task if you're not sure how to do it yourself. Doing the job the wrong way wastes time and money. It's important to write down a telephone order correctly. Printing the wrong letter or number in an order can foul-up the order and waste time and money correcting the error. It's important to thank customers for their business. Expressing appreciation will encourage them to continue doing business with you.

To communicate clearly on the job, you need three basic communication skills: listening skills, speaking skills, and writing skills. Workers with good communication skills usually have little difficulty succeeding and advancing on the job.

LISTENING SKILLS

Some people never seem to listen. They become so wrapped up in what they have to say that they do not bother to listen to others. Have you ever encountered people who seem to be thinking about something else when you are talking to them? Do you ever do the same thing to others?

There is a difference between hearing and listening. Hearing is done with the ear only. Listening involves understanding what you hear. For communication to occur, a message must be sent and received. Therefore, if a person is not listening when a message is sent, communication does not take place.

People often fail to listen when they are in the following situations.

They are interrupted. A person's ability to listen is affected when someone walks into the room, an airplane flies over the building, or other people are talking nearby.

They think they know what's going to be said. Sometimes people only listen to part of a conversation because they think "I've heard this before."

They don't agree with what's being said. When people don't agree with what's being said, they often block the information out of their minds. They refuse to listen to what the speaker is saying.

They are having difficulty hearing. People do not listen when they can't hear well. For example, you may stop listening when someone is speaking so softly you cannot understand what is being said.

They are distracted by the speaker. Sometimes the speaker has distracting mannerisms, speaks in a monotone, or does not make eye contact with the audience. This discourages listening.

They do not understand the words. Not knowing the meanings of words used by the speaker handicaps the listener.

They start thinking about something else. When people allow their minds to wander, they fail to concentrate on what is being said.

To be a good listener, the main thing you need to do is concentrate on what is being said, 4-1. Do not let other things distract you from the speaker. Block out everything except the voice of the speaker. Do not interrupt the speaker unless you do not understand what is being said. Then ask the speaker to explain in more detail what he or she is trying to say. Being a good listener will help you be a better worker. Consider listening a skill that you can improve with practice.

How good a listener are you? After reading about Quentin, how would you rate his listening skills? How can you and Quentin become better listeners?

ARE YOU LISTENING, QUENTIN?

At a department meeting, Quentin's supervisor introduced a new process that their company is going to begin using in the manufacture of their products. He explained that the

4-1 A good listener pays attention to what is being said and shows a sincere interest in what the speaker is saying.

new process would require a new processing machine. In order to make room for the new machine, all the other machines in the department would have to be relocated. He said, "This new, large semi-automatic machine will be aligned with the east wall. All other machines will be placed along the north and west walls."

The supervisor went on to explain how the heavy equipment should be moved. Suddenly, Quentin said, "Why don't we put the new machine along the east wall?"

It was quiet in the room until the supervisor explained to Quentin that he had already discussed that idea. Quentin was embarrassed but declared he had not heard it discussed. Everyone at the meeting laughed at him. Why didn't Quentin hear his supervisor? He did hear him, but he wasn't listening to him.

SPEAKING SKILLS

When you began talking as a young child, you probably learned one or more new words every day. Now that you are older, you know thousands of words which you use from day to day. By putting words together, you form combinations to communicate with others. Some people are able to form combinations of words more easily than others. Therefore, some people have better speaking skills than others.

How good are your speaking skills? Do you practice the following guidelines when you speak to others?

Speak clearly and distinctly. Avoid running words together such as "whydoncha" for "why don't you." If necessary, talk more slowly. If you have a tendency to mumble, try opening your mouth a little wider when talking. Always be sure not to talk with food or anything else in your mouth.

Speak to the listener. Look directly at the person or people with whom you are talking. Making eye contact will help hold the listener's attention and show that you are interested in talking to him or her, 4-2.

Speak with a friendly and courteous tone. Try to phrase what you want to say in a positive way. When you find it necessary to criticize, be ready to offer a constructive idea. Avoid arguing and complaining.

4-2 Speaking directly to a person and making eye contact will help hold the listener's attention.

GENERAL ELECTRIC

Use standard English. This means you should use standard grammar and pronunciation when speaking as well as when writing. "Bob came here yesterday" is standard English. "Bob come here yesterday" is not. Since standard English is the same everywhere, it is the language form that is best to use at work and in any business situation. The person who uses standard English on the job appears more competent and better educated.

Talk "with" the listener, not "to" the listener. Keep messages short and understandable. Make sure your messages are received correctly. You may want to ask questions like "What do you think?" or "What are your feelings about this?" This will give the listener a chance to give you feedback on what you've said. From the listener's comments, you will be able to tell if your messages have been understood.

Talking on the telephone

Jennifer dials a business telephone number. After the telephone rings five times, she hears someone pick up the receiver. Then she hears voices in the background, but nobody speaks to her. Eventually, a voice says, "Hulooo."

"Is this the Acme Company?" Jennifer asks.

"Yeah."

"This is Jennifer Jones. I would like to speak to Gordon Brown, please."

"Whatcha wan hem fir?"

If you were Jennifer, what type of mental picture would you have of the person who answered the phone? Would this person's behavior influence your opinion of the Acme Company? What do you think the person who answered the telephone at Acme should have said to Jennifer?

Using the telephone in the working world is one of the quickest ways to communicate. A one minute telephone call, if handled properly, can save hours or even days in communication time. If you have a job where you answer or talk on the telephone, it is important that you learn good telephone manners. The way you communicate over the telephone can help or hurt your employer. Here are some pointers to improve your telephone skills at work.

When the telephone rings, answer it immediately. Greet the caller pleasantly and give the name of your company, the name of your department, or your own name. You may want to say something like this: "Good morning, the Acme Company, may I help you?"

When talking, hold the phone about one inch from your lips and speak directly into the transmitter. Speak clearly, and say each word distinctly. Do not eat, drink, or chew gum while speaking on the phone. Always be courteous to the caller, even if it is a wrong number. See 4-3.

Be sure to keep a message pad or paper and pen close to the telephone so you can write down messages. When taking a message, write down the date, the time of the call, who the message is for, who the message is from, and the message itself. After writing down the message, read it back to the caller to make sure you recorded the information correctly. If you are not sure how to spell a person's name or a company's name, ask the caller to spell it for you. It's important for you to copy down the message exactly right.

When you're calling other people, plan your call in advance. For example, if you are placing an order for company supplies, be sure you have all the facts you need in front of you. Know what you want to say and how you want to say it.

When any business call comes to a close, end the conversation pleasantly. You may want to thank the person for calling if the person called you or the company. If you made the call, you may want to thank the person for their assistance or cooperation. Remember, the impressions you make on others will influence the impressions they will have of you and your company.

Speaking to a group

At school you have probably been asked or required to speak in front of a group. You have probably given oral reports in some of your classes. Or maybe you have spoken in front of a club or participated in a public speaking contest.

Many occupations also require some public

speaking. As an employee you may be asked to explain to a tour group how a certain machine works. You may be asked to present an idea to a group of workers. You may be asked to make a sales pitch to a group of buyers or to speak at a union meeting. Regardless of the type of work you do, having the ability to speak in front of a group will help you be a better communicator on and off the job.

Many people are afraid to speak in front of a group because they are afraid they might say or do something foolish. But that should never be a problem for you if you speak on a topic that you know about. You may be thinking you don't know much about anything, but you do. You are the expert on yourself. You could talk confidently about where you live, where you go to school, where you work, and what your interests and hobbies are. You are the expert on what you do at your training station—the tasks you perform and the skills you learn. Knowing your subject is half the work in public speaking. The other half is preparing your presentation.

When preparing your speech, outline the main items you want to get across to your audience. Try to limit yourself to five main points or less. Then organize your points in a logical order. For example, suppose you are going to be speaking to a group about how to refinish furniture, a hobby of yours. You decide there are three main points you want to include:

1. The different types of finishes that can be used.
2. A step-by-step explanation of how to refinish furniture.
3. The material and equipment needed for refinishing.

After looking over these three points, you decide the most logical point to talk about first is a step-by-step explanation of

4-3 Be sure to use good telephone manners whenever you are on the job.

INGALLS MEMORIAL HOSPITAL

how to refinish furniture. Next, you decide you should describe the material and equipment needed for refinishing. Then discuss the different types of finishes that can be used. Therefore, you decide to organize your points like this:

1. A step-by-step explanation of how to refinish furniture.
2. The material and equipment needed for refinishing.
3. The different types of finishes that can be used.

Now you have a speech, but how do you deliver it? Here's one easy rule to follow: Tell them what you're going to tell them. Tell them. Then tell them what you told them.

When telling your audience what you're going to tell them, it's important to catch their attention. You may want to tell a funny story that is related to your subject or that will lead into your subject. Or you may want to tell about a personal experience that is related to the subject. When telling your audience what you have to tell them, begin with point one. Then go through each point. When telling them what you have told them, summarize your main points.

Before giving your speech, practice! Practicing will help you know what you want to say when you want to say it. You'll also want to time your talk to make sure your speech is not too long. If you are not given a time limit, do the limiting yourself. It's best not to ever speak over twenty minutes.

When delivering your speech, avoid reading it from note cards. Use notes instead. You should speak to your audience, not read to them. As you speak, project your voice so that everyone can hear you clearly. It's also important to look at the people to whom you are talking. Making eye contact will help you hold your audience's attention and get across your message.

Your appearance is also important when making a presentation. Dress appropriately for the group to whom you are speaking. If you're speaking to your classmates in your English class at school, dress as you would for school. If you're speaking to a group of employers about your cooperative work experience, dress in your casual best. Always make sure you look nice, clean, and neat.

Remember, when you're giving a speech, you simply have a message you want to tell others. Give it with confidence and enthusiasm. See 4-4.

WRITING SKILLS

Many employers consider written communication skills one of the most important job skills an employee can have. Why? One reason is that there are so many people who do not communicate well. Poor communication can cause employers to lose business and lose money. Therefore, the ability to write a message clearly and accurately is an important skill to have in the working world.

Writing skills become especially important as you advance on the job. Written business communication is commonly done through business letters, memorandums, and reports.

BUSINESS LETTERS

Writing a business letter is different from writing a personal letter to a friend or relative. When writing a personal letter, you can use your own style of writing. You can write just as you would talk to the person face to face. You can write on bright red stationery or yellow paper with polka dots. And you don't have to keep a copy of every personal letter you write.

However, letters written in the working world are more formal. There are certain styles for writing business letters. There are certain parts that should be included in business letters. There are certain ways business letters should appear. And it's important to keep a copy of any business letter you write.

Types of business letters

Business letters are usually written for one of three reasons:

1. To request information, merchandise, or service.
2. To give good news or a neutral message.
3. To give bad news.

Therefore, there are three main types of business letters: request letters, good news and neutral message letters, and bad news letters. The type of letter you are writing will determine what you should write and how you should write it. Here are guidelines for writing each type of letter.

Request letters. When the main purpose of your message is to ask the reader to do something, you are writing a request letter. When writing a request letter, there are three things that are important to tell the reader. First, introduce your request and state why you are making the request. Second, include any details that are necessary for the reader to respond to your request correctly. For example, if you are ordering merchandise, it is important to include the name of the merchandise, the quantity wanted, the order or catalog number, the size, the color, and any other important information. Third, state clearly what action you want the reader to take and when. Once again, if you are ordering merchandise, give the reader the name and address to whom the merchandise should be sent. Tell the reader when the order is needed and how it will be paid.

In the closing paragraph, you should also include a statement of appreciation. You might want to say something like this: "I will appreciate your mailing this order within the next two weeks." See 4-5.

Good news and neutral message letters. Letters that answer requests, grant favors, express appreciation, or make announcements about events, policies, and procedures can be written by the good news/neutral message letter plan. These types of letters are usually easy to write because you are telling the reader something that is pleasant or that is neither good nor bad.

In a good news/neutral message letter, there

NATIONAL VICA

4-4 Smiling, gesturing, and being enthusiastic will get your audience interested in what you have to say and help hold their attention.

are three important things to tell the reader. First, tell the reader the good news or the main idea. Second, explain any details, facts, or reasons that relate to the good news or main idea. For example, suppose you are filling a mail order for a customer. If the customer ordered four items and you only have three items in stock, explain when the other item will be sent. And third, end the letter on a positive and friendly note. In the mail order example, thank the reader for the order. Let the reader know you will be glad to fill future orders. If your company is sending information to readers about a new product or service, tell them how they can order or receive the product or service. Let your readers know you are willing to help them further. See 4-6.

Bad news letters. Acknowledging orders you can't fill, turning down requests, announcing bad news about prices or services are examples of bad news messages. The wording of bad news letters is very important. You want to be able to tell the reader the bad news without the reader forming a bad impression of your company.

Usually there are four important things to tell the reader. First, say something positive that is of interest to the reader, yet related to the bad news. For example, thank the reader for making a request although you must decline it. Second, explain why the request cannot be granted or explain why the situation must be different from the way the reader wants it. For example, if an order cannot be filled for a customer, explain why. Third, offer a constructive suggestion or an alternative. For example, maybe your company does not carry the exact item requested, but you do have a very similar product that may interest the reader. Or maybe you can direct the reader to the company that does carry the item. And lastly, end the letter on a friendly and positive note. Express continued interest in the reader. Or invite the reader to contact you in the future. See 4-7.

Parts of a business letter

Most business letters have eight standard parts: the return address, the date, the inside address, the salutation, the body, the complimentary close, the signature and typed name, and reference initials. Each part is described below and identified in 4-8.

Return address. The return address tells the reader where the letter is from. Most companies have their return addresses printed on their stationery which is called a letterhead. If you are typing a business letter on blank paper, you will need to type in the return address.

Date. The date tells the reader when the letter was written.

Inside address. The inside address includes the name, business title, and address of the person to whom the letter is being sent. It is the same address that is typed on the envelope.

Salutation. The salutation is the greeting that comes before the body of the letter. The most widely used salutation is "Dear Mr. (Mrs., Ms., Miss) Jones." If writing to a group of men or women, you can use "Gentlemen" or "Ladies." If you know the person on a first name basis, you can write "Dear Terry." A colon (:) is typed after the salutation.

Body. The body contains the message.

Complimentary close. Most business letters have one of the following closings: "Sincerely," "Yours truly," or "Cordially." A comma is typed after the closing.

Signature and typed name. Your name should be typed in and signed. If you have a business title, it can be typed directly below your typed name. Then you should sign your name in ink above your typed name. Sign both your first and last name unless you are on a first name basis with the person to whom you are writing.

Reference initials. Your initials as writer of the letter and those of the typist should be typed below your typed name and business title. The writer's initials usually appear in all capital letters, and the typist's initials in lower case letters. The common forms used are MLD/ch and MLD:ch.

Appearance of a business letter

Although the typist is usually responsible for the appearance of a letter, the writer also

H. B. JONES WELDING
812 N. 7th Avenue
Kansas City, Missouri 65100

November 18, 19__

Mr. Albert Romero, Manager
Winston Welding Supplies
1020 North 8th St.
Springfield, Mo 65802

Dear Mr. Romero:

Please ship the following order as quickly as possible and charge to our account no. 65100-02.

Quantity	Description	Unit Price	Total
100 lbs.	No. 1102 flux	$1.00 lb.	$100.00
500	No. 35 corner supports, iron	$2.00 ea.	1000.00
250	No. 68 hinges, steel	$1.50 pr.	375.00
		TOTAL	$1475.00

Since most of our flux was ruined during yesterday's rainstorm, we need these supplies immediately. Your prompt delivery will be greatly appreciated.

Sincerely,

Jackie Jones

Jackie Jones
Purchaser

JRJ/ra

4-5 The main purpose of a request letter is to get the reader to do something for you.

ACME WELDING SUPPLY
999 Camden Street
St. Louis, Missouri 63000

November 20, 19__

Ms. Jackie Jones, Purchaser
H. B. Jones Welding
812 N. 7th Ave.
Kansas City, MO 65100

Dear Ms. Jones:

Thank you for your letter requesting information about our
new Acme welding machine. Enclosed is a booklet describing the machine to familiarize you with its exceptional
features.

Ken Adams is our Acme welding machine representative in
the Kansas City area. He would be happy to demonstrate the
welding machine to you and answer any questions you may
have about its use for your company. Ken will be calling
you this week to arrange a visit.

Again, thank you for your interest. Ken will be happy to
fulfill an order for you if you decide the Acme welding
machine or any of our other products will meet your
needs.

Sincerely,

Larry Smith

Larry Smith
Sales Manager

LS/rb

4-6 The good news or neutral message letter is written when
answering requests, granting favors, expressing appreciation, or
making announcements about events, policies, and procedures.

ACME WELDING SUPPLY
999 Camden Street
St. Louis, Missouri 63000

December 2, 19__

Mr. J. T. McRae
McRae & Sons Construction
110 East Rd.
Independence, Mo 65923

Dear Mr. McRae:

Thank you for your order for three Acme welding machines.

Since the demand for this newest welding device has far exceeded our sales expectations at this time of year, we are temporarily out of stock. However, our production manager has assured me that a new supply of welding machines will be available within ten days.

You can plan on receiving a rush shipment of your welding machines by December 15. We are confident that you and your workers will like using these new lightweight welding machines, and that they will help you get your jobs done faster.

Sincerely,

Larry Smith

Larry Smith
Sales Manager

LS/rb

4-7 The main purpose of the bad news letter is to tell the reader unfavorable news without the reader forming a bad impression of your company.

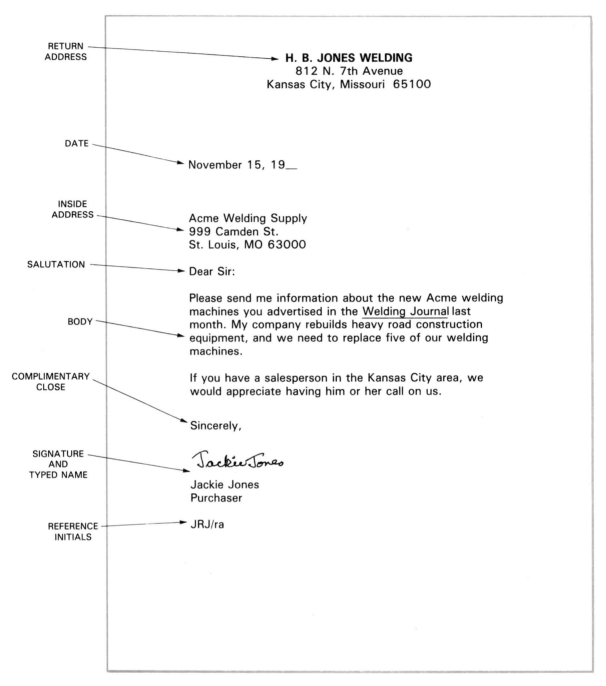

RETURN ADDRESS →

H. B. JONES WELDING
812 N. 7th Avenue
Kansas City, Missouri 65100

DATE →

November 15, 19___

INSIDE ADDRESS →

Acme Welding Supply
999 Camden St.
St. Louis, MO 63000

SALUTATION →

Dear Sir:

BODY →

Please send me information about the new Acme welding machines you advertised in the Welding Journal last month. My company rebuilds heavy road construction equipment, and we need to replace five of our welding machines.

If you have a salesperson in the Kansas City area, we would appreciate having him or her call on us.

COMPLIMENTARY CLOSE →

Sincerely,

SIGNATURE AND TYPED NAME →

Jackie Jones

Jackie Jones
Purchaser

REFERENCE INITIALS →

JRJ/ra

4-8 Most business letters have eight standard parts.

needs to know how a business letter should look. Most business letters are arranged in one of two ways: block form and modified block form.

With the *block form,* all parts begin at the left margin. Paragraphs are not indented. This is the fastest style to type. The good news letter in 4-6 is typed in block form.

With the *modified block form,* all parts begin at the left margin except the return address (if typed in), date, complimentary close, and typed name and signature. The bad news letter in 4-7 is typed in modified block form. These parts begin near the center of the page. A variation of this form is the modified block with paragraphs indented.

Another factor that influences the appearance of a letter are the margins (white space around a letter). A letter needs top, side, and bottom margins. The top margin is usually formed by the company's letterhead. The left and right margins should be equal in width. Most side margins range from 1 1/4 inches for long letters to 2 1/4 inches for short letters. The width of the bottom margin depends on the length of the letter. The longer the letter, the narrower the bottom margin will be. However, the width should never be less than 1 1/4 inches.

The placement of letter parts is also important. If the return address is typed in, it is usually placed on line 12 with the date typed directly below it. On letterhead stationery, the date should be typed about two lines below the last line of the company letterhead, which is usually line 14. The inside address is placed two to eight lines below the date, depending on the length of the letter. The shorter the letter, the more lines you should leave between the date and the inside address. The salutation is typed two lines below the inside address. The body of the letter begins two lines below the salutation. It is typed single-space, with double spacing between paragraphs. The complimentary close is typed two lines below the last line of the body. Your typed name and business title should appear about four lines below the complimentary close. And the reference initials should be typed two lines below your name and business title.

Most business letters are typed on white or off-white typing paper, 8 1/2 x 11. They should appear neat and clean with no smudges or finger prints.

MEMOS

When you want to send a written message to someone at work, you don't send a business letter, you send a memorandum. A *memorandum* or memo is an informal written message from one person or department to another person, persons, or department in the same company. It may be a short note to remind others of a coming event or to explain a new company regulation. Memos are usually short messages because they usually deal with only one subject. Therefore, they tend to be fast and easy to write.

Parts of a memo

The standard parts of a memo are: date, to, from, subject, and body. Each part is described below and shown in 4-9.

Date. The date tells the reader when the memo was written. It can be written out as November 10, 198X or abbreviated as 11/10/8X. The abbreviated date is more informal. The style to use depends on the situation and your company's style.

To. After "To:" you type the person, persons, or department to whom the memo is written. If you work closely with the person, you may use just their first name or nickname. For example, you may just type "To: Jennifer." However, you may need to refer to your reader by title and position if the reader is a superior, if you don't know the reader very well, or if the memo needs to be filed as a record. In these situations, it may be best to type "To: Ms. Jennifer Jones" or "To: Jennifer Jones, Personnel Manager."

From. After "From:" you type your name or the person or department sending the memo. Whether you use your first name only, your first and last name, or your first and last name and your business title depends on the situation. In more formal situations, type your first and last name and your business title.

Subject. After this heading, you state the purpose or the content of the memo in a few words. For example, suppose you're writing a memo to the business department to request certain office supplies. The subject of your memo might read "Office supplies needed."

Body. The body of the memo contains the message. The same general guidelines that apply to writing business letters also apply to memos.

Appearance of a memo

Many businesses have a special type of stationery they use for typing memos. The stationery may have the words "Office Memorandum" and the company's name printed across the top of the page. Along the left margin may be printed: Date, To, From, Subject, and sometimes Message.

If your company does not have memo stationery, regular typing paper can be used.

DEPARTMENT OF INDUSTRIAL TECHNOLOGY

MEMO

DATE: October 22, 19___

TO: Jim Jenkins, Director
               Warehouse Chemical Stores

FROM: Joe Larks, Foreman
               Production Lab - Room 30

SUBJECT: Sulfuric Acid . . . RUSH!

We are on the last bottle of acid today. Please send 20 gallons of concentrated sulfuric acid to our department by 10:00 a.m. tomorrow.   Thanks!

4-9 Memos are usually short, informal messages that deal with one subject.

Although there are no set guidelines for typing memos, here are some tips for memo placement. The words DATE, TO, FROM, and SUBJECT should be typed flush with the left margin in all capitals and followed by colons. There should be double-spacing between each heading. The body of the memo should begin a double or triple-space under the subject line, regardless of the length of the message. It is usually typed single-space.

BUSINESS REPORTS

Business reports are written to account for work that has been done, to present a new idea, or to explain a problem that needs action. They are usually written to help the receiver understand a significant business situation, solve a business problem, or make executive decisions. Business reports are commonly classified as formal and informal.

Formal reports are usually long and about complex problems. They include certain parts such as a cover, a title page, a table of contents, an introduction, the body, a summary, and a bibliography. They often include graphs, tables, and illustrations to explain specific points.

Informal reports are generally short and usually include only the body, like the body of a letter or a memo. Sales reports, work progress reports, laboratory reports, and reports of business calls are examples of informal reports. They are often typed on company reporting forms.

As with letters and memos, you will need to plan what you want to write in a report before you begin writing. First, define the purpose. Why are you writing the report? What do you need to tell the receiver? Second, consider who will receive the report. Who wants or needs the report? How much detail will they prefer? Third, determine what ideas to include. What points will you need to cover to accomplish the report's purpose?

When preparing any report, write clearly, concisely, and accurately. Present the facts objectively. This means you should make sure you don't let your personal feelings toward the subject influence what you write about it.

to Review

1. Why is good communication so important in the working world?
2. What is the difference between hearing and listening?
3. When do people often fail to listen to what is being said?
4. Name five guidelines that are important to follow when speaking to others.
5. What is the proper way to handle a business call?
6. What information should you write down when taking a telephone message?
7. What is an easy rule to follow to help you deliver a good speech?
8. Why should you practice before giving a speech?
9. How do most businesses communicate in writing?
10. What are the three main reasons for writing business letters?
11. Name four examples of good news and neutral message letters.
12. How does writing a good news letter differ from writing a bad news letter?
13. Why is it important to word bad news letters so carefully?
14. What is a memorandum? When would you send a memorandum instead of a business letter?
15. What is the purpose of a business report?

to Discuss

1. On a scale from one to ten with ten being the highest, how would you rate your listening skills? What can you do to become a better listener?
2. Why is it possible to talk to someone but not communicate?
3. How should you end a business call? Why?
4. Name some of the occupations that require some public speaking. Is your future occupation one of them?
5. How do you feel about speaking in front of others? Do you get nervous before giving a speech?
6. What things can you do to help you deliver a good speech?
7. Why are good writing skills important skills to have in the working world?
8. Why is it sometimes best to send a business letter instead of telephone?
9. How does the appearance of a business letter differ from the appearance of a memo?
10. Before you begin writing a business letter, memorandum, or business report, what do you need to do first?

to Do

1. Practice your listening and speaking skills by having a conversation with another classmate about any topic. When one person is speaking, the other listens. Neither person may respond to any statement without first summarizing what the other person has said. Incorrect summaries must be clarified before the conversation continues.
2. Demonstrate the correct way to:
   a. Answer the telephone at work.
   b. Take a telephone message.
   c. Place a telephone order for company supplies.
3. Prepare a three to five minute speech on how to give a speech and present it to the class.
4. Write a business letter to a manufacturing company requesting information on a new product that your company might be interested in buying.
5. You go to work on Monday morning and discover that one of the company's machines is broken. Your supervisor asks you to send a memorandum to the maintenance department requesting the repair of the machine. Write the memo.

WENDY'S

Being able to operate a cash register is an
important skill to have for many jobs.

5

Math skills

After studying this chapter, you will be able to:

- ☐ Perform basic math operations and figure percentages.
- ☐ Operate a calculator properly.
- ☐ Explain how to count change correctly.
- ☐ Explain the difference between gross pay and net pay, and describe the deductions that may be made from your paycheck.
- ☐ Describe how to take inventory and order supplies.
- ☐ Measure accurately with a ruler.
- ☐ Explain how to measure in metrics and make metric and conventional conversions.

Some people think that math is just a course taught in school or a function performed by calculators and computers. However, the principles of math are used by people at home, work, and school every day. Many small tasks such as figuring sales tax, understanding your paycheck, making change, and measuring distances require basic math skills. Also a computer or calculator can do nothing without a person who knows how to program or operate it correctly.

To be successful on and off the job, you need to be able to master basic math skills. You also need to understand the metric system of measurement.

BASIC MATH OPERATIONS

The four basic math operations are: addition, subtraction, multiplication, and division. Each operation can be expressed and written in various ways.

Addition is the process of combining two or more numbers to find out the total number. The total number is called the *sum* or *total*. The plus sign (+) is used to indicate that numbers are to be added. Numbers to be added may be written:

$$6 + 8 + 2 + 4 = 20 \text{ or } \begin{array}{r} 6 \\ 8 \\ 2 \\ +4 \\ \hline 20 \end{array} \text{ (sum)}$$

Subtraction is the process of taking away one number from another number. The difference between the two numbers is called the *remainder* or *difference*. The minus sign ($-$) is used to indicate that one number is to be subtracted from the other. Numbers to be subtracted may be written:

$$984 - 231 = 753 \text{ or } \begin{array}{r} 984 \\ -231 \\ \hline 753 \end{array} \text{ (remainder)}$$

Multiplication is a short-cut method of adding the same number over and over again. For example, instead of adding $76 + 76 + 76 + 76 + 76 + 76 + 76 + 76 + 76 + 76 + 76$ to get the number 836, you can multiply 76 by 11 and get the same number. In multiplication, the answer is called the *product*.

The times sign is used to indicate that two numbers are to be multiplied. Numbers to be multiplied may be written:

$$76 \times 11 = 836 \text{ or } \begin{array}{r} 76 \\ \times 11 \\ \hline 76 \\ 76 \\ \hline 836 \end{array} \text{ (product)}$$

Division is the operation used to find out how many times one number is contained in another number. For example, to find out how many times 22 is contained in 682, you divide 682 by 22. The answer (31) is called the *quotient*. If a number does not divide evenly into the other number, the amount left over is called the *remainder*.

The divide sign ($\div$) is used to indicate that one number is to be divided into another. Numbers to be divided may be written one of three ways:

$$682 \div 22 = 31 \text{ or } \begin{array}{r} 31 \text{ (quotient)} \\ 22\overline{\smash{)}682} \\ \underline{66} \\ 22 \\ \underline{22} \\ 0 \end{array}$$

$$\text{or } \frac{682}{22} = 31$$

Working with fractions and decimals

A fraction is one or more parts of a whole number, 5-1. Fractions are written with one number over or beside the other:

$$\frac{1}{3} \text{ or } 1/3 \qquad \frac{13}{15} \text{ or } 13/15 \qquad \frac{5}{9} \text{ or } 5/9$$

The number below or after the line in a fraction is called the denominator. The *denominator* is the number of parts the fraction is divided. The number written above or before the line is the numerator. The *numerator* is the number of parts present in the fraction.

$$\frac{4}{5} \quad \begin{array}{l} \text{numerator} \\ \text{denominator} \end{array}$$

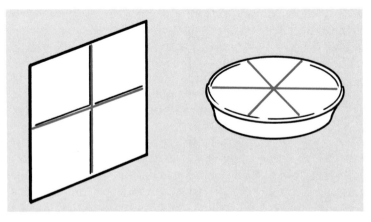

5-1 Shown at left is a window with four equal-sized panes and a pie cut into six equal pieces. One window pane would be 1/4 of the window. One piece of pie would be 1/6 of the pie.

When reading a fraction, you always read the numerator first, then the denominator. The fraction 4/5 is read four fifths.

A decimal fraction is a fraction with a denominator of 10 or multiple of 10 such as 100, 1000, and 10,000. When writing a decimal fraction, you omit the denominator and place a dot, called a decimal point, in front of the numerator. Therefore, the fraction 7/10 becomes .7 as a decimal fraction. Both are read the same, seven tenths.

The number of numbers to the right of the decimal point lets you know what multiple of 10 the denominator is. When there is one number to the right of the decimal point, the decimal is read as tenths. Two numbers to the right of the decimal point are read as hundredths. Three numbers to the right of the decimal point are thousandths; four numbers are ten thousandths.

.7	7/10	seven tenths
.07	7/100	seven hundredths
.007	7/1000	seven thousandths
.0007	7/10,000	seven ten thousandths

Decimal fractions are usually easier to work with than common fractions, and they are used in many ways. They are used to figure sales tax, measure the amount of fuel pumped at service stations, and calculate the number of miles you travel. Decimals are also used in our money system to separate dollars from cents. Can you think of other ways decimals are used?

Since decimals are easier to write and compute than fractions, fractions are often changed into decimals to figure math problems. To change a fraction into a decimal, you divide the denominator into the numerator. Therefore, to change 5/8 into a decimal you would divide 5 by 8.

$$
\begin{array}{r}
.625 \\
8\overline{)5.000} \\
\underline{4\,8} \\
20 \\
\underline{16} \\
40 \\
\underline{40}
\end{array}
$$

When changing a fraction to a decimal, the number of decimal places in the quotient must be the same as the number of zeros you add to the numerator. If the division does not come out even, you carry it out as many decimal places as needed for the answer. Carrying the division to four or five decimal places is usually the most you would ever need.

Figuring percentages

The term percentage is used every day in business and industry. A percentage is an easy way to express a decimal fraction. Instead of saying all men's suits are reduced .30, most people would say all men's suits are reduced 30%. Sales taxes, interest on bank accounts and loans, discount sales, and comparisons are all expressed as percentages, 5-2.

5-2 A discount sale is one of the many things expressed as a percentage.

A percentage is a part of a hundred. One percent of a number is 1/100 part of the number. Two percent of a number is 2/100 parts of the number. Thirty-six percent of a number is 36/100 parts of the number.

To find 1% of a number, you multiply .01 or 1/100 times the number. For example, to find 1% of 225, you multiply .01 times 225. The answer is 2.25.

$$\begin{array}{r} 225 \\ \times\ .01 \\ \hline 225 \\ 000 \\ \hline 2.25 \end{array}$$

Now try this problem. How much sales tax would you pay for a $7.00 book if the sales tax rate is 5%? To find 5% of $7.00 you would multiply $7.00 by .05.

$$\begin{array}{r} \$7.00 \\ \times\ .05 \\ \hline 3500 \\ 000 \\ \hline \$\ .3500 \end{array}$$

You should come up with the answer .35. Therefore, you would pay 35 cents in sales tax.

But, what if the $7.00 book is on sale at a 15% discount? What would be the price of the book? How much sales tax would you have to pay at the discounted price? To find the price of the book, you multiply $7.00 by .15 and subtract that amount from $7.00.

$$\begin{array}{r} \$7.00 \\ \times\ .15 \\ \hline 3500 \\ 700 \\ \hline \$1.0500\ \text{(the 15\%} \\ \text{discount)} \end{array} \qquad \begin{array}{r} \$7.00 \\ -1.05 \\ \hline \$5.95\ \text{(the discount} \\ \text{price)} \end{array}$$

To figure the sales tax, you multiply $5.95 by .05. The amount of sales tax would be 30 cents. Therefore, the total cost of the book would be $6.25.

$$\begin{array}{r} \$5.95 \\ \times\ \ .05 \\ \hline 2975 \\ 000 \\ \hline \$\ .2975\ \text{or .30 (sales} \\ \text{tax)} \end{array} \qquad \begin{array}{r} \$5.95 \\ +\ .30 \\ \hline \$6.25\ \text{(discount} \\ \text{price plus} \\ \text{tax)} \end{array}$$

USING A CALCULATOR

An instrument that can help you solve math problems more quickly is the calculator. It can add, subtract, multiply, and divide as well as perform other math operations. A pocket calculator is inexpensive and easy to learn how to use, 5-3.

To operate a calculator properly, you need to be able to enter information and instructions into it correctly. You enter information by pressing certain numbers and symbols on the keyboard. The information you enter appears above the keyboard in the display box.

Here are the most common symbols you will find on a calculator and the function each performs.

C	key	Clears calculator.
CE	key	Clears last entry.
•	key	Enters the decimal point.
+	key	Adds.
−	key	Subtracts.
×	key	Multiplies.
÷	key	Divides.
%	key	Gives the percentage.
=	key	Provides the answer.

Are you ready to try some problems? Get a calculator. Turn the switch to "on." Then follow the steps below to add, subtract, multiply, and divide 63 and 21

Addition
To add 63 and 21:
1. Enter 63 by pressing the 6 and then the 3. The number 63 should then appear on display.
2. Press the (+) key.
3. Enter 21 by pressing the 2 and the 1. Now the number 21 should appear on display.
4. Press the (=) key. Look for the sum on display. It should be the number 84.

Try adding these problems, and see if you come up with the right answers. Remember, you must press the add sign (+) before entering the second number.

792	1934	7317	639
+136	+ 928	+1834	354
928	2862	9151	+417
			1410

Subtraction

To subtract 21 from 63:

1. Enter 63.
2. Press the ($-$) key.
3. Enter 21.
4. Press the ($=$) key. The remainder should be 42.

Now try these subtraction problems. You should come up with the answers below. Remember, you must press the minus sign ($-$) before entering the second number.

967	4315	2398	$73.46
-238	$- 876$	-1993	$- 19.99$
729	3439	405	$53.47

Multiplication

To multiply 63 by 21:

1. Enter 63.
2. Press the ($\times$) key.
3. Enter 21.
4. Press the ($=$) key. The product should be 1323.

Here are some multiplication problems to work. Do you come up with the same answers? Remember, you must press the times sign ($\times$) before entering the second number.

12	692	7846	439.5
$\times 13$	$\times 34$	$\times 622$	$\times 548.2$
156	23,528	4,880,212	240,933.9

Division

To divide 63 by 21:

1. Enter 63.
2. Press the ($\div$) key.
3. Enter 21.
4. Press the ($=$) key. The quotient should be 3.

Try these division problems. Your answers should match the ones below. Remember, you must press the divide sign ($\div$) before entering the second number.

$$7/\overline{19} = 2.71$$
$$722 \div 4 = 180.5$$
$$9490 \div 36 = 263.61$$

5-3 Many students use calculators to help them solve math problems more easily and quickly.

COUNTING CHANGE

For some jobs, workers have the responsibility of using a cash register and counting change. Whether you make change on your job or receive change when you buy goods and services, you need to know how to count change accurately.

Here is one way to make change. Count out the change by adding the change to the purchase price until it equals the amount of money given. For example, suppose you are given a $10 bill for a $2.36 purchase. You would say, "Two dollars and thirty-six cents from $10, your change is:

2.40," (Hand back four pennies.)
2.50," (Hand back one dime.)
2.75, 3.00," (Hand back two quarters.)
4.00, 5.00," (Hand back two $1.00 bills.)
10.00." (Hand back one $5.00 bill.)

The total amount of change you should hand back is $7.64.

Another way to count change is to state the amount of change due and count back the change beginning with the largest bill or coin. This has become a more common way to count change since many cash registers automatically figure the change for the cashier. Using the same example above, the cashier would say, "Seven dollars and sixty-four cents is your change:

Five," (Hand back one $5.00 bill.)
Six, seven," (Hand back two $1.00 bills.)
25, 50," (Hand back two quarters.)
60," (Hand back one dime.)
Four." (Hand back four pennies.)

UNDERSTANDING YOUR PAYCHECK

Your first pay day finally arrives. You have worked 40 hours for the week. You are to earn $4.00 per hour. What will your pay be? You might expect to be paid $160.00 since 40 × $4.00 = $160.00. However, $160.00 would be your gross pay, not the amount of your paycheck.

Gross pay is the total amount you earn for a pay period before any deductions are subtracted from your paycheck. The actual amount of pay you receive is called net pay or take-home pay. *Net pay* is gross pay minus deductions. How much money is deducted from your gross pay? At least two deductions are made by your employer — social security tax and federal income tax.

When you begin a job, your employer will ask you to fill out a *W-4 Form*. This form is called the Employer's Withholding Allowance Certificate, 5-4. It tells your employer how much tax to withhold from your paycheck. The amount of social security tax withheld is a set percentage of your income. The amount of federal income tax withheld depends on how much you earn and the number of exemptions you are allowed. An *exemption* is a source or an amount of income on which you do not have to pay tax. Every taxpayer can take a $1000 personal exemption. This means you do not have to pay tax on $1000 of your income. Additional exemptions can be claimed for people over 65, for a spouse, and for dependents.

On your paycheck, the amount of social security tax withheld appears under "social security" or "FICA." FICA stands for the Federal Insurance Contributions Act which began the social security tax. The amount of federal income tax deducted will appear under "federal tax."

Other deductions may be withheld from your paycheck. If your state has a state income tax, that too will be deducted. Like social security and federal income taxes, state income taxes are usually based on a percentage of your income and the number of exemptions you have. If your company has a retirement plan, a certain amount from each paycheck may be contributed to a retirement fund for you and matched with company funds. With your permission, other deductions such as insurance premiums and union dues may also be withheld from your paycheck.

In 5-5 is a check stub which shows the deductions for a weekly gross pay of $160.00. After deductions were made for state, federal, and social security taxes, the net pay came to $128.48. What percentage of $160.00 was deducted for taxes? To find this answer, add the three deductions together and divide the total by $160.00. The answer would be 19.7%.

Form **W-4** (Rev. January 1983)	Department of the Treasury—Internal Revenue Service **Employee's Withholding Allowance Certificate**	OMB No. 1545–0010 Expires 8–31–85

1 Type or print your full name	2 Your social security number

Home address (number and street or rural route)	3 Marital Status	☐ Single ☐ Married ☐ Married, but withhold at higher Single rate **Note:** If married, but legally separated, or spouse is a nonresident alien, check the **Single** box.

City or town, State, and ZIP code

4 Total number of allowances you are claiming (from line F of the worksheet on page 2) . . . .

5 Additional amount, if any, you want deducted from each pay . . . . $

6 I claim exemption from withholding because (see instructions and check boxes below that apply):

  a ☐ Last year I did not owe any Federal income tax and had a right to a full refund of **ALL** income tax withheld, **AND**

  b ☐ This year I do not expect to owe any Federal income tax and expect to have a right to a full refund of   Year

    ALL income tax withheld. If both a and b apply, enter the year effective and "EXEMPT" here . . ▶

  c If you entered "EXEMPT" on line 6b, are you a full-time student? . . . . ☐ Yes ☐ No

Under the penalties of perjury, I certify that I am entitled to the number of withholding allowances claimed on this certificate, or if claiming exemption from withholding, that I am entitled to claim the exempt status.

Employee's signature ▶ _____   Date ▶ _____ , 19____

7 Employer's name and address (Employer: Complete 7, 8, and 9 only if sending to IRS)	8 Office code	9 Employer identification number

5-4 An employee must fill out a W-4 Form when he or she begins working for an employer.

TOTAL HOURS	YOU EARNED AND WE PAID →			TOTAL	WE PAID OUT THESE AMOUNTS FOR YOU						NET AMOUNT	PERIOD ENDING
	REGULAR	OVERTIME			F.I.C.A.	FEDERAL WH/TAX	STATE WH/TAX					
40	160 00			160 00	10 72	16 00	4 80				128 48	6/10

EMPLOYEE'S STATEMENT OF EARNINGS AND DEDUCTIONS. RETAIN.

The Goodheart - Willcox Company, Inc.   South Holland, ILL.   60473

5-5 This check stub shows the deductions made for state, federal, and social security taxes from a weekly gross pay of $160.00.

```
$ 4.80 state tax              .197  (19.7%)
 16.00 federal tax     160/31.520
 10.72 FICA                 16 0
$31.52                      15 52
                            14 40
                             1 120
                             1 120
                               00
```

Now figure what percentage of $160.00 was deducted for each tax. To do this, divide each tax amount by $160. Are you surprised to find such a large percentage of your income is deducted for taxes?

```
            .03  (3% for
   160/4.80   state taxes)
      0 0
      4 80
      4 80
        00
```

```
            .10  (10% for
  160/16.00   federal taxes)
     16 0
       00
       00
       00
```

```
            .067  (6.7% for
  160/10.720    FICA)
     00 0
     10 72
      9 60
      1 120
      1 120
        00
```

TAKING INVENTORY AND ORDERING SUPPLIES

"What are you going to do at work today?" asked John.

"Take inventory," replied Sue.

John looked puzzled, "What's inventory?"

Sue answered, "Well, when we take inventory at our store, it means we count everything that is for sale. That includes everything on the store shelves and in the storeroom. After inventory, the manager decides which merchandise items to order so the store will be stocked for next week's customers."

Every business has some form of inventory. Why have inventories? Inventories are a way of keeping track of goods and supplies. Without inventories, a store would probably run out of the goods wanted by consumers. A factory would run out of the supplies needed for production.

Stock refers to the goods and supplies that are available and ready for immediate use or sale. *Inventory control* is the process of keeping up-to-date records of how many goods and supplies are in stock, how many have been ordered and received, and how many have been sold. Inventory is usually taken on a regular basis such as once a month. Some companies use inventory control sheets to record inventories, but more and more companies are using computers to help them do the job more efficiently, 5-6.

In the retail store where Sue works, inventory is kept on each item in every department of the store. This enables the store to know what supplies are in stock and what supplies need to be ordered. Sue works in the department where nurses' uniforms are sold. One of her job responsibilities is filling out an inventory control sheet for nurses' caps as shown in 5-7. On the control sheet, Sue records the number of small, medium, and large caps in stock at the first of the month, the number ordered the first of the month, the number received during the month, and the total number sold for the month. Keeping an inventory control sheet helps Sue decide how many caps to order at the beginning of each month.

Before filling out an order form for caps, Sue reviews the number of caps ordered and sold over the previous months. She notes that on the average 8 small caps, 15 medium caps, and 4 large caps were sold each month. With 22 small caps in stock and only 7 sold the previous month, Sue decides not to order any small caps for April. With only 8 medium caps in stock and 15 medium caps sold the previous month, she orders two dozen of the medium size. (Sue can only order caps in units of 12.) With 2 large

GENERAL ELECTRIC

5-6 Many companies use a computer for inventory purposes.

Supplier: Uniform Sales, Inc. P.O. Box 2191 Chicago, IL 65000			Item ___Nurses' caps___ Number: 6023 Units of: 12 (1 doz.)		
Month	Sizes	In stock 1st of month	Number ordered 1st of month	Number rec'd. during month	Number sold
January	S	11	12	12	8
	M	5	24	24	16
	L	15	0	0	3
February	S	15	12	0	10
	M	13	12	12	10
	L	12	0	0	5
March	S	5	12	24	7
	M	15	12	12	19
	L	7	12	0	5
April	S	22			
	M	8			
	L	2			

5-7 Inventory control sheets help a store or company know what supplies are in stock and what supplies need to be ordered.

caps in stock and only four caps sold the previous month, Sue orders just one dozen of the large size. In 5-8 is the purchase order Sue submitted for April.

After Sue writes the order, she sends the original copy to the supplier and keeps a carbon copy for the store's files. If the store has any problem with the order, Sue can pull out her copy of the order, call the supplier, and refer to the order number. The order number is printed in the upper right hand corner of every order form. For example, suppose there was a problem with the order Sue just prepared. She would call the supplier, Uniform Sales, and say, "My name is Sue Smith from Mr. T's Retail Store. I'm calling in reference to order number 545." Then the supplier could quickly locate the order and help solve the problem.

Why wouldn't it just be better for the store to order 12 dozen of each cap size about once a year? If the store did this for every item, imagine how much money it would need to buy such large supplies. Think of the extra space the store would need for storage. And think of what would happen if new products were manufactured that customers would rather buy instead of the items the company has in stock? The company would be stuck with a lot of merchandise it couldn't sell. With these disadvantages and variables, most companies find it best to order merchandise and supplies every month or every few months.

MEASURING DISTANCES

"How far is far?"

"I don't know, but it is farther than near."

"Well then, how far is near?"

"It is closer than far, but it doesn't touch here."

When you say something is near or far away, you are expressing a form of measurement, although it is not a very accurate form. If you say something is six feet away, you are expressing a precise measurement of distance. Distance is measured in inches, feet, yards, and miles. In many skilled and unskilled jobs, you may be asked to measure distances. Being able to

ORDER FORM   Order No. 545

SUPPLIER: Uniform Sales, Inc.   PURCHASER: Mr. T's Retail Store
          P.O. Box 2191   3568 W. Moline
          Chicago, IL 65000   Lincoln, NE 68510

Quantity	Description	Unit Price	Total Price
2 doz.	Nurses' caps, 6023 M	$39.00	$ 78.00
1 doz.	Nurses' caps, 6023 L	39.60	39.60
			$117.60

5-8 A purchase order is a typed order for supplies that is sent to a supplier.

measure distances is a math skill everyone needs to have.

Some of the tools used to measure distances include rulers, yardsticks, measuring tapes, carpenter's squares, and micrometers. However, the ruler is the basic measuring tool.

A ruler is divided into equal parts or inches. Each inch is divided into equal fractional units—halves (1/2), quarters (1/4), eighths (1/8), and sixteenths (1/16). Some rulers have inches that are divided into fractions as small as thirty seconds (1/32) and sixty fourths (1/64).

The drawing in 5-9 (size has been enlarged) shows an inch divided into halves, fourths, eighths, and sixteenths. Note that the one inch line is the longest. The 1/2 inch line is next in length, then the 1/4 inch line and the 1/8 inch line. The 1/16 inch line is the shortest.

When measuring, it is usually best to measure to the smallest fraction on the ruler you are using. Most rulers are divided into sixteenths. Unless you need to make extremely precise measurements, measuring to within 1/16 of an inch is acceptable. Another point to remember—fractional measurements are always reduced to lowest terms. For example, a measurement of 12/16 should be read as 3/4, 4/16 should be read as 1/4, and 2/4 should be read as 1/2.

The best way to become accurate at measuring is to practice! Begin now by measuring the three lines below with a ruler.

a. _____

b. _____

c. _____

You should get the following measurements: a. 2 7/16, b. 1 1/4, and c. 2 5/8.

THE METRIC SYSTEM

To measure distance, weight, volume, and temperature, European countries and many other countries use the metric system of measurement. They use the meter to measure distance, the gram to measure weight, the liter to measure volume, and the degree Celsius to measure temperature. Although the United States has talked a great deal about converting to the metric system, it still uses the conventional system of measurement. Inches, feet, yards, and miles are used to measure distance. Ounces and pounds are used to measure weights. Pints, quarts, and gallons are used to measure volume, and degree Fahrenheit is used to measure temperature. However, many U.S. manufacturers use the metric system in order to compete in the world market. Speedometers on U.S. cars show kilometers per hour as well

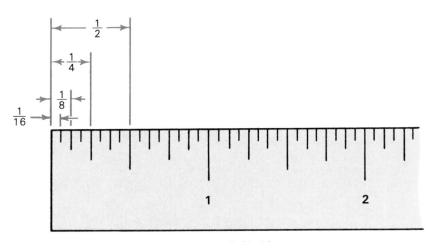

5-9 On most rulers, inches are divided into halves, fourths, eighths, and sixteenths.

as miles per hour. U.S. manufactures 35 millimeter film for 35 millimeter cameras not 1.365 inch film for 1.365 inch cameras. Soda pop is bottled in liter bottles, not gallon bottles. Many businesses have also learned the metric system so they can repair and service foreign products.

Since metrics are a widely used system of measurements, you may work with metrics on the job. Therefore, you need to become familiar with the metric system and learn how to measure in metrics and make metric conversions.

How the system works

The metric system is based on a decimal system like our money system. This means metric units increase and decrease in size by 10s. To increase the amount, you move the decimal point one place to the right or multiply by 10. To decrease the amount, you move the decimal point one place to the left or divide by ten. For example, think about how you write one dollar ($1.00). If you move the decimal point one place to the right, you increase the amount 10 times and make it ten dollars ($10.00). Move the decimal point one more place to the right,

and you have one hundred dollars ($100.00). This is ten times more than $10.00. Any metric unit works the same way. In 5-10 you can see how dollars and meters are similar.

The metric system has seven basic units. Four of these units are used in our daily lives: meter, gram, liter, and degree Celsius. The other three are used by scientists, mathematicians, and engineers. In the metric system, one of six prefixes can be added to a meter, gram, or liter to show its level of value, 5-11. Deci, centi, and milli can be added to identify smaller measurements. Deka, hecto, and kilo can be added to identify larger measurements. The most commonly used prefixes are milli, centi, and kilo.

Meter. The meter is used to measure distance or length. A meter (m) is just a little longer than one yard. It is used to measure the dimensions of a room, the length of a race track, and fabric lengths. A kilometer (km) is just over a half mile, or 5/8 of a mile. It is used to measure the distance between cities and the altitude of a plane. A centimeter (cm) is about the length of one half inch. Body measures, such as chest, waist, and hip measurements are given in centimeters. One millimeter (mm) is about the thickness of a dime. It is used to measure short

OUR MONEY SYSTEM COMPARED TO THE METRIC SYSTEM

DOLLARS		METERS	
$1000.00	1000	1000 m	1 kilometer — km
100.00	100	100.0 m	1 hectometer — hm
10.00	10	10.00 m	1 dekameter — dam
1.00	1	1.000 m	1 meter — m
.10	1/10	.1000 m	1 decimeter — dm
.01	1/100	.0100 m	1 centimeter — cm
.001	1/1000	.0010 m	1 millimeter — mm

5-10 The metric system is similar to our money system because they are both based on a decimal system. Here, dollars are compared to meters.

lengths such as camera film and small hardware.

Gram. The gram is the metric unit used to measure weight or mass. One gram (g) is a very small weight, much smaller than one ounce. A United States dollar bill weighs about one gram. The gram is used to measure small amounts such as the weight of small cans of food and spices. A kilogram (kg) is about 2.2 pounds (35 ounces). Body weight and freight weights are figured in kilograms. Very, very small things such as a grain of sand or minute portions of chemical substances are measured in centigrams (cm) or milligrams (mg).

Liter. The liter is used to measure volume. A liter (L) is a little more than a quart. Gasoline and motor oil are sold by the liter, so are bottles of soft drinks and cartons of milk. Large tanks of liquids are measured in kiloliters (kl). Volumes less than a liter such as paint, cooking oil, and recipe ingredients are usually measured in milliliters (ml).

Degree Celsius. The degree Celsius (deg. C) is the metric unit used to measure temperature. One degree Celsius is a little more than two degrees Fahrenheit.

Water freezes at 0 deg. C instead of 32 deg. F, and water boils at 100 deg. C instead of 212 deg. F. A comfortable room temperature is about 20 deg. C, and a warm, sunny day is about 25 deg. C. Normal body temperature is 37 deg. C instead of 98.6 deg. F.

Making conversions

The best way to learn the metric system is to "think metric." This means learning to measure in metric and not measuring by the conventional system and changing to metric. However, there may be times when you may need to change a conventional measure to a metric measure or vice versa. This is called making conversions. Chart 5-12 shows you how to make conventional and metric conversions. To use the chart, look up the conventional or metric unit you know in the left column and multiply it by the number given. Your answer will be approximately the number of units in the right column.

Suppose you needed to find out how many meters are in 15 yards of fabric. According to the chart, you would multiply 15 by 0.9144 to find the number of meters in 15 yards. The answer would be 13.716 meters.

UNITS OF MEASURE IN THE METRIC SYSTEM

PREFIX	NUMBER	DISTANCE	WEIGHT	VOLUME
kilo	1000	kilometer (km)	kilogram (kg)	kiloliter (kl)
hecto	100	hectometer (hm)	hectogram (hg)	hectoliter (hl)
deka	10	dekameter (dam)	dekagram (dag)	dekaliter (dal)
	1	meter (m)	gram (g)	liter (L)
deci	.1	decimeter (dm)	decigram (dg)	decaliter (dl)
centi	.01	centimeter (cm)	centigram (cg)	centiliter (cl)
milli	.001	millimeter (mm)	milligram (mg)	milliliter (ml)

5-11 The six prefixes indicate different levels of value.

MAKING CONVERSIONS

CONVENTIONAL TO METRIC

WHEN YOU KNOW	MULTIPLY BY	TO FIND
Distance		
inches	25.40	millimeters
inches	2.54	centimeters
feet	0.3048	meters
yards	0.9144	meters
miles	1.6093	kilometers
Weight		
ounces	28.350	grams
pounds	454.00	grams
pounds	0.454	kilograms
Volume		
ounces	29.573	milliliters
pints	0.473	liters
quarts	0.946	liters
gallons	3.785	liters
Temperature		
Fahrenheit	5/9 (after subtracting 32)	Celsius

METRIC TO CONVENTIONAL

WHEN YOU KNOW	MULTIPLY BY	TO FIND
Distance		
millimeters	0.039	inches
centimeters	0.394	inches
meters	3.2808	feet
meters	1.0936	yards
kilometers	0.6214	miles
Weight		
grams	0.035	ounces
grams	0.002	pounds
kilograms	2.2	pounds
Volume		
milliliters	0.034	ounces
liters	2.1	pints
liters	1.056	quarts
liters	0.264	gallons
Temperature		
Celsius	9/5 (then add 32)	Fahrenheit

5-12 This chart can help you convert conventional measures to metric measures and metric measures to conventional measures.

to Review

1. What are the four basic math operations?
2. How do you read a fraction? How would you read the fraction 9/16 and the decimal fraction .9?
3. How do you write 8/100 as a decimal fraction?
4. How are decimal fractions used?
5. How do you change a fraction into a decimal?
6. What is a percentage? How do you find 6% of 40?
7. Explain how to make change when a purchase is made.
8. What is the difference between gross pay and net pay?
9. At least two deductions are made from an employee's paycheck. What are they? What other deductions may be withheld?
10. What is inventory control? Why is it important for businesses to take inventories?
11. What are the basic units of measure for distance, weight, volume, and temperature in the conventional system of measure? In the metric system?
12. Why do many U.S. manufacturers and businesses use the metric system or know how to use it?

to Discuss

1. Why is it important for everyone to learn basic math skills?
2. Does your state charge a sales tax on goods and services purchased? If yes, what percentage of each dollar is taxed?
3. Name some of the tasks at home and at work for which people use calculators.
4. Do you check to make sure you are given the correct change when you make a purchase? Why is it important to do so?
5. What deductions are made from your paychecks? What percentage of your gross pay is each deduction?
6. Why do most companies find it best to order merchandise and supplies every month or every few months instead of once a year?
7. Discuss the advantages and disadvantages of the metric system of measurement.
8. Do you think the U.S. should convert to the metric system? Why?

to Do

1. If you are given a $50 bill for a $21.15 purchase, how much change would you hand back to the customer? How would you count the change to the customer?
2. At the beginning of next month, Bob will receive a 10% raise. If his hourly wage is now $3.60, how much will his new wage per hour be? How much more money will he earn per eight-hour day? How much more money will he earn per 40-hour week?
3. Estimate the length and width of your cooperative education classroom in feet and inches and in meters. Then measure the two distances with a yardstick and meter stick. What were your estimated conventional and metric measurements? What were the actual conventional and metric measurements? Did you do better at estimating conventional measurements or metric measurements? What are the reasons for your answer?
4. With the help of a classmate, measure your height in centimeters.

Your personal appearance can
influence your success on the job.

6

Looking good on the job

After studying this chapter, you will be able to:

☐ Explain how your health habits, grooming habits, and clothes influence your appearance and influence the way other people see you.
☐ Describe the grooming habits you need to practice to stay neat and clean every day.
☐ Evaluate your wardrobe and make wise clothing selections for school, work, and other occasions.
☐ Evaluate the construction of clothes, the fabric used to make clothes, and the clothing care label when shopping for clothes.
☐ Care for clothes properly so they will look nicer and wear longer.

When you meet someone for the first time, what do you notice first? Most people notice a person's appearance. In fact, people tend to form first impressions about others based on their appearance. That includes employers. Many employers assume that people who take pride in their appearance are likely to take pride in their work as well.

Looking good on the job involves more than wearing the "right clothes." Your health and grooming habits, as well as your clothes, influence your appearance. What impressions do you think others form of your appearance? The impression you should want to make at work is, "I want to succeed at this job." You can do this by keeping yourself in good physical condition, keeping neat and clean, and dressing appropriately.

GOOD HEALTH

Looking good on the job begins with a healthy you. Good grooming and nice clothes will make very little difference if you're in poor physical health. That's because your health affects everything about you. It affects the way you look and feel.

To stay physically healthy, there are three guidelines you should follow. You need to eat well-balanced meals, get adequate sleep, and exercise regularly, 6-1. Following these guidelines will not only make you look more attractive, it will help you be more alert and productive on the job.

GOOD GROOMING

Good grooming is essential to getting and keeping a job. When it comes to good grooming, there are two words you need to remember—cleanliness and neatness. You need to be clean and neat from your head down to your toes, every day on the job.

Clean body

To help you stay clean, you need to bathe or shower and use a deodorant or antiperspirant every day. Everyone perspires, even in winter. When you perspire, bacteria act on the perspiration and cause body odor. Frequent bathing with soap and water removes the bacteria and the odor. However, you can't go around bathing all day. That's why it is important to use a deodorant or antiperspirant.

Both deodorants and antiperspirants help control body odor by interferring with the growth of bacteria. Antiperspirants also help reduce the flow of perspiration. A deodorant or antiperspirant should be applied after you bathe. You may want to use a roll-on, solid,

6-1 Bicycling is a fun exercise you can do with friends to help you stay physically healthy.

or aerosol—scented or unscented. Experiment to find out which brand will work best for you.

A smooth shave

To shave or not to shave is a decision both men and women have to make. Men need to decide if they want to shave their facial hair or to grow a mustache, beard, or both. Women need to decide if they want to shave their legs and underarms.

Some men want to have a mustache or beard. Yet there are some employers who object to facial hair, especially beards. They prefer the "clean shaven" look. These employers often think a clean shaven man gives a better impression of their company.

Whatever decision you make, the general rule is to be neat and clean. If you want the "clean shaven" look, keep your face neatly shaved. Don't go to work with a stubble on your face. For most men, this means they must shave every day. See 6-2. If you choose to have a beard or mustache, wash it regularly with a mild soap and keep it neatly combed and shaped. An unkempt beard or mustache will certainly give a sloppy appearance. Also be sure the style of beard or mustache you choose is becoming to your hairstyle and face shape.

Most young women in the United States choose to shave their legs and underarms because they think it gives a neater and more attractive appearance. Women who don't shave may be considered less concerned about their appearance or less attractive. Shaving under the arms also can help reduce perspiration odor.

The decision to shave or not to shave is

6-2 For the "clean shaven" look, most men must shave every day.

yours. Do whatever feels the most comfortable for you.

Healthy complexion

Sometimes your complexion can be the most difficult part of your body to keep looking good. That's because many young people often have problems with oily skin which contributes to skin problems such as pimples and acne. Regardless of the type of skin you have — normal, oily, dry, or a combination of oily and dry — you can keep it looking clean by caring for it properly.

Proper skin care begins with proper cleansing. All skin types should be cleansed regularly with warm, soapy water or a cleanser to keep the skin free of bacteria, dirt, and oils. After washing, people with oily skin may want to rinse with cold water or use an astringent. This will help shrink the skin pores and temporarily delay the skin from producing more oil. After rinsing, people with normal, dry, and combination skin may want to use a moisturizer or lotion to prevent dryness and chapping. If your skin is extremely oily and acne becomes a problem, you should see a dermatologist. A dermatologist is a doctor who specializes in treating skin. This type of specialist will be able to recommend the best cleansers and cosmetics for your skin. If your skin is very dry, you also may need special cleansers and moisturizers to help keep your skin soft and pliable.

Clean hair

The hair has often been called a person's "crowning glory" because it either enhances or distracts from a person's appearance. That's why it is so important to keep your hair clean and neatly styled. Hair care involves three major steps: shampooing, conditioning, and styling.

How often you should shampoo your hair depends on the type of hair you have. Dry hair may only need washing once a week. Oily hair may need shampooing daily. If you have a problem with dandruff or scalp infections, you may need to use a special type of shampoo and shampoo more often.

After a thorough shampoo and rinse, you may want to condition your hair. Conditioning can make hair look healthier and help it have more body.

Once hair is cleaned and conditioned, it needs to be styled. You should choose a style that will suit the texture of your hair, the shape and size of your face, and your life-style. For example, if your hair is very thin and limp, you may want to have it permed to add body and fullness. If you have a round face shape, you may want to choose a style that will add height to your face. If you are very active in sports, you may want to choose a hairstyle that will be super easy to maintain and that will not interfere with the sports you play.

A good hairstyle begins with a good haircut, 6-3. You may want to consult a hairstylist to help you choose the best style for you. Hairstylists are trained to analyze hair and facial features and to cut and style it accordingly. Whatever style you choose, make sure it is one you can care for easily.

Handsome hands

Since your hands are in sight most of the time, they are an important part of your appearance. You need to keep your hands and fingernails clean and manicured.

If your hands and nails get heavily soiled on the job, like a mechanic's, you may need to use a special soap to get them clean. A nail brush also can help you wash away dirt and oil from under and around the nails. After cleansing, dry each fingernail separately, pushing back the cuticles (skin around the nail) gently. To keep your cuticles and hands soft and pliable, you will probably need to use a cuticle conditioner or a hand lotion.

When your nails are completely dry, file and shape them with an emery board. A manicure once a week should keep your nails looking neat and well-groomed.

Fresh breath

Your mouth plays an important role in your appearance. Your mouth talks for you, eats for you, smiles for you, and frowns for you. Since the mouth draws a lot of attention, it needs to look attractive and have a pleasant odor.

Teeth are an important part of your mouth, your breath, and your smile. To help keep your teeth clean and healthy, your breath fresh, and your smile bright, you need to brush your teeth regularly. You also need to floss your teeth often and visit your dentist regularly, 6-4.

In addition to brushing, some people find it helpful to gargle with a mouthwash to avoid bad breath. You may want to try a mouthwash as well. Whatever insures good breath for you, do it daily! You don't want to be caught with bad breath on the job—especially if you work closely with others.

DRESSING FOR THE JOB

Many people feel they have a right to wear whatever they want to work. And they do have that right. However, employers also have the right to expect employees to dress appropriately for work. If an employee chooses not to dress

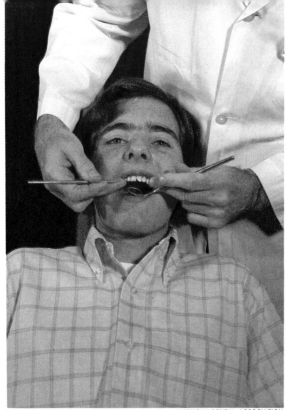

AMERICAN DENTAL ASSOCIATION

6-4 Regular checkups are an important part of dental care.

6-3 A good haircut will help you have nicely groomed hair.

appropriately, the employer can always hire another worker who will.

You'll be dressed right for the job if you wear clean clothes that are properly fitted and appropriate for the work you do. The question you may be asking is "What is appropriate?"

To help you decide what is appropriate to wear to work, think about the responsibilities you will have on the job. Will you be doing a lot of physical labor? Will you be handling food? Will you be working at a desk in an office?

If you are going to be doing physical work where you are likely to get dirty and greasy, you'll need clothes that are appropriate for those conditions, 6-5. For example, an auto mechanic needs tough clothes to withstand wear, tear, grease, and oil. Similar clothing is needed for service station workers, carpenters, plumbers, factory workers, farmers, and construction workers.

Outside workers need clothes that will protect them from rain, snow, cold, and the sun. Other workers may need to wear safety clothing such as a hard hat, safety shoes, eye goggles, or ear plugs. Outdoor and safety clothing are usually needed for miners, welders, chemists, brick masons, and some construction and factory workers.

For health reasons, hospital workers, food handlers, and dental assistants must take extra care to stay clean and wear clean clothes. Many of these workers wear uniforms or lab coats that can be cared for easily. Workers who handle food may also be required to wear hair nets to make sure no hair falls into the food.

Clothing choices become more important for office and business workers such as salespeople, receptionists, office clerks, and cashiers because these workers come in contact with the public. A company wants workers who will make a good impression on customers and the general public so they will form a good impression of the company.

In general, female office workers should wear nice slacks with a blouse or sweater or a skirt or dress with hose. Male workers should wear nice slacks; a shirt and tie, shirt and sweater, or a tieless shirt; and possibly a sports jacket. Workers should avoid inappropriate clothes such as tight pants, unbuttoned shirts, and miniskirts.

Another good way to help you decide what's best to wear is to observe what others wear to work. If most of the workers tend to dress conservatively, you may want to dress this way also. If many of the employees wear nice jeans to work, you may feel comfortable wearing jeans as well. If you're still in doubt about what's appropriate, ask your work supervisor or coordinator. He or she should be able to give you some good suggestions.

SELECTING CLOTHES FOR YOUR WARDROBE

Before each season of the year, you will need to take an inventory of your wardrobe. A *wardrobe inventory* is a list of all the clothes, shoes, and accessories you have for school, work, and all other occasions. Taking an inventory will help you clear out the clothes and accessories you no longer wear or need, 6-6. It will also help you decide what clothes you need to add to your wardrobe.

As you examine each wardrobe item, make a decision as to whether or not you will keep it, discard it, or replace it. Some garments you may have outgrown. Others may have gone out of style. Try on each garment to help you make your decisions. Some of the garments may only need a little altering to make them fit. Others may only need a new belt, tie, or scarf to update their style.

If you come across items you cannot or will not wear, clear them out of your wardrobe. If the clothes are still wearable, give them to an organization, charity, or resale shop so they can be passed along to others.

Once you've decided what you're going to keep and what you're going to discard, think about the items you'd like to replace or add to your wardrobe. Using your inventory, identify the gaps you need to fill. Then make a list of the items you need to fill those gaps.

Before you buy any new clothes or accessories, estimate the price of the items. Do a little window shopping, and price the items you need and want to buy. Window shopping will also give you an opportunity to study the new styles, fashions, and colors for the season.

Now figure out how much you have to spend for clothing. Compare that dollar figure with your estimated total for new clothes. If you can afford everything you want, great! If not, you'll need to reconsider the items on your list. Decide which items are most important, and buy those items first. Very few people have enough money to buy all the clothes they want. You will need to buy clothes according to what you and your family can afford.

One way to cut clothing costs is to bargain hunt. Try shopping at clothing warehouses, surplus shops, discount stores, and secondhand stores. Also, watch for sales at regular clothing stores. However, don't buy a great-looking sweater or shirt just because it's on sale at a really low price. A sale item will only be a good buy if it's an item you really need, if it will go well with the other clothes you have, and if it fits and looks nice on you.

6-5 This auto mechanic is dressed appropriately for his job.

6-6 At the start of each season, take a wardrobe inventory. Remove the items that you no longer wear and do not need.

Keep in mind that having a large wardrobe is not necessary to be well dressed. A small, well-chosen wardrobe can work very well for you. It's certainly better than a large assortment of clothes that do not mix and match. With careful planning and wise buying, you can have a well-rounded wardrobe that is stylish, colorful, and well-coordinated.

SHOPPING FOR CLOTHES

When shopping for clothes, there are three important factors you need to evaluate closely before buying:
- The construction of the garment.
- The fabric used to make the garment.
- The garment care label.

Clothing construction

The construction of garments, the way they are cut, sewn, and finished, affect their appearance, fit, and durability. That's why poorly constructed clothes often become worn and unattractive after only a few wearings. Better constructed clothes usually cost more, but, with proper care, they continue to look attractive for a much longer time.

You can evaluate clothing construction by inspecting the seams, stitching, hems, collars, lapels, buttonholes, reinforcements, zippers, pockets, and other construction features. Follow the guidelines in 6-7 to help you select quality clothing.

Fabrics

The type of fabric used to make clothes also affects the appearance of clothes, as well as their performance, comfort, price, and care. Most fabrics are made from fibers, either natural fibers or manufactured fibers. Cotton, linen (flax), wool, and silk are the *natural fibers*. Polyester, rayon, nylon, acrylic, and acetate are the most common *manufactured fibers*. In general, fabrics made from natural fibers are absorbent and comfortable to wear. Fabrics made from manufactured fibers are generally strong and wrinkle-resistant.

A fabric made from two or more fibers is called a *blend*. Blends are designed to offer the best features of the different fibers used. Cotton/polyester is a popular blend. It combines the absorbent, comfortable properties of cotton with the strong, wrinkle-resistant properties of polyester. Blends such as cotton/polyester and cotton/nylon are ideal for most work clothes.

To find out the fiber content of a garment, check the label inside the garment. The label should state the fiber content in percentages. For example, a label for a cotton/polyester blend might read: 50% polyester and 50% cotton. This would mean the fabric was made from half polyester fibers and half cotton fibers.

The way fibers are made into fabrics also affects a fabric's appearance and performance. Weaving and knitting are the common methods for constructing fabrics. In general, woven fabrics are durable and hold their shape well. Knit fabrics are wrinkle-resistant and comfortable to wear.

In addition to fiber content and fabric construction, finishes are another factor which affect fabrics. A finish is a treatment applied to a fabric to achieve certain characteristics. For example, a permanent press finish applied to a fabric helps the fabric resist wrinkling after washing and drying. A soil-release finish makes it possible to remove oily stains from permanent press fabrics. Fabrics with a permanent press or soil-release finish are excellent fabrics for durable work clothes.

Care labels

In addition to reading clothing labels for fiber content, you need to read them for care information, 6-8. Before buying, you should always find out how the garment should be washed, dried, and ironed. Should it be machine washed in warm water, hand washed in cold water, or dry cleaned? Can it be dried in a dryer, or should it drip-dry on a hanger? Should it be ironed with a cool iron or not ironed at all?

It would be impractical for a child care worker or telephone repair person to buy work clothes that must be dry cleaned. Unless you're in a job where you must wear suits, buy work clothes that can be machine washed and dried. Wash and wear and permanent press clothes are great for work because they are easy and inexpensive to keep clean.

CARING FOR CLOTHES

Even the best quality clothes will not look good if you do not care for them properly. Taking proper care of your clothes will help them look better and last longer. Clothes that are clean, neatly pressed, and mended will also help you have an attractive appearance.

Caring for clothes on a routine basis will keep clothes in good condition and ready to wear. For example, don't just pull off your clothes, wad them up, and throw them on the floor. Take that one extra minute to remove your clothes carefully and put them away properly. Be sure to undo buttons, snaps, and zippers before removing a garment. This will help you avoid tearing or stretching the garment out of shape.

After each wearing, check clothes for stains, tears, and missing buttons. It's best to remove any stains right away. The longer the stain stays in a fabric, the harder it will be to remove. Small sewing repairs such as sewing on a button or mending an untacked hem do not take long. Everyone can learn how to do these simple mending jobs.

If clothes do not need cleaning or mending, you may want to air them in an open room before storing. Then fold knits and sweaters neatly and store them in drawers or on shelves. Hang blouses, dresses, shirts, skirts, trousers, and jackets.

When clothes and accessories need cleaning, be sure to follow the directions on clothing care labels, laundry products, and washers and dryers. Washing clothes the correct way will keep them from fading, shrinking, and wrinkling unnecessarily.

SHOPPING FOR QUALITY CLOTHING

1. Seams should be flat, even in width, and finished to prevent raveling.
2. The stitching should be straight and even.
3. Hems should be even in width and invisible from the right side.
4. Collar points should be neatly finished.
5. Lapels should roll softly and lie flat to the chest.
6. Buttonholes should appear sturdy and properly spaced.
7. Points of strain such as armholes and crotches should be reinforced with double stitching or overcast seams.
8. Zippers should be inserted neatly, securely stitched, and operate smoothly.
9. Pockets should be flat, smooth, and well-matched.
10. Buttons, hooks and eyes, and snaps should be properly placed and firmly attached.

6-7 As you examine garments, keep these guidelines in mind.

Newcombe ™

ACTIVE SPORTSWEAR
65% POLYESTER
35% COTTON

| STYLE | 969 | WAIST | 30 |
| COLOR | LT. BLUE | # | 23 |

organically grown SWEATERS

65% POLYESTER
35% COTTON
MACHINE WASH WARM
(40°C)
DO NOT BLEACH
DRY FLAT
MEDIUM IRON
MADE IN HONG KONG
RN 60121

S

PURE WOOL ®

The sewn-in Woolmark label
is your assurance of quality-tested
fabrics made of the world's best
...Pure Wool.

The Woolmark is the registered certification
mark of The Wool Bureau, Inc.

• FULL PILE LINING •

SIZE 7/8   STYLE 5001
COLOR: BROWN
CONTENT: 100% COTTON
RN 59561

Norton McNaughton

50 % COTTON
50% POLYESTER

MACHINE WASH

RN 57909

STYLE 1019

6   V

WASHING INSTRUCTIONS

65% POLYESTER
35% COTTON

HAND OR MACHINE
WASH COLD.
LINE DRY. DO NOT
WRING, BLEACH
OR DRY CLEAN.

STYLE: 1125

SIZE :   S

LOT :

MADE IN KOREA

bon jour ®

6-8 Clothing labels and hangtags provide many kinds
of information about garments such as fiber content,
care information, brand name, size, and style number.

84

to Review

1. What do many employers assume about a person who has a nice appearance?
2. What three factors influence your appearance?
3. What is the impression you should want to make at work?
4. Name the three guidelines you should follow to stay in good physical health.
5. Name the two major things you need to do every day to keep your body clean.
6. What three factors do you need to consider when choosing a hairstyle?
7. Why is it a good idea to take an inventory of your wardrobe before each season of the year?
8. What three important factors do you need to evaluate closely before buying clothes?
9. Name at least five clothing features you should check for quality construction.
10. What is a blend? Which blends tend to be ideal for most work clothes?
11. Why is it important to read clothing labels before buying a garment?
12. Why is it important to remove stains from clothes as soon as possible?

to Discuss

1. How can the clothes you're wearing influence a person's first impression of you?
2. What do you do to help yourself stay in good physical health?
3. Why is good grooming essential to getting and keeping a job?
4. Why do you think some employers object to beards?
5. How do you decide what is appropriate to wear to work?
6. Why are clothing choices especially important for office and business workers such as salespeople, receptionists, office clerks, and cashiers? List three different outfits that would be appropriate for a female office worker to wear and three different outfits that would be appropriate for a male office worker to wear.
7. What clothes do you like most in your wardrobe? Why do you like them the best?
8. What do you need to consider before making any additions to your wardrobe?

9. Name ways you can cut clothing costs.
10. List ways you can care for clothes on a routine basis.

to Do

1. Invite a personnel manager from a company to speak on the importance of good grooming in getting and keeping a job.
2. Make a daily and weekly schedule of good grooming habits.
3. Invite a hairstylist to conduct a class workshop on proper hair care and styling.
4. Take an inventory of all the clothes, shoes, and accessories that you have. List items that you no longer wear, need, or want, and list places where you can sell, trade, or dispose of these items. Then make a list of items that you need to complete your wardrobe for school, work, and other occasions.
5. Obtain a well made garment and a poorly made garment to inspect and compare in class. Identify the construction features that make the one garment well constructed and the other garment poorly constructed.
6. Prepare a bulletin board to illustrate what people need to do to "look good on the job."

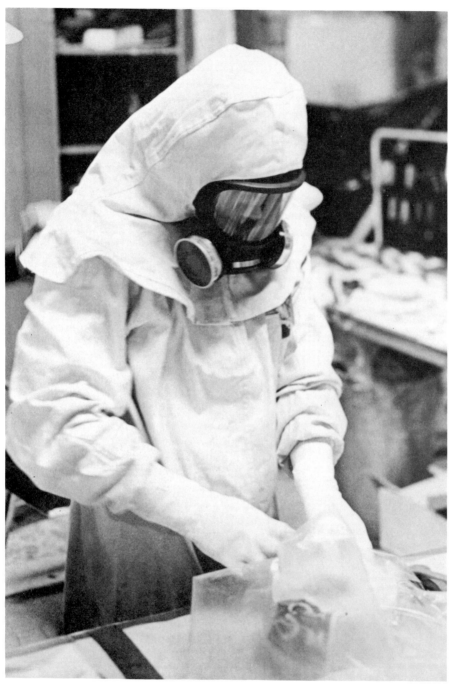

This worker is properly dressed to investigate
a radiation leakage in a nuclear plant.

7

Safety on the job

After studying this chapter, you will be able to:

☐ Describe the causes of accidents on the job.
☐ Explain what the Occupational Safety and Health Administration does to protect workers on the job.
☐ Identify things workers can do to avoid and prevent accidents.

Accidents and injuries are not pleasant. No one wants to get hurt or see anyone else get hurt. Accidents can damage equipment as well as people. Injured workers and damaged equipment cost the employer time and money.

Working safely is every worker's and employer's responsibility. It is much better to prevent an accident than to live with the results of a serious one. Although jobs in mining, construction, farming, and manufacturing tend to have the highest accident rates, accidents can and do happen on any job. People are not perfect. However, many accidents can be prevented when workers are alert, careful, and knowledgeable about their jobs.

WHAT CAUSES ACCIDENTS?

Directly or indirectly, people cause accidents. Accidents most often occur because of environmental hazards, lack of knowledge or skills, poor work attitudes, and unsafe behavior.

Environmental hazards

The working environment can influence the number of accidents that are likely to occur on the job. For example, it's not surprising to read that more accidents occur in construction jobs than in office jobs. Construction workers come in contact with more environmental hazards (dangers) such as heavy equipment, hand tools, hot substances, and motor driven vehicles. The only environmental hazard office workers may face is riding the elevator in the office building where they work.

Environmental hazards also exist in mining; logging; roofing; meat processing; excavating; and operating elevators, hoisting apparatuses, saws, and power-driven machines. See 7-1. Although these hazards cannot be eliminated, there are safety regulations to help prevent employee accidents. The *Occupational Safety and Health Administration* (OSHA) is the federal government administration that sets and enforces job safety and health standards for workers. OSHA makes it mandatory for each employer to furnish all its employees with a place of employment that is free from hazards that can cause death or serious physical harm.

7-1 Can you identify the environmental hazards in these working environments?

SOUTHWEST FOREST INDUSTRIES

STANDARD OIL OF CALIFORNIA

BUCYRUS-ERIE

OSHA has also set forth rules for employees to follow. These include the following:

- Abide by OSHA's safety standards and your employer's standards.
- Report any injury that occurs on the job.
- Wear personal protective equipment when required. A list of some of the most common protective devices and the protection each provides is given in 7-2.
- Use safety devices properly.
- Participate in fire drills and other safety practices.
- Report unsafe working conditions and practices. If your employer does not correct the situation, request OSHA to make an inspection.

Laws and regulations cannot prevent accidents, but employers and employees working together safely can.

Lack of knowledge and skills

The worker who has not been trained to do his or her job accurately and safely is most likely to make mistakes and have accidents.

EXAMPLES OF PERSONAL PROTECTIVE DEVICES

DEVICES	PROTECTS AGAINST
Leather gloves and apron shields	Welding burns
Gloves	Cuts and abrasions
Safety goggles and face shields	Eye injuries
Hard hats and safety shoes	Injuries from falling objects
Rubber gloves, aprons, and face shields	Burns from acids, caustics, and alkalies
Asbestos gloves and leggings	Burns from flames and hot metal
Ear plugs and ear muffs	High frequency sounds
Masks and respirators	Harmful gases

7-2 Some employees are required to wear certain types of clothing and devices to protect them from environmental hazards.

Knowledge and skill are especially important when working with machinery and equipment. Workers who operate machinery should learn as much as possible about the equipment before they begin operating it, 7-3. They should know

7-3 Workers can avoid many accidents if they learn how to operate machines before they try operating them.

NATIONAL VICA

exactly what to do if the machine appears to be overheating or if something gets caught in the machine. They should not even attempt to operate any piece of machinery that they have not been trained to use.

Lack of knowledge and skill can cause accidents in any job—not just machine-operating jobs. For example, consider what happened to Bob. Bob just became a waiter at a nice restaurant. All the waiters there carry their trays of orders high on their shoulders and gracefully place them on stands for serving. When Bob picked up his first order, he attempted to do the same thing. However, half his tray of food ended up scattered across the floor and the other half across his table of customers. Bob tried to perform a task before he developed the skill to do it.

You need to be aware of the things you can and cannot do. Don't pretend to know how to do something when you don't. Seek out information about a job you don't know how to do. Make sure you have the knowledge and the skills to perform the task correctly and safely before you begin.

To learn a new skill, watch a skilled worker perform the task. Then ask the worker to show you step-by-step how to do the task. Next, perform the task slowly yourself. Have the skilled worker watch you to make sure you do each step the right way. Afterwards, practice doing the task until you can do it safely and accurately.

Poor work attitudes

Not taking the right attitude toward safety can put you and others in danger. Read what happened to these workers.

Joan decided to stop wearing her work goggles when drilling metal at work. She said they were too hot and uncomfortable to wear. The next week a metal chip flew into her eye. She had to have surgery.

One of David's jobs at the warehouse where he works is to stack boxes of merchandise. When the stack of boxes reaches a certain height, David is supposed to start another stack. One day David didn't bother to start a new stack. Later that day the stack of boxes fell on another worker and gave him a nasty bump on the head.

Karen works in an office as a word processor. One afternoon while she was on break, she tossed a lighted match into an office wastebasket. She said there wasn't an ashtray close by. Karen's little match started a fire. Fortunately, the office manager was able to put out the fire with a fire extinguisher before it got out of control.

You and every worker need to "think safety." Safety rules are developed to protect you and others. Get into the habit of doing tasks the safe way. Wear the proper clothes and equipment. See 7-4 and 7-5. Follow the safety procedures exactly. Don't give yourself the opportunity to slip up and cause an accident.

Unsafe behavior

An office worker takes a file from the bottom drawer of the file cabinet and doesn't bother to close the drawer. Another worker walks around the corner and trips over the open drawer, 7-6.

After mopping the hallway, the worker forgets to put up the signs, "Caution—Wet Floor." A customer walks in, slips on the wet floor, and injures his back.

A file clerk decides to climb the shelves in the storage room to get a box of file folders instead of using a stepladder. The clerk loses her footing, falls backward, and fractures her elbow, 7-7.

Near the end of a workday, two woodworking employees start horsing around with each other. No one bothers to turn off the circular saw. Jokingly, one worker pushes the other worker. The worker loses her balance and falls against the circular saw. She gets a nasty cut on her arm.

These stories are all examples of unsafe behavior. Being inconsiderate like the office worker, careless like the cleaning worker, impatient like the file clerk, and reckless like the woodworkers are threats to everyone's safety.

7-4 This welder knows that wearing the proper clothing and equipment is crucial for his safety. To protect himself from the hot, blinding sparks, he must wear an arc welding helmet, a leather apron, leather gloves, and safety shoes.

7-5 For the safety of others, food service workers need to follow certain safety rules such as wearing hair nets and washing their hands before handling food.

Safety on the job 91

7-6 The employee on the left set the trap, and the employee on the right falls for it.

7-7 Makeshifts make mishaps.

to Review

1. Why do accidents most often occur?
2. What does OSHA do?
3. According to OSHA, what rules should employees follow to insure a safe working environment?
4. If you don't know how to operate a machine or perform a task, what should you do before trying to do it on your own?
5. Describe a good way to learn a new skill.
6. Give three examples of workers not taking the right attitude toward safety.

to Discuss

1. What are the costs to the employer when workers are injured or equipment is damaged due to accidents on the job?
2. Discuss the environmental hazards workers face in mining; logging; roofing; meat proccessing; excavating; and operating elevators, hoisting apparatuses, saws, and power-driven machines.
3. Why are knowledge and skill so important to job safety?
4. What can workers do to prevent many accidents from occurring on the job?
5. How does a person's attitude affect job safety?
6. Discuss the examples of unsafe work behavior described in the book. Then describe examples of unsafe work behavior you've seen on the job or heard about from other workers.

to Do

1. List two examples of accidents that have occurred in your type of work. Write a paragraph about each one, describing what happened. Then write another paragraph about each, explaining how the accident might have been prevented.
2. Using classroom or library resources, locate the OSHA office nearest you.
3. Write to your nearest OSHA office and ask what a worker should do if unsafe working conditions or practices exist at the worker's company and the employer has made no attempt to correct these conditions or practices.

Career planning

Learning about yourself—becoming aware of your interests, aptitudes, and abilities—will help you identify careers that will be interesting to you.

8

Learning about yourself

After studying this chapter, you will be able to:

- ☐ Describe how your interests, aptitudes, and abilities relate to your career decisions.
- ☐ List several personality traits and explain how they may influence career choices.
- ☐ Explain how identifying your values, goals, standards, and resources can help you understand yourself more fully.

Choosing a career involves more than pulling a job out of a hat. It's a matching game. The object of the game is to match yourself with the "right" career.

To be successful at the game, you need to get to know all about yourself. What skills do you have? What do you do well? What type of work appeals to you? Do you have the aptitudes or abilities to become successful in a business, health, or sports career? Is your personality more suited to that of a teacher, a construction worker, or an X-ray technician?

What are the principles and beliefs that you consider important? In other words, what do you value? Do you value earning a lot of money? Do you value having a challenging and responsible job? Do you value having a family? Do you value being honest and loyal?

What are your goals in life? What do you want to achieve? What resources do you have to achieve your goals?

Your answers to these questions are important ones. They are the bases from which you make all your many decisions. Therefore, the more you know about yourself, the better prepared you will be to make decisions about your career and your future.

WHAT ARE YOUR INTERESTS?

To know and understand yourself, you need to be aware of your interests. What do you enjoy doing the most? How do you like to spend your time? What are your hobbies? What do you like most in school? What would you do if you had an hour to kill—an afternoon, a day, or a weekend? Make lists for each answer. Your lists of answers should help you identify careers that will be interesting to you.

Sometimes people have a hard time determining their interests. One day a person may have a strong interest in becoming a teacher, but later have little interest in teaching. Interests tend to change as people mature, meet new people, and participate in new activities. That's why it's important for you to take it upon yourself to get interested in people, in things, and in activities. Interests are learned, so unless you have tried something, you do not know for sure if you have an interest in it. You are likely to develop new interests as you experience new activities, 8-1.

In your cooperative work experience, you may be discovering new career interests. Or you may be realizing you're not as interested in a particular occupation as you thought you were. Having a work experience or observing others on the job can help you understand what a job

UTAH TRAVEL COUNCIL

8-1 After taking skiing lessons, many of these people developed a keen interest in the sport of snow skiing.

involves. Learning about different careers and occupations helps you determine what careers interest you.

If you find it hard to identify your interests, talk to others. Listen to those who know you well. Your friends and family members may be able to help you recall the activities you have enjoyed the most or the projects you have done well. Also ask others about their career interests and how they chose their occupations. "Why did you decide to become a photographer?" "What's your job like?" "What do you like most about your job?" "What don't you like about your job?"

Another way to become more aware of your interests is to take an *activities preference inventory*. Most high school guidance departments are prepared to give preference tests to students. The inventory is designed to help you determine if you prefer working with people, objects, or ideas. The inventory is similar to a multiple choice test. You are given several activities and asked to select the one activity that appeals to you most. After completing the inventory, you are given a key to interpret the results.

If the inventory indicates you would enjoy working with people, you may want to consider a career in social work, teaching, sales, or health care services. If the inventory points to objects, you might want a job as a fashion illustrator, an auto mechanic, a baker, or a machine operator. An interest in ideas would suggest careers in publishing, advertising, and marketing. Listed here are only examples of the types of careers related to people, objects, and ideas. There are many, many more.

Keep in mind that no one person or test can tell you what to do with your life. They can only provide direction and help you consider possibilities of which you may not have been aware. It's up to you to make the final decisions about your occupational interests. Chart 8-2 may help you become more aware of your interests and understand how interests relate to choosing an occupation.

CAREER INTERESTS

CONCEPTS	EXAMPLES
There are many interest areas in a career.	A grain farmer may have an interest in growing things, working for himself, and operating machinery. The farmer might also have an interest in athletics or upholstering, but these interests are not needed in farming.
People have interest areas in which they do not want to work.	A mechanic may have gardening as a hobby, but does not want an occupation as a farmer or horticulturist.
Interest is important for success in any career.	Working at something you like is more pleasant.
Everyone has many interests.	A person may have interests in music, athletics, mechanical things, and in working with people.
Different careers may involve similar or the same interests.	A salesperson, a politician, a teacher, and a lawyer are interested in working with people and, in some way, influencing them.

8-2 As you think about your career interests, consider these basic concepts.

WHAT ARE YOUR APTITUDES?

To be successful in a career, you need to have more than an interest in a career. You also need to have an aptitude or an ability for it.

Aptitudes are your natural physical and mental talents for learning. If you have an aptitude for a certain skill, you will be able to learn the skill easily and perform the skill well.

For example, if you have an aptitude for singing, you would have a good chance for success as a singer. If you are naturally talented at writing, perhaps you could become a successful television writer. On the other hand, if you do not have an aptitude for typing, you would have a poor chance of becoming a fast and accurate typesetter.

Be realistic about your aptitudes. Become

APTITUDES MEASURED BY THE GATB

APTITUDE	TESTS
GENERAL LEARNING ABILITY: The ability to "catch on" or understand instructions and underlying principles. The ability to reason and make judgments.	Three-dimensional space Vocabulary Arithmetic reason
VERBAL APTITUDE: The ability to understand the meanings of words and to use words effectively. The ability to comprehend language, to understand relationships between words, and to understand the meaning of whole sentences and paragraph.	Vocabulary
NUMERICAL APTITUDE: The ability to perform arithmetic operations quickly and accurately.	Computation Arithmetic reason
SPATIAL APTITUDE: The ability to think visually of geometric forms and to comprehend the two-dimensional representation of three-dimensional objects. The ability to recognize the relationships resulting from the movement of objects in space.	Three-dimensional space
FORM PERCEPTION: The ability to perceive detail in objects or in pictures or graphics. The ability to make visual comparisons and discriminations. The ability to see slight differences in shapes and shadings of figures and widths and lengths of lines.	Tool matching Form matching
CLERICAL PERCEPTION: The ability to perceive detail in verbal or tabular material. The ability to observe differences in copy, to proofread words and numbers, and to avoid errors in arithmetic computation.	Name comparison
MOTOR COORDINATION: The ability to coordinate eyes and hands or fingers rapidly and accurately in making precise movements with speed. The ability to make a movement response accurately and swiftly.	Mark making
FINGER DEXTERITY: The ability to move the fingers and manipulate small objects with the fingers rapidly or accurately.	Assemble Disassemble
MANUAL DEXTERITY: The ability to move the hands easily and skillfully. The ability to work with the hands in placing and turning motions.	Place Turn

8-3 Here are the nine aptitudes measured by the GATB and the tests given to measure each one.

aware of your mental and physical limitations as well as your strengths.

To learn more about your aptitudes, ask your guidance teacher if your school gives the General Aptitude Test Battery (GATB). The GATB is a series of tests to measure nine aptitudes. See 8-3 and 8-4. By taking these tests, you will get a better idea of the kinds of careers in which you have the best chances for success.

WHAT ARE YOUR ABILITIES?

You are born with certain aptitudes, but you must develop your abilities. Everyone has abilities of some kind. *Abilities* are your physical and mental powers to perform a task or skill well. They are learned through training and practice.

Abilities are developed more easily if you have related aptitudes. For example, if you have physical aptitudes for rhythm and coordination, you will probably excel quickly in a ballroom dancing class. If you have very little aptitude for dancing, hard work and genuine interest can help you overcome low aptitudes and develop abilities. By taking dancing lessons on a regular basis and practicing dancing, you can develop the ability to dance.

Your abilities, aptitudes, and interests all need to be considered in career planning. Most people are usually interested in the activities they do best, but sometimes that may not be

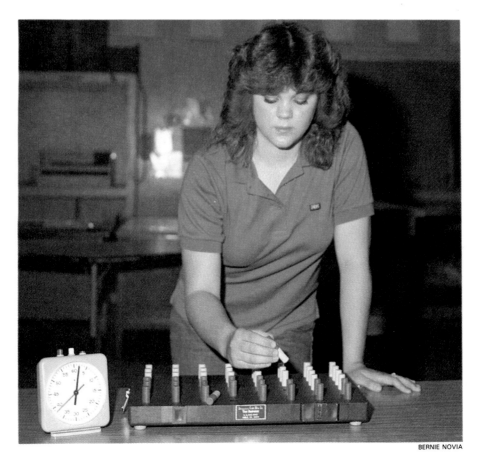

BERNIE NOVIA

8-4 This student is taking a finger dexterity test to measure her ability to manipulate small objects rapidly and accurately with her fingers.

the case. A person may want to become a professional basketball player but not have the physical aptitude for the sport. Or a person may have the ability to play a musical instrument but not have the interest to do so. The ideal situation is to have the mental and physical aptitudes and abilities that relate to a career that interests you, 8-5.

YOUR PERSONALITY

Do you know someone who has no personality? You do? Wrong! Everyone has a personality. Your personality is a combination of your emotional and behavioral traits that make you distinct and separate from everyone else. Your personality influences how you think and feel. It influences how you interact with different people in different situations. And your personality influences the way other people feel about you.

Different careers require different personality traits. That is why it is important to consider your personality when choosing a career. Suppose you have a quiet, reserved personality and like to spend much of your time alone woodworking. In this case, you probably would not enjoy a career in sales. To be successful in sales, a person needs to be outgoing and friendly and willing to spend a lot of time talking with people.

Personality traits

Employers also consider personality when they are choosing an applicant for a job. Employers not only want employees who can get the job done, they also want employees who can work well with others. Employers also tend to hire people with warm, friendly, outgoing personalities for positions of managers, directors, and supervisors and pay them larger salaries.

What are your personality traits? A number of traits are listed below. Which of these traits describe your personality?

Attitude. Your attitude is the way you feel about yourself and about others. It's your outlook on life. Your attitude is revealed in the way you do things, say things, and react to things. For example, if you like your work experience and work hard to do a good job, your behavior will imply that you have a positive attitude about your job. However, if you waste time at work and complain about your job, your behavior will imply that you have a negative attitude about your work experience.

Most everyone likes a person with a positive attitude. People with positive attitudes are cooperative, friendly, and responsible. They like themselves, they smile, and they enjoy living.

Dependability. Being dependable means being reliable and responsible for the things you are expected to do. A person who is dependable can be trusted to get the job done. The worker who is always at work and always on time is a dependable employee. The employer knows the employee will always be on the job unless there's an emergency. The employee who often misses days of work for no good reasons is not considered dependable.

Friendliness. A person who is considered friendly is usually considered to have a good personality. People like other people who are pleasant, sociable, and courteous. Friendly people speak to others and smile, 8-6. They show an interest in the activities and welfare of others. A smile and a warm hello are much more inviting than a frown and a grouchy greeting.

Honesty. Honest people are truthful and sincere. They keep the promises they make and deal with people fairly. Being honest is very important in your work and in your relationships with others. Dishonesty is not a desirable trait to have, especially on the job. An employer doesn't want an employee who cannot be trusted on the job.

Initiative. Being aware of what needs to be done and taking action to do it shows initiative. Employers like employees with initiative. Employees with initiative look to see what else needs to be done when they complete their work. They don't sit back and wait for their employer to come to them with a new work assignment. They go to their employer and ask about the next assignment.

PHELPS DODGE CORP.

8-5 This worker combined his interest in helping
people with his life-saving skills and became a paramedic.

WENDY'S

8-6 Being pleasant and friendly are positive personality
traits to have at work and in your personal life.

Learning about yourself   103

Loyalty. People who are faithful to themselves, to others, or to their employers exhibit loyalty. Employers consider loyalty an important trait for workers to have. Loyal workers respect their employers and speak well of them to others.

Open-mindedness. Open-minded people are interested in hearing the ideas and opinions of others, even though they may not agree with what they have to say. They don't always assume that their opinions are the only logical ones. They look at "both sides of the coin." Open-minded people also are willing to accept constructive criticism and to make improvements.

Self-confidence. People with self-confidence believe in their ability to do things. They have the desire and drive to succeed on the job. They feel confident about the way they look, the way they talk, and the skills they have. People who appear self-confident tend to cause others to have confidence in them as well.

Self-control. How do you react when things go wrong? Do you stay in control of your emotions? Having self-control means having the patience, willpower, or the self-discipline to cope with a stressful situation. When you're in control of your emotions, you don't lose your temper when someone doesn't agree with you. And you don't eat a hot fudge sundae when you're trying to lose weight.

Sense of humor. Having a good sense of humor is being able to laugh at the dumb little things you may do. The person who is always so serious and never cracks a smile has little or no sense of humor. People like other people who enjoy a good laugh and see the humor in everyday situations, even when the joke is on them.

Your personality traits are traits you acquire over the years. You are not born with a trait for friendliness or a trait for honesty. You learn how to be or how not to be friendly or honest from the people around you. Therefore, anyone can change and improve their personality, 8-7. For example, suppose you have a bad temper, but want to acquire self-control. You can change your behavior if you have a strong desire to do so. For instance, the next time something goes wrong or someone offends you, don't react immediately. Think before you act. Figure out other ways of handling the problem besides yelling at the top of your lungs or slamming the door. Work out the problem calmly and logically.

Habits

When you do something the same way every time, it is said to be a habit. Your daily life includes many habits such as the way you stand, sit, talk, walk, and gesture when speaking. The habits you have formed are a part of your personality, and they influence the way others see you.

Habits can be good or bad. For example, being on time for work everyday is considered a good habit. An employer can trust the employee to be on the job at the same time each day. Being late for work everyday is considered a bad habit. An employee with this habit is not dependable.

Examine your habits. Do you have good grooming habits? Do you have any annoying mannerisms? What new habits would you like to establish? What old habits would you like to change?

WAYS TO IMPROVE YOUR PERSONALITY

AVOID	TRY
Being sarcastic to others.	Understanding others.
Not caring about others.	Being sensitive to the feelings of others.
Losing your temper.	Controlling your temper.
Refusing to help others.	Showing good manners.
Being gloomy.	Being bright and happy.
Being pessimistic and sour.	Being optimistic and pleasant.
Constantly changing your mind and loyalties.	Being confident and consistent in your thoughts and feelings.
Mumbling your words.	Speaking clearly.

8-7 If you are unhappy with your personality, here are a number of ways you can improve it.

When beginning a new job, it's important to learn good work habits from the very beginning. Learn a skill correctly, and do it the same way each time. Once learned, a skill becomes a habit and it is not easily changed or forgotten. That's why it's important to learn a skill the correct way and continue doing it the same way until it becomes habit.

VALUES

Another important aspect of yourself is your values. *Values* are the principles and beliefs that you consider important. The values you have influence your decisions and actions. That's why it is important for you to become aware of your values. Most people value friendship, honesty, good health, and nice clothes. Many people also value education, popularity, new cars, a happy family life, and money. What do you value? Why do you value these things?

Identifying the ideals and objects that are important to you will help you choose a meaningful and satisfying career, 8-8.

For instance, if you value being able to wear blue jeans and casual clothes, you probably wouldn't be happy working at a job where you have to wear suits or dress clothes. Or if you value a quiet, comfortable environment, you would probably dislike a job working in a noisy, bustling factory.

Take the time now to identify your values. Then rank your values from most to least important. As you rank your values in the order of their importance to you, you create a *value system*. Your value system guides your behavior and helps you develop a sense of direction in your life. It also simplifies the process of making career decisions. For example, suppose you have listed a challenging job and a well-paying job as two of your values. However, you have ranked a challenging job near the top of your

ARIZONA COMMISSION ON THE ARTS

8-8 If you value spending time with young children, you would probably enjoy a career working with or teaching children.

list and a well-paying job lower down. Therefore, you would probably decide that having a challenging job would be more important than taking a nonchallenging job just because it paid more money.

GOALS

Goals are the things you want to attain. A person's goals are usually based on his or her values. For example, John values listening to music on a good stereo system. However, John's system does not work very well anymore. Therefore, John has set a goal to buy a new stereo system in a year by saving a portion of each paycheck. As this example shows, goals and values are related. Values express thoughts and feelings, and goals put values into action. Like values, goals influence and shape the decisions you make.

Have you thought about your goals? What do you want to do with your life? What do you want to accomplish?

The first step in setting and achieving goals is to make a list of the things you really want out of life. Be sure to include both short-range goals and long-range goals. *Short-range goals* are the goals you want to reach tomorrow, next week, or within a few months. Getting an A on your next English assignment, becoming an officer in one of the school clubs, and improving your tennis game are examples of short-range goals. *Long-range goals* are those goals that may take several months or several years to achieve. Completing school, starting a career, and buying a car are examples of possible long-range goals. See 8-9.

One important factor to remember when setting goals is to be realistic. Do you really want to reach that goal? Is it possible for you to reach? What will it cost in terms of time, energy, money, and other resources? Is the goal in keeping with your values? Setting well-defined, realistic goals can help you develop a sense of direction and purpose in life.

8-9 Getting married after you complete your education and begin your career is an example of a long-range goal.

STANDARDS

Standards are accepted levels of achievement. There are standards for dress, standards for cleanliness, standards for food and drug safety, and standards for school grades. Electrical products must meet certain safety standards before they are given a seal of approval. People in professions such as law and medicine must meet certain standards before they can practice their professions, 8-10.

Individuals also have their own standards — personal standards of living. A person's standard of living refers to the goods and services he or she considers essential for living. For some, a college education, gourmet food, and the theater are essential. Other people's standard of living may be based on a high school diploma, simple home-cooked meals, and TV shows.

Standards are closely related to values and goals. The things you value and set goals to achieve are the things for which you will have high standards. For example, if you value making the school honor roll and set aside time to study regularly, your standards for grades would be high. On the other hand, if you place little value on clothes and pay little attention to the quality and style of clothing you wear, your standards for clothes would not be high.

What are your standards for living? Do you strive to do your very best on the job or do you just put in your hours? Do you have high standards for the way you look and dress? What are your standards for education? Knowing your own standards and what you expect from life can help you understand yourself more fully. And this can help you make satisfying career decisions.

RESOURCES

Resources are all the things you have or can use to help you reach your goals. To know yourself well, you need to recognize your resources. What resources do you have? What

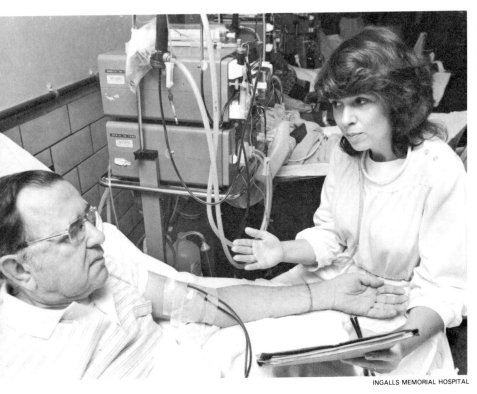

8-10 Health care professionals must pass certification tests in order to practice their professions.

are your human resources? What are your nonhuman resources? *Human resources* are the resources you have within yourself such as skills, knowledge, experience, and time, 8-11. Determination, motivation, and imagination are also valuable human resources. *Nonhuman resources* are the material things you have or can use to achieve goals such as money, tools, clothes, and community resources.

Identifying your resources helps you identify your strengths and weaknesses. For example, if you know you have artistic talents (a human resource), you know you will probably be successful pursuing a career in art. If you want to go to college but know you don't have the money (a nonhuman resource) to pay the expenses, you will have to try to get a scholarship, take out a loan, or work part-time. Knowing your strengths and limitations can help you set realistic goals for your life and career.

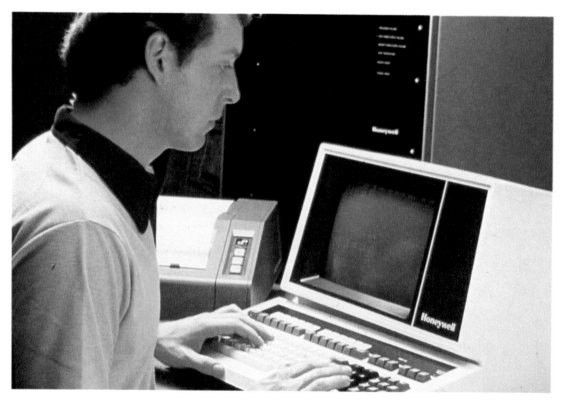

8-11 Being knowledgeable about computers is a human resource that may help you get a job in the future.

to Review

1. Why is it important for you to learn as much about yourself as possible at this point in your life?

2. When does a person's interests tend to change?

3. What two things can you do to help you identify your interests?

4. What is an activities preference inventory?

5. Explain the difference between aptitudes and abilities. Give an example of each.

6. How is it possible to overcome low aptitudes?

7. Why is it important to consider your personality when choosing a career?

8. List and describe five personality traits.

9. What is a value system and what does it do?

10. Explain the difference between values and goals.

11. How are standards related to values and goals?

12. What are resources? Give examples of human and nonhuman resources.

to Discuss

1. How can participating in new activities and meeting new people help you determine your interests?

2. Of the nine aptitudes measured by the GATB, on which ones do you think you would score high?

3. What abilities would you need to have to be successful in the careers that interest you?

4. Why do you need to consider your abilities, aptitudes, and interests in career planning?

5. How would you describe your personality? How do you think others would describe it?

6. How can a person change his or her personality?

7. How can your habits have a negative or a positive influence on the way others see you?

8. Why are values and goals different for different people?

9. Why do people's values and goals usually change as they grow older?

10. What do you consider your most valuable human and nonhuman resources?

to Do

1. List twelve things you like to do. Beside each activity on your list, note whether it involves mainly people, objects, or ideas. Evaluate your responses to see if you can form any conclusions about your interests and how they might influence your job choices.

2. Ask your guidance counselor about taking the GATB or another type of aptitude test. If available, take an aptitude test and discuss the results of the test with your counselor.

3. Describe how people could show that they value the following: honesty, friendship, education, good health, responsibility.

4. List several short-range and long-range goals you might want to achieve over the next five years.

A career center can help you learn about the many careers and jobs from which you have to choose.

9

Learning about careers

After studying this chapter, you will be able to:

☐ Discuss the many different types of career clusters.
☐ Describe the wide range of jobs within career clusters.
☐ Identify careers and occupations that interest you.

The working world is quite complex. Just think, there are over 20,000 different job titles. One way to learn about the thousands of jobs in the world is to read about them in career clusters. A career cluster is a group of jobs that are similar to each other. For example, a nurse, physician, dental hygienist, orderly, and pharmacist can be grouped into the same cluster because they are all related to the health field. Classifying occupations into clusters can help you identify jobs that are of interest to you. It can also help you learn about the range of jobs within a career area.

Jobs can be grouped in different ways. Here they are grouped into fifteen career clusters according to their area of interest:

- Agriculture.
- Arts and humanities.
- Business and office.
- Communications.
- Construction.
- Health.
- Home economics.
- Hospitality and recreation.
- Manufacturing.
- Marine science.
- Marketing and distribution.
- Natural resources & environmental control.
- Personal services.
- Public service.
- Transportation.

AGRICULTURE

This cluster includes occupations in farming, ranching, logging, and horticulture. Workers in these occupations mostly work outside with plants and animals.

Farmers need skills in planning, planting, fertilizing, cultivating, and harvesting crops. Farmers or ranchers who raise animals are responsible for feeding and caring for their animals properly. Horticultural workers grow and maintain plants, shrubs, and trees in nurseries and greenhouses. Loggers have the job of cutting and hauling trees. Other workers in lumber mills process trees for use in the paper, construction, and furniture industries. Workers in both farming and logging need to be able to operate and maintain machinery correctly and safely.

Many workers who choose occupations in farming grew up on farms themselves. They may have received all or most of their training through experience. However, young farmers are finding it beneficial to receive additional training at a two or four year college to keep up with modern farming techniques. Most jobs in logging and lumber mills do not require previous training. Entry-level jobs can be learned on the job from experienced workers. High school subjects related to agriculture are horticulture, agricultural mechanics, animal science, and forestry.

AGRICULTURE

MAJOR CATEGORIES	EXAMPLES OF CAREERS		TYPICAL PLACES OF EMPLOYMENT
Production	Field crop farmer Dairy farmer Poultry farmer Livestock rancher Ranch worker General farmer	Fruit farmer Farm equipment operator Beekeeper Animal breeder Animal inspector	Farm Ranch U.S. Department of Agriculture Landscaping firm Nursery
Horticulture	Greenhouse manager Landscape contractor Groundskeeper Greenskeeper	Landscape gardner Tree surgeon Lawn-service worker	Florist shop Golf course Lumber mill Paper mill Forest service Christmas tree farm
Logging	Sawyer Logger Chainsaw operator	Faller Log marker Log inspector	

Logger

Field crop farmer

Farm equipment operator

Cattle rancher

Learning about careers   113

ARTS AND HUMANITIES

People who are creative and imaginative often choose a career in the arts or humanities to express their ideas and talents. Musicians, sculptors, artists, writers, dancers, and actors and actresses are just a few of the many different occupations in this field.

Careers in the arts and humanities require a great deal of self-discipline. This means that people who choose a career in drama, music, dance, or writing must be prepared to work hard to perfect their talents. For example, to become a classical pianist, you will need to receive the proper training and be willing to spend many hours practicing each week. For those who have the interest, ability, and determination to develop their talents, a career in the arts can offer great personal satisfaction.

Training for such a career usually begins at an early age. A professional ballet dancer may have started taking ballet lessons at the age of four. However, the amount of training or education does not always determine how talented a person is. A person's ability to become employed as a performing artist is determined by the quality of his or her performance, not by the number of years the person has trained.

High school subjects related to the arts and humanities include art, drama, literature, creative writing, band, and orchestra.

ARTS AND HUMANITIES

MAJOR CATEGORIES	EXAMPLES OF CAREERS		TYPICAL PLACES OF EMPLOYMENT
Performing artists	Actor/actress Musician	Conductor Dancer	Theater Drama troupe Band Orchestra
Artists	Illustrator Painter Sculptor Potter Photographer	Art director Graphic designer Fashion designer Set designer Costume designer	Advertising agency Choral group Dance company Art studio
Performing arts production	Stage manager Director Producer	Choreographer Sound technician Lighting director	Dance studio Movie studio Recording studio Clothing manufacturer
Writers	Novelist Playwright	Screen writer Cartoonist	Publishing company Newspaper TV studio Radio station Museum

Actor and actress

Musicians

Potter

Dancer

BUSINESS AND OFFICE

Office workers perform many tasks to keep businesses and organizations running smoothly on a day-to-day basis. Office occupations include clerical, computer, banking, insurance, and administrative jobs. Clerical workers, such as bookkeepers, secretaries, and clerks, type office correspondence, maintain files, operate office machines, and ship and receive merchandise. Professional and technical office employees prepare financial reports, design computer systems, arrange bank loans, and purchase merchandise.

Office work involves a variety of skills. Clerical workers need to pay close attention to detail in order to maintain accurate records and files. Professional workers need to be able to solve problems, analyze data, and make company decisions. All office workers need to be good communicators when writing, talking over the phone, or speaking to others in person.

Many workers are employed in office occupations, and employment in this field is expected to increase in the years ahead. A high school education with a strong business emphasis may be all the education you need for some clerical jobs. Professional and administrative jobs in computers, banking, and insurance will probably require an occupational or college education. You can prepare yourself for an office occupation in high school by taking classes in typing, data processing, office machines, and bookkeeping.

BUSINESS AND OFFICE

MAJOR CATEGORIES	EXAMPLES OF CAREERS		TYPICAL PLACES OF EMPLOYMENT
Clerical	Secretary Bookkeeper Cashier Shipping, receiving, and stock clerks Typist	Receptionist Bank teller File clerk Office machine operator	Bank Insurance office Hospital Post office Government office Law office Retail store Publishing company Business office
Computer related	Computer operator Typesetter	Programmer Systems analyst	
Insurance related	Actuary Underwriter	Claims representative	
Administrative	Office manager Personnel manager Buyer	Purchasing agent Accountant Lawyer	

Cashier

Office manager

BERNIE NOVIA

File clerk

GENERAL ELECTRIC

Typesetter

COMMUNICATIONS

Watching television, reading a newspaper or book, talking on the telephone, or going to the movies would not be possible without workers in communication occupations. The communications field involves jobs in radio, television, motion pictures, printing, publishing, photography, and communication systems.

Some occupations in communications such as newspaper writers, magazine editors, and newscasters, require skills in writing, editing, and producing information. Other jobs, such as broadcast engineers, camera operators, and lithographers require technical skills. Technicians are responsible for operating, maintaining, and repairing the equipment needed to broadcast radio and television programs; to print newspapers, books, and magazines; and to transmit telephone and satellite signals.

Most technical jobs in communications will require training at a technical institute or college or training through an apprenticeship. High school and vocational school training in art, graphic arts, photography, chemistry, electronics, and mathematics are also helpful. The writing and creative jobs will usually require advanced training in journalism, English, broadcasting, and production. Some jobs also require knowledge in specific areas, such as sports, international affairs, or home economics in addition to writing skills. High school courses in speech, creative writing, journalism, and drama can help you prepare for a career in communications.

COMMUNICATIONS

MAJOR CATEGORIES	EXAMPLES OF CAREERS		TYPICAL PLACES OF EMPLOYMENT
Publishing	Editor Newspaper reporter Photoengraver	Lithographer Printing press operator Bindery worker	Newspaper Magazine publisher Book publisher
Radio, television, motion pictures	Camera operator Broadcast technician Disc jockey Director	Producer Announcer Film, tape, and sound editors	Advertising agency Radio station TV station Motion picture studio Police station
Communication systems	Telegrapher Radio dispatcher Telephone operator	Equipment installer Line installer Telephone repairer	Telegraph company Telephone company

Line installer

Printing press operator

Telephone operator

Camera operator

Learning about careers   119

CONSTRUCTION

The construction industry includes more occupations than most people realize. It involves the construction of homes, bridges, industrial plants, dams, hospitals, highways, pipelines, and shopping centers.

Architects are the workers who design the structures to be built. Architects spend much of their time in the office at the drawing board. Engineers supervise the building of structures and make sure construction plans are structurally sound. The actual building of structures is done by carpenters, bricklayers, roofers, plumbers, electricians, and other skilled workers.

Some construction jobs require workers to work outside in dusty, noisy, and potentially dangerous conditions. They may also have to work in rain or snow to get the job done.

To be an architect or engineer, you must complete at least four years of college. Other construction jobs can be learned through apprenticeships, vocational training, or through experience. High school courses in carpentry, plumbing, drafting, masonry, welding, and electricity can help you prepare for a construction occupation.

CONSTRUCTION

MAJOR CATEGORIES	EXAMPLES OF CAREERS		TYPICAL PLACES OF EMPLOYMENT
Metalworking	Welder Plumber	Pipefitter Sheet-metal worker	Building contractor Sheet metal shop
Electrical	Electrician Electrical inspector	Electrical engineer	Plumbing firm Electrical firm Construction company
Woodworking	Carpenter Cabinetmaker	Form builder Roofer	Mobile home factory Concrete and block layer company
Masonry	Bricklayer Stonemason Cement mason	Blocklayer Tilesetter Plasterer	Swimming pool company Interior design company Flooring company
Finishing	Drywall installer Glazier Painter	Paperhanger Floorcovering installer	Architectural firm
Construction related	Architect Drafter Civil engineer Elevator installer	Operating engineer Construction laborer Building inspector Heavy equipment operator	

Blocklayer

DEL E. WEBB CORP.

Roofer

GENERAL ELECTRIC

Drafter

Heavy equipment operator

HEALTH

Workers in health occupations have the job of helping keep people healthy or helping heal people who are injured or ill. The field of health is quite broad and the need for health care workers keeps growing. Many workers in health occupations find their work very rewarding because of the personal satisfaction they receive from helping others.

Registered nurses, physicians, pharmacists, and dentists are the most common health care professionals. Veterinarians and therapists are also professional health care workers. Other workers include technicians, dental hygienists, practical nurses, and orderlies. Hospitals employ about half of all workers in the health field. Other workers are employed by clinics, pharmacies, nursing homes, public health agencies, and private offices.

Physicians, veterinarians, and dentists must usually complete seven to ten years of education to become licensed doctors. Registered nurses, medical technicians, dental hygienists, and practical nurses can become qualified workers after two to three years of training. Some registered nurses train four years at a college and receive a bachelor's degree in nursing. Other jobs such as orderlies, nurse's aides, and hospital attendants require no specific training and can be learned on the job. High school courses in health, biology, health occupations, and psychology can orient you to the field of health.

HEALTH

MAJOR CATEGORIES	EXAMPLES OF CAREERS		TYPICAL PLACES OF EMPLOYMENT
Dental	Dentist Dental laboratory technician	Dental hygienist Dental assistant	Dentist's office Doctor's office Hospital
Medical practitioners	Physician Osteopathic physician Veterinarian	Optometrist Chiropractor	Clinic Medical laboratory Drug store
Nursing	Registered nurse Licensed practical nurse	Nursing aid, orderly, and attendant	Ambulance service Optical shop
Medical technologists, technicians, and assistants	Medical technologist Radiologist Emergency medical technician X ray technician	Respiratory therapy worker Electrocardiograph technician Optometric assistant	
Therapy and rehabilitation	Occupational therapist Occupational therapy assistant Physical therapist	Physical therapist assistant Speech pathologist Audiologist	
Other	Pharmacist Paramedic	Dispensing optician	

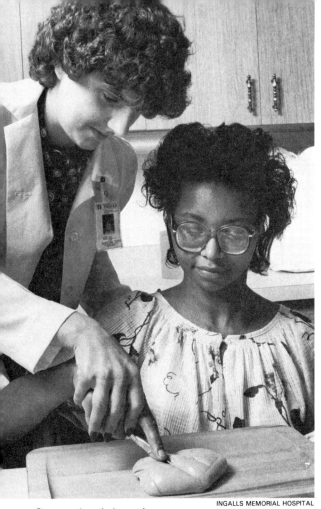

Occupational therapist

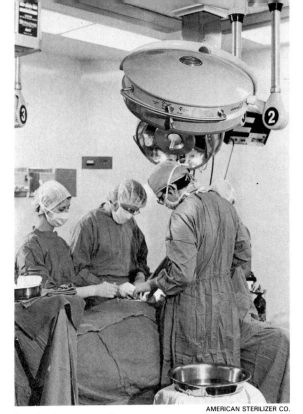

Surgical nurse and surgeons

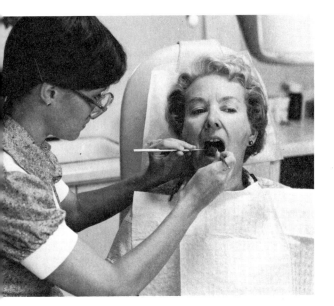

Dental hygienist

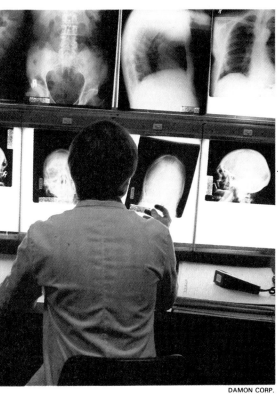

Radiologist

HOME ECONOMICS

Careers in home economics focus on ways to improve the quality of individual and family life. Child care workers, dietitians, fashion designers, interior designers, food editors, consumer communications specialists, and home economics teachers are some of the many occupations in home economics. Their place of work may be a classroom, a day care center, a retail store, a home, or a company.

The professional home economics worker is called a home economist. Home economists have at least a four-year college degree in one or more home economics subject areas. These areas include child development and family relations, food and nutrition, home economics communications, clothing and textiles, family economics and home management, housing and interior design, and home economics education. Dietitians and home economics teachers are home economists. Many fashion buyers and designers, food editors, family counselors, interior designers, and consumer service representatives are also home economists.

Other home economics related occupations such as nutrition aides and child care workers may only require a high school diploma or vocational training. Some fashion designers and clothing buyers may receive their training through a two-year program at a school of fashion design or technology.

High school courses in home economics, child development, clothing, food and nutrition, consumer education, interior design, and family living can help you prepare for a career in home economics.

HOME ECOMONICS

MAJOR CATEGORIES	EXAMPLES OF CAREERS		TYPICAL PLACES OF EMPLOYMENT
Food and nutrition	Dietician Nutrition aide Food technologist Food stylist	Test kitchen specialist Food editor Food service manager	Food company Appliance manufacturer Hospital Nursing home Newspaper Publisher
Clothing and textiles	Clothing buyer Fashion designer Bridal consultant Patternmaker	Seamstress Quality control specialist for textile firm	Retail clothing store Clothing manufacturer Textile manufacturer Bridal shop
Child development and family relations	Child care facility manager	Child care worker Family/marriage counselor	Child care center Nursery Mental health center
Interior design	Home designer Furniture designer	Commercial designer	Family counseling center Interior design shop
Family economics and home management	Family financial counselor	Consultant	Agricultural extension service
Education and consumer services	Consumer communications specialist Teacher	Consumer services representative Extension agent Product specialist	Public and private schools and colleges

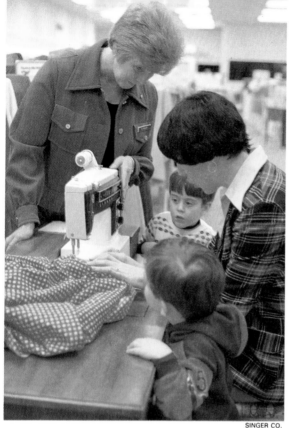

Consumer services representative

Interior designer

Child care worker

Food technologist

HOSPITALITY AND RECREATION

People who work in hospitality and recreation occupations have jobs that are designed to help others enjoy themselves. Since more people are having more free time for leisure, the outlook for jobs in this area is very good.

Travel agents, hotel managers, chefs, sports instructors, and professional athletes are just a few of the careers in this cluster. Travel agents help people plan trips and make room and travel reservations. Hotel managers, with the assistance of reservationists, bellhops, housekeeping assistants, and front desk clerks, check guests in and out, keep the hotel clean, and see to the needs of all the guests. Chefs, with the help of cooks, waiters and waitresses, and host and hostesses prepare and serve food. Sports instructors teach others how to play sports and coach athletes.

Some hospitality and recreation jobs are seasonal because some hotel resorts are only open certain times of the year. For example, ski resorts are only open during the cold months when it snows. Therefore, being a ski instructor or a ski lift operator would be a seasonal job. Also, some hospitality and recreation jobs require working weekends, nights, or holidays—the times when most people are vacationing from their jobs.

Many jobs in hospitality and recreation require no specific education. Workers such as front desk clerks, housekeepers, and waiters and waitresses are often trained on the job. However, managers of large resorts, hotels, restaurants, amusement parks, and recreation facilities usually have a college degree or other advanced training.

HOSPITALITY AND RECREATION

MAJOR CATEGORIES	EXAMPLES OF CAREERS		TYPICAL PLACES OF EMPLOYMENT
Food service	Bartender Chef Cook	Waiter/waitress Food counter worker Dishwasher	Restaurant Bar School or hospital cafeteria
Recreational services	Park caretaker Greenskeeper Camp manager Country club director	Sports pro such as golf pro and tennis pro Bowling alley manager	Country club Golf course Park Camp
Hotel industry	Front desk clerk Hotel manager Food and beverage manager	Housekeeper Bellhop Bell captain	Bowling alley Sports club Amusement park Hotel Resort center
Tourism	Travel agent	Tour guide	Travel agency

Chef

Bellhop

Travel agent

Waitress

MANUFACTURING

Almost everything you use at school, work, and home is manufactured. Workers in manufacturing occupations process foods and chemicals and knit and weave textiles. They also help produce thousands of other products such as machinery, automobiles, household appliances, and food products.

Many workers in manufacturing occupations operate machinery, install and maintain machinery, and move and store materials for manufacturing. These employees are often called blue-collar workers. The white-collar workers are the professionals who oversee production and carry out product research and development. Engineers, scientists, technicians, and production managers make up a large share of the professional workers.

Most manufacturing employees work indoors in factories or plants. Since machinery is used to manufacture goods, many employees work in noisy conditions. Employees who work with dangerous equipment and substances may be required to wear special clothing or use safety devices to guard against possible accidents.

Many blue-collar workers often train on the job to become machine operators. Skilled jobs such as machinists, inspectors, and welders are usually learned through an apprenticeship or training at a technical or vocational school. College degrees are required for jobs such as engineers, scientists, and production managers. Some of the school subjects related to manufacturing occupations are welding, drafting, electricity, machine shop, sheet metal, cabinetmaking, and chemistry.

MANUFACTURING

MAJOR CATEGORIES	EXAMPLES OF CAREERS		TYPICAL PLACES OF EMPLOYMENT
Machining	Machinist Instrument maker	Tool-and-die maker	Electronics manufacturer
Foundry	Patternmaker Molder Coremaker	Furnace operator Extruder	Automotive manufacturer Food processing company Aircraft manufacturer
Other industrial production	Sewing machine operator Cutter Presser	Assembler Automobile painter Welder	Toy manufacturer Furniture manufacturer Appliance manufacturer
Product development	Industrial designer Drafter	Laboratory technician	Ore refinery Steel mill
Management	Supervisor Quality control manager	Production manager Safety inspector	

Sewing machine operators

Furnace operator

Safety inspectors

Quality control managers

MARINE SCIENCE

The lakes, seas, oceans, and rivers are valuable sources of food, fossil fuels, and minerals. They also influence the weather, serve as transportation routes, and offer many kinds of recreation. Workers in marine science work with these bodies of water and their resources.

Oceanographers are scientists who study the movements, the physical properties, and the plant and animal life of oceans. This research helps develop fisheries, forecast weather patterns, and mine ocean resources. Many oceanographers work in laboratories on land. Others explore the ocean at sea. Research at sea requires oceanographers to be away from home for weeks or months at a time.

Fish farmers, oil rig workers, and marine biologists work to get plants, animals, and fuels from the oceans. They work on fishing boats, research ships, and oil rigs.

A career as an oceanographer or a marine biologist requires at least a four-year college degree in oceanography or marine science. Fishing and oil rig workers usually require no special training. They learn on the job from other workers.

MARINE SCIENCE

MAJOR CATEGORIES	EXAMPLES OF CAREERS	TYPICAL PLACES OF EMPLOYMENT
Oceanography	Oceanographer Marine biologist Marine geologist	Navy National Oceanic and Atmospheric Administration College or university Fishery Fishery laboratory Cannery Oil company Well drilling company
Fishing and fish farming	Fisher Fish farmer Fish grader	
Petroleum exploration and extraction	Petroleum engineer Well-drill operator Rotary driller Mud-analysis operator Oil rig worker	

Marine biologist

Oil rig worker

Oceanographer

Fish farmer

MARKETING AND DISTRIBUTION

Marketing and distribution refers to the buying, selling, promotion, and delivery of goods and services. Since a company's success depends on the buying and selling of goods and services, occupations in this cluster are usually found in all businesses.

Sales jobs employ many of the workers in marketing and distribution. There are sales jobs in retail trade, wholesale trade, manufacturing, insurance, real estate, and securities. Generally, a manufacturer's representative sells to wholesalers, retailers, or other companies. Wholesalers sell to retailers. And retailers sell to consumers. Workers in sales need to be personable and outgoing. They also need to be able to meet people easily and relate to them effectively.

Other marketing and distribution jobs include purchasing agents and buyers. These workers have the responsibility of buying supplies, equipment, and products that their companies need to continue business successfully. They meet with salespeople and suppliers to compare the price and quality of goods and services.

Training requirements for sales work varies. The salesperson who sells complex goods or services such as electronic or medical equipment probably will need a college education or some advanced training. Others may be trained on the job by an experienced salesperson. Most buyers and purchasing agents at large companies need a degree in business or merchandising. Small companies may have less educational requirements because they often buy less goods. An associate degree program in purchasing or merchandising may be adequate for an entry-level job. High school courses in business, economics, marketing, and merchandising can help you prepare for a career in marketing and distribution.

MARKETING AND DISTRIBUTION

MAJOR CATEGORIES	EXAMPLES OF CAREERS		TYPICAL PLACES OF EMPLOYMENT
Buying and selling	Buyer Purchasing agent Retail store manager Retail store clerk Industrial sales representative	Manufacturer's sales representative Wholesale sales representative Real estate agent	Retail store Grocery store Manufacturing company Wholesaler Real estate agency School Government office Warehouse
Promotion	Marketing research worker Advertising manager	Copywriter Public relations worker	
Distribution	Shipping clerk Local route driver Loader	Forklift driver Packer	

Forklift driver

Marketing research worker

Manufacturer's sales representative

Clothes buyer

Learning about careers   133

NATURAL RESOURCES AND ENVIRONMENTAL CONTROL

Conservationists, environmentalists, foresters, and ecologists are a few of the careers related to natural resources and environmental control. These workers focus on ways to improve the present and future quality of life. Foresters plan and supervise the growing, protection, and use of trees. Conservationists and environmentalists help people and communities make the best use of their land, water, and air without damaging them or other natural resourses. They also conduct studies to resolve problems related to land use, pollution, solid waste disposal, conservation of natural resources, and the preservation of wildlife.

Most of these occupations require two or more years of technical study, but some may be learned on the job. Professional careers in forestry, conservation, and environmental control require a four-year college degree. School subjects related to environmental control include agriculture, biology, geography, health, industrial arts, and sociology.

NATURAL RESOURCES AND ENVIRONMENTAL CONTROL

MAJOR CATEGORIES	EXAMPLES OF CAREERS	TYPICAL PLACES OF EMPLOYMENT
Environmental engineering	Chemist Geologist Meteorologist Environmental engineer	Mining company Oil company Weather bureau Waste water treatment plant Forest service City council Environmental Protection Agency
Environmental health	Sanatation laboratory tester Pollution control engineer Waste water treatment operator	
Environmental planning	Ecologist Conservationist Forester Botanist Urban planner	

SANTE FE RAILWAY

Pollution control engineer

SOUTHWEST FOREST INDUSTRIES

Forester

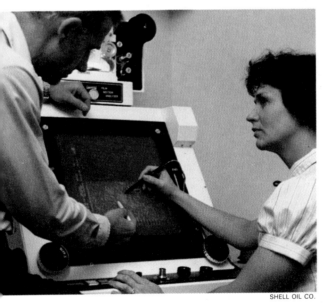

SHELL OIL CO.

Geologist

GENERAL ELECTRIC

Chemist

PERSONAL SERVICES

Workers in personal services help others enjoy their lives and make their lives more comfortable. Occupations in this field include cosmetologists, barbers, dry cleaners, child care workers, funeral workers, and exercise instructors.

Workers in personal services need to be able to perform their services well and to deal effectively with their customers. The impression they make on their customers will determine their success on the job.

Some personal service occupations require special skills that must be learned through formal training. Others require skills that can be learned on the job. For some jobs, such as funeral directing and hairstyling, most workers must obtain a state license after completing a training program or apprenticeship.

PERSONAL SERVICES

MAJOR CATEGORIES	EXAMPLES OF CAREERS		TYPICAL PLACES OF EMPLOYMENT
Grooming services	Cosmetologist Barber Manicurist	Pedicurist Colorist	Hair salon Barber shop Beauty salon
Clothing care	Dry cleaner Laundry worker Shoe repairer	Tailor Seamstress	Dry cleaner Laundry service Clothing store Shoe repair shop
Health care	Exercise instructor Karate instructor	Yoga instructor Masseur/masseuse	Health club Health salon YMCA/YWCA
Domestic care	Cook Butler	Housekeeper Chauffeur	Park district Private household
Child care	Child care worker	Babysitter	Day care center
Animal care	Kennel manager Dog groomer	Animal trainer	Kennel Pet shop
Other	Minister	Funeral director	Funeral home Church

Cosmetologist

Dry cleaner

Funeral director

Exercise instructor

PUBLIC SERVICE

People in public service occupations work for local, county, state, or federal government offices or agencies to provide a variety of services to the community. Postal workers, police officers, sanitation workers, firefighters, teachers, and librarians are all public service occupations.

Postal workers sort and deliver mail. Police officers, firefighters, and safety and health inspectors enforce laws, fight fires, and make inspections. They have the jobs of helping people stay safe and comfortable. Social service workers help individuals, families, and communities solve problems. Teachers, teacher's aides, and librarians help educate people of all ages.

Some public service workers such as teachers, librarians, social workers, and FBI agents must have college degrees. The other occupations in this group usually require at least a high school diploma. Police officers and firefighters must undergo a formal training program and get on-the-job experience before they are fully qualified. To qualify for some government jobs, workers must pass a civil service test.

PUBLIC SERVICE

MAJOR CATEGORIES	EXAMPLES OF CAREERS	TYPICAL PLACES OF EMPLOYMENT
Federal services	Mail carrier Mail clerk Armed services worker Social security clerk Internal Revenue Service worker FBI agent CIA agent USDA meat inspector	Post office Armed Forces Social Security Administration Other federal government offices School State government offices Local and city government offices Library
State and local services	Teacher Teacher's aide Firefighter Police officer Sanitation worker Librarian Social worker Correction officer Coroner Health and safety inspector	

Mail clerk

JOE WALTERBACH

Librarian

BERNIE NOVIA

Teacher

JOE WALTERBACH

Police officer

TRANSPORTATION

Transportation by land, water, and air offers many opportunities for employment. Many workers in this cluster provide transportation by driving cabs, buses, and trucks; flying aircraft; or operating trains and ships. Other employees assist in the transportation of people and cargo. Flight attendants and reservation agents assist airline passengers. Railroad station agents arrange to transport cargo for businesses. Car, bus, truck, plane, railroad, and ship mechanics keep transportation equipment in good working condition.

Workers who drive trucks and buses and who fly planes must be alert and ready to act if something goes wrong. They are responsible for getting their passengers or cargo to their destinations safely. Most states require bus and truck drivers to have a chauffeur's license, which is a commercial driving permit. Airplane pilots must have a commercial pilot's license from the Federal Aviation Administration. Flying can be learned in military or civilian flying schools. Airlines and many businesses prefer pilots who have trained in the Armed Forces because these pilots usually have jet aircraft experience.

Ship officers must have licenses as well. They can be earned with sea experience or by graduating from an approved training program at a merchant marine academy.

Many railroad workers such as brake operators, conductors, and locomotive engineers are trained on the job. Apprenticeship training is the most common way of learning to become railroad repairers. These skilled workers are employed in railroad yards, terminals, engine houses, and locomotive repair facilities. Other transportation repairers and mechanics learn their job skills in a high school, a trade school, or an apprenticeship program.

TRANSPORTATION

MAJOR CATEGORIES	EXAMPLES OF CAREERS		TYPICAL PLACES OF EMPLOYMENT
Land transportation	Bus driver Truck driver Cab driver Railroad worker Brake operator	Conductor Locomotive engineer Diesel mechanic Auto mechanic Traffic dispatcher	Busing company Public or private school system Trucking company Cab service Railroad company Service station Truck stop Airline company Airport Delivery company Shipping company Cruise line Federal government
Air transportation	Airline pilot Airline attendant Reservation agent	Airplane mechanic Air flight controller	
Water transportation	Ship captain Ship officer Deck mate	Merchant marine Ferry boat operator	

Truck driver

AMERICAN STEAMSHIP CO.

Ship officer

AMERICAN AIRLINES

Airline attendant

GREYHOUND LINES, INC.

Reservation agent

Learning about careers   141

KPNX-TV (NBC) PHOENIX

Under which career cluster would
you classify this man's job?

to Review

1. What is a career cluster? How are the fifteen career clusters in this chapter grouped?

2. What careers are found in the arts and humanities cluster? Give at least six examples of careers in this field.

3. What one skill do all office workers need to have?

4. Describe the job duties of communication technicians.

5. How many years of education are required to become a physician, veterinarian, or dentist? How many years of training are needed to become a registered nurse, medical technician, dental hygienist, or practical nurse?

6. What is a home economist? What are the educational requirements for this career?

7. Explain the special working conditions that workers in the hospitality and recreation cluster may face.

8. Explain the difference between blue-collar workers and white-collar workers.

9. What do workers in the marine science career cluster do for a living?

10. What role do the marketing and distribution careers play in business?

11. What does a worker need to be able to do to be successful in a personal services career?

12. Give at least six examples of jobs found in the public service career cluster.

to Discuss

1. What career cluster or career clusters interest you the most? Explain why.

2. People who pursue agricultural careers usually have interests in what areas?

3. Why do most careers in arts and humanities require a great deal of self-discipline?

4. How would you describe the advantages and disadvantages of a business or office career?

5. Describe the working conditions some construction workers may face on the job.

6. Why has there been a decline in some of the jobs in manufacturing?

7. Describe some of the careers related to natural resources and environmental control.

8. What would the working hours be like for many workers in the transportation industry such as airline pilots, truck drivers, railroad conductors, and cab drivers?

to Do

1. Sponsor a career day or career week for the class. Select several careers that interest class members. Then invite people to come and tell about their personal experiences in those jobs.

2. List at least five jobs from any of the career clusters that you would be interested in having. Then list the school subjects that relate to each job. Have you taken any of these subjects or plan to take them in the future? In what other ways could you prepare yourself for these jobs?

3. Prepare a bulletin board illustrating the fifteen career clusters.

Be sure to take advantage of the many
career sources available to you at libraries.

10

Researching careers

After studying this chapter, you will be able to:

☐ Explain how to research careers and occupations.
☐ Evaluate careers based on educational requirements, working hours, working conditions, and pay.

Perhaps you are thinking, "There are so many occupations, how do I find the one that is best for me?" Research is the answer. You need to research the careers that are similar to the job interests and skills you have and the job opportunities you want.

Many sources are available to help you research careers: libraries, career information guides, school counselors, and career conferences and consultations. However, it's up to you to do the learning. You must take the initiative to find information about the careers that interest you. The more information you can learn about occupations, the easier it will be for you to plan your career.

Libraries

Your school and public libraries are both important sources of career information. Many books, brochures, magazines, and audio-visual materials are available on occupations, careers, job training, and job hunting. Once you begin your information search, you'll probably be amazed at the number of sources available to you.

A good place to begin your library research is the card catalog. For general information, look in the card catalog under "careers" or "vocations." If you are interested in a certain career field, such as computers, auto mechanics, or fashion merchandising, look under that topic.

Next, check the periodical section. Magazine articles are one of your best sources for current information. The *Readers' Guide to Periodical Literature* indexes articles which appear in major magazines. The guide lists the articles alphabetically by subject (such as "careers"). It gives the title of the article, the name and date of the magazine, and the page number.

Some libraries have pamphlet files for specific occupations. These files often contain career booklets published by large companies or professional associations. They may also contain current newspaper articles related to careers.

Other sources of occupational information include nonprint materials such as films, filmstrips, cassette tapes, and kits. And some libraries have computerized occupational information systems which allow you to obtain career information instantly.

If you have any trouble locating any information, do not hesitate to ask a librarian for help. If you know what occupations you're interested in, a librarian can help you locate the materials related to your interests.

Career information guides

The U.S. Department of Labor publishes a number of career information guides to help people identify occupations and career options. Three common guides are the *Dictionary of Occupational Titles,* the *Occupational Outlook Handbook,* and the *Guide for Occupational Exploration.* These guides can usually be found in your local library, school library, or school guidance office.

The *Dictionary of Occupational Titles* (DOT) provides standard descriptions for over 20,000 jobs. Jobs are described in terms of general duties and work characteristics needed for the job. This information can help you learn about different careers and help you match your skills, abilities, and interests to

specific job descriptions.

The *Occupational Outlook Handbook* describes hundreds of occupations including the training and education needed for each occupation, expected earnings and working conditions, and job prospects for the future. It provides up-to-date information for most any job to help individuals choose fulfilling careers.

The *Guide for Occupational Exploration* groups thousands of occupations by interests and by abilities and traits required for successful job performance. For example, all jobs that involve the operation of heavy machinery and equipment are grouped together under the heading "Equipment Operation." The guide is designed to help people see themselves realistically in regard to their ability to meet job requirements.

School counselors

School counselors also play an important role in providing career information. When you want to know more about a specific occupation, a counselor can direct you to the information you need. Many counselors keep career files in their offices that contain up-to-date information about different occupations and their educational requirements.

If you are in the process of trying to determine a career interest, a counselor can help you explore your options. A counselor will help you consider career possibilities in relation to your abilities and personal goals. He or she can also answer questions about entry requirements and costs of schools, colleges, and training programs that offer the education you need to prepare for a specific career.

Career conferences and consultations

Schools often have career days where representatives from a variety of occupations, professions, and colleges are available to speak to interested students, 10-1. Be sure to participate in these programs and talk with company and college representatives.

If possible, consult workers who are in jobs that interest you. Having a chance to actually see and talk with workers will give you insight into their occupations. Most people will be glad to talk with you about their jobs and careers. By asking the right questions, you can find out what kind of training is important and how workers got their first jobs. You can also ask workers what they like most and least about their jobs. Informal interviews with people will help you learn more about a specific occupation. They will help you learn more about the business world. They will help you make future job contacts, and they will give you practice at interviewing.

EVALUATING CAREERS

As you research the careers that interest you, be sure to evaluate each one closely. There are certain questions you should be able to answer about each career. What educational requirements would you need for the career? What would be the working hours? Under what conditions would you be working? How much pay could you expect to earn from the career? Finding the answers to these questions will help you choose a more satisfying and rewarding occupation.

Educational requirements

Education is often the most important consideration when evaluating careers. The career you choose will determine the training and education you need. You may already be in the process of learning skills for an occupation in your high school classes. However, most occupations require further training after high school.

Does the occupation or occupations you're

INGALLS MEMORIAL HOSPITAL

10-1 Attending career fairs can help you discover careers that are similar to the job interests you have and the job opportunities you want.

interested in require further education? How much time, effort, and money are you willing to spend on your education? Can you receive the education you need through occupational training? Could you learn the skills you need through an apprenticeship? Will you need a college degree? Should you consider career training through the Armed Forces? Remember, the amount of training and education you obtain will influence your earnings and your opportunities for job advancement.

Occupational training. Occupational training prepares a person for a job in a specific field, 10-2. Training can be received through occupational schools, skill centers, community colleges, company training programs, and correspondence programs. Since the quality of training can vary from one source to another, it's important to investigate a training program before you enroll.

If you choose to attend an occupational school, skill center, or a community college, be selective. Make sure the school has up-to-date equipment and facilities to provide you with up-to-date training. There are many fine occupational schools with excellent instructors. There are also schools that will be willing to take your money but fail to provide you with the training you need. Your guidance counselor or coordinator can probably help you evaluate occupational schools and help you choose an appropriate one for you.

Some companies will train prospective employees for specific skills that are needed within their companies. Company training may be offered through regular class instruction by company instructors. Or trainers from outside the company may be brought in to provide instruction. Company training offers new employees an opportunity to develop new skills, and it helps older employees improve the skills they have.

If you live in an isolated area, you may find correspondence courses a good way to further your education. These courses are often offered through local high schools, community colleges, and universities and through private correspondence schools. Students complete the course requirements at home and mail their work to the school for evaluation and

10-2 These students are training to be drafters at a vocational skill center.

course credit. Be sure to consider taking correspondence courses carefully before enrolling. Educating yourself by this method usually requires a great deal of self-discipline since there is no teacher close by to give direction and assistance.

Apprenticeships. Another way to learn the skills for an occupation is through an apprenticeship. An apprenticeship is a type of education in which a worker learns the knowledge and skills for a trade or craft while working on the job. Skills are actually learned by doing them under the supervision of a highly skilled tradesperson. See 10-3.

Over 350 apprenticeships are registered in the U.S. Bureau of Apprenticeship and Training, a division of the U.S. Department of Labor. They range from carpentry to auto mechanics. A high school diploma or equivalency certificate is the general requirement for applying for an apprenticeship. However, application requirements may differ in various states and from one trade to another.

Not all of an apprentice's training is learned on the job. Apprentices also take classroom instruction. Apprentice programs require that the apprentice learn the entire trade, not just parts of it. This is accomplished by breaking down each trade or craft into basic skill blocks. As apprentices complete each block, their skill and understanding of the trade grow and their pay increases. Most apprenticeships take about four years to complete.

If you like to work with your hands and want to learn a specific craft, an apprenticeship may be right for you. Employment opportunities and earnings are good for those who complete apprenticeships.

A college education. A high school education or occupational training is adequate for many occupations, but a college education is often necessary to be a professional in a certain occupational field. For example, two years of training at an occupational school or two-year college can prepare you to be an architectural drafter. An architectural drafter is

10-3 Through an auto mechanics apprenticeship, this young woman is learning skills on the job under the supervision of a highly skilled mechanic.

someone who makes drawings of buildings to be built. However, it takes five or six years of college with two to three years of work experience to become a registered architect. An architect is the person who designs buildings. Although the two occupations are in the same field, the job of an architect requires advanced training. Since the architect has more training and education than an architectural drafter, the architect has more skills to offer. Therefore, the architect is able to earn a higher salary.

If college is a part of your career plans, be sure to choose a college or university that can help you achieve your career goals. For example, if you want to become a mechanical engineer, choose a school that has a reputable engineering department. To find out which colleges offer the programs you're interested in, begin by talking with your guidance counselor. A guidance counselor can help you review college catalogs and evaluate the programs they offer. Compare different colleges and universities on the basis of reputation, entry requirements, cost, and convenience. Then apply to the school or schools that you would like to attend. Sometimes it's best to apply to more than one school. You may or may not be accepted by all schools because of certain entry requirements. Also, applying to more than one school gives you time to reconsider the alternatives you have. A college education is an investment in your future; make your choice carefully.

Armed Forces. Each year the Armed Forces provide thousands of men and women educational training that can be used in both military and civilian careers. Training is given for clerical and administrative jobs, skilled construction work, electrical and electronic occupations, auto repair, and hundreds of other specialties, 10-4.

Receiving educational training through a branch of the Armed Forces has a number of advantages. There is little or no cost to the student for training. The student gets paid a generous salary while being trained. And the student receives many benefits such as paid vacations, paid health care programs, free housing, and opportunities for travel and advancement. However, military life does have its disadvantages. It is more disciplined than civilian life. People in the military must do what they are told, wear what they are told, and go where they are told. When a person joins a branch of the Armed Forces, that person must stay for three, four, or six years or until the end of his or her contract. People in the military cannot just drop out or resign before the end of their terms if they decide they do not like military life.

Joining the military may be right for you if you want education and training beyond high school but cannot afford to pay for it. You also must be willing to conform to the military way of life and work well with others.

Working hours

In the working world, people work a variety of hours. As some people are going to work, others are leaving their jobs to go home. A baker may start work at one o'clock in the morning. A night security guard may go to work at ten o'clock at night.

What working hours would you like to have? Would you mind working long or irregular hours? Would you prefer a seasonal occupation? Since the occupation you choose will determine your working hours, it's important to consider working hours in your career planning. For example, if you know you want to work daytime hours during weekdays only, you may not want to consider a career in nursing. As a nurse, you may be required to work afternoon and night shifts as well as weekends and holidays. If the thought of being in an office building nine to five, five days a week has no appeal to you, an occupation that is less confining may be better. A career in sales, construction, or police work would enable you to move around from place to place.

Most employees work forty hours a week. Office workers usually work from nine o'clock to five o'clock, Monday through Friday. Factory and service workers work in eight hour shifts. They may work the morning shift, 7:00 a.m. to 3:00 p.m.; the afternoon shift, 3:00 p.m. to 11:00 p.m.; or the night shift, 11:00

p.m. to 7:00 a.m., five days a week.

Other working plans also exist. Some employees work ten hours a day, four days a week. One work plan allows workers to select their own working hours. For example, an office worker could choose to work 7:30 a.m. to 3:30 p.m. instead of the usual nine to five.

Many occupations require people to work irregular hours, 10-5. People in real estate and insurance sales often work evening hours in order to schedule appointments with their clients. Some doctors also may work irregular hours. An obstetrician may be called to deliver a baby any time of the day or night.

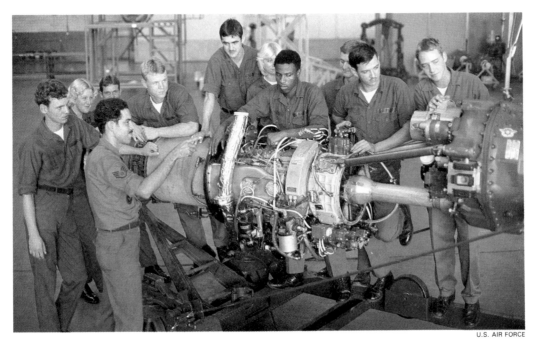

U.S. AIR FORCE

10-4 The Air Force and other branches of the Armed Forces offer a variety of educational opportunities and training programs.

WENDY'S

10-5 A manager of a fast food restaurant can expect to work irregular hours.

Some occupations are seasonal such as farming field crops, playing professional sports, and operating a ski resort. Farmers usually work their longest hours when the crops must be planted, fertilized, and harvested. Professional football players work long and hard hours during the practice and play seasons and are off the rest of the year. Ski resort owners only operate when there's snow which is usually during the winter and early spring months.

Working conditions

When evaluating occupations, you should also consider the conditions in which you will be working. Are there certain environmental, physical, or mental conditions that you would object to? Would you be opposed to working in dusty, dirty, noisy, hot, or cold conditions? Would you be opposed to lifting boxes, climbing ladders, or sitting at a desk all day? Would you be opposed to following a set routine, meeting work deadlines, or supervising and directing others? See 10-6.

Do you want to do the same job over and over like an assembly line or factory job? Or do you want a variety of job responsibilities? Do you prefer to work alone or to work with others as a team?

Every occupation has desirable and undesirable working conditions. You'll want to choose the one that will be the most satisfying to you.

The pay: starting and potential

Although an occupation should not be selected just on the basis of earnings, pay is an important aspect to consider. How much money do you want to earn? How much do you want to be earning fifteen years from now?

Find out about the wages or salaries you can expect to earn in the occupations that interest you. What is the starting pay? How much do experienced workers earn? Can you support yourself on that amount of income? Could you support a family?

The amount of the paycheck is not the only financial consideration. Does the company provide any fringe benefits? *Fringe benefits* are financial extras in addition to the regular paycheck. Medical and life insurance coverage, paid vacations, bonuses, and retirement plans are examples of fringe benefits. You may find a lower paying job with excellent benefits to be as beneficial or more beneficial than a higher paying job with fewer or no benefits.

10-6 Climbing tall poles to work on high-powered electrical lines would be an undesirable working condition for many people.

ARIZONA PUBLIC SERVICE

to Review

1. What sources are available to help you research careers?
2. Where is a good place to begin your library research?
3. How can the *Readers' Guide to Periodical Literature* help you in your career search?
4. Name three common guides published by the U.S. Department of Labor that can help you identify occupations and career options.
5. How can a school counselor help you learn more about careers?
6. What do you have to gain by talking to people who are working in jobs that interest you?
7. What four questions can help you evaluate careers that interest you?
8. Where can you receive occupational training?
9. What is an apprenticeship?
10. What are the advantages and disadvantages of receiving educational training through a branch of the Armed Forces?
11. Why is it important to consider working hours in your career planning?

12. What are fringe benefits? Why should they be considered as well as wages or a salary when selecting a career?

to Discuss

1. Why is it important to research careers before choosing a career?
2. What types of career planning information are available in your school's guidance office?
3. Does your school have career days or career conferences? If yes, when will they be held? Which company or college representatives would you talk with to find out more about the career or careers in which you are interested?
4. What are the educational requirements for the careers in which you are interested?
5. Why is it important to be selective when choosing an occupational school, skill center, or college? What factors should you consider when choosing a school?
6. What working hours would you like to have on the job?
7. What working conditions would you object to in a job? Describe the ideal working conditions.
8. Why is it important to look not only at the starting salary but at future salary expectations as well when researching careers?

to Do

1. Choose three careers which interest you. Then go to your school or local library, look in the *Readers' Guide to Periodical Literature,* and write down two magazine articles that directly relate to each career. Read one of the six articles and write a one-page report about it.
2. Look up the same three careers you identified above in the *Occupational Outlook Handbook.* Find out the training and education needed for each career, expected earnings and working conditions, and job prospects for the future.
3. For each one of the three careers you identified above, locate one successful person in that career and interview that person about the work he or she does. Ask questions to find out about the following:
   - Duties of the job.
   - Skills needed for the job.
   - Education or training needed for the job.
   - Working hours.
   - Working conditions.
   - Future of the job and career.

Career decisions are major decisions that need
to be made with careful thought and planning.

11

Making career decisions

After studying this chapter, you will be able to:

☐ Explain the decision-making process.
☐ Use the decision-making process to help you make career decisions and other important decisions.

Rick is sitting at the kitchen table. He shakes his head as he stares at the blank paper before him. Rick has an assignment to do for his English class. The assignment is to write a two-page paper about the career he wants to pursue.

Rick is seventeen, and he has never seriously thought about a career for himself. Now, this assignment is forcing him to sit down and think about his future. But Rick has no idea what he wants to do when he graduates. He thinks there must be some logical way to make such an important decision, but he doesn't know the process.

Rick is right. There is a logical way to make important decisions. It's called the decision-making process.

THE DECISION-MAKING PROCESS

Making decisions is something you do every day. From the minute you get up in the morning, you begin making decisions. You decide what to wear, what to eat, and what time to leave for school. These decisions are so routine and minor that you probably don't even know you are making them. You just make them automatically. See 11-1.

Then there are other decisions which take a little more thought such as deciding which movie to see or what album to buy, 11-2. These decisions usually take a little more time, but they are still easy to make.

Then there are the major decisions. Major decisions are the tough ones—the ones that guide your career and personal life. Deciding whether or not to go to college, to get married, or to buy a car are major decisions because they tend to have long lasting effects, 11-3.

If you become a manager or supervisor on the job, you will also have major decisions to make. You may have to decide whether or not to hire or fire an employee. Or you may have to decide how to sell and market a new product. These are decisions that not only affect you. They also affect the company and the people with whom you work.

If you make a wrong decision about something that is not very important, the decision normally does not affect your life to any great extent. For example, Bill decided to buy his father a blue shirt for his birthday, but he bought the wrong size. Although Bill chose the wrong size, he was able to take the shirt back and exchange it for the right size. A wrong decision was made, but it was corrected with little effort and time.

On the other hand, if you make a wrong decision about something that is important, the

AMERICAN DENTAL ASSOCIATION

11-1 Deciding to brush your teeth is a routine decision that most people make automatically.

THE RECORD BAR, INC.

11-2 Deciding what album to buy is a decision most people would find easy to make.

decision may influence your life a great deal. For example, Diane decided to be a dentist just because her father is a dentist. She went through college and dental school and then realized she had made a big mistake. Being a dentist the rest of her life was the last thing she wanted to do. In fact, she only chose denistry because she didn't take the time to investigate other careers.

Now Diane has realized that forestry is the career for her, and she wants to return to college for a forestry degree. Although an education never hurt anyone, Diane spent most of her college years unhappy about her career deci-

sion. Her parents also spent a lot of money on an education Diane doesn't want to use. Since Diane's parents are now paying tuitions for her younger sister and brother, Diane will have to pay her own tuition. She will have to work a couple of years as a dentist to pay for her college expenses or else take out a loan. Diane's quick career decision influenced her a great deal. It caused her much unhappiness as well as future financial problems.

When you have important decisions to make, you need to approach them carefully and logically. The decision-making process helps you do this. Here are the steps to follow when

11-3 Deciding what type of car to buy is considered a major decision for most people because it usually involves a large sum of money.

you face big decisions.

1. Define the problem. Determine the decision to be made and its importance to your life.
2. Establish goals. Set specific goals for yourself. Then establish what you want to accomplish from the decision you are about to make.
3. Identify resources. Make a list of all the things available to you that you can use to help you reach your goals. Include your human resources such as your aptitudes and abilities as well as your nonhuman resources like money, property, and equipment.
4. Consider the alternatives. Explore all the options that are available to you, and weigh the advantages and disadvantages of each. A good way to test alternatives is to ask yourself the following questions. Would this decision have a bad effect on me or anyone else? Will this decision help me reach my goals? Would this decision be illegal or against the law? Will I be happy with the decision I make?
5. Make a decision. Choose an alternative that will help you reach your goals. If you have followed all of these steps and have thought out the situation very carefully, you will probably be happy with the decision you make.
6. Implement the decision. Carry out the decision you have made. In other words, turn your words into action.
7. Evaluate the results. Look back on the decision and judge its success. Did the decision solve the problem? Are your goals being met? Are you satisfied with the results of the decision? Evaluating the results of a decision will help improve your future decision-making skills.

CAREER DECISIONS

Some of the hardest decisions to make are career decisions. Many people have no idea what they want to do for a living. They just go from job to job and never take the time to select a career and make plans to pursue it.

Your own career is too important for that. Career decisions are major decisions that influence your entire future. They need to be made with careful thought and planning. The work you choose will largely determine the way you live, the people you meet, the money you earn, and the satisfaction you get out of life. See 11-4.

You probably know some people who never really made career plans, they just ended up in a job. Some just took any job and hoped that it would lead to a fulfilling career. Some let their parents pick a career for them. And some chose the same career their best friends selected. But do you really think you would be satisfied letting someone else make your decisions for you and not take the time to make them yourself? With the decision-making process, choosing a career can be made easy and a great deal of fun. In the following case studies, each person solves his or her career problems by using the decision-making process.

WHAT CAREER FOR ALICIA?

Alicia, a senior in high school, is a very talented person, especially in art. She sketches, water colors, and paints with oils. Many of her illustrations have been printed in the school newspaper. Alicia designs and makes her own clothes. She also has designed the costumes for all the school plays that have been given over the past two years. Alicia has done well at every subject she has studied and every activity she has pursued. That's part of her problem. Alicia has so many interests and skills that she's having a hard time deciding what career to choose. She is only sure of one thing; she wants to go to college.

The problem

Alicia's problem is deciding what career she wants to pursue so she can select the best college for that career.

The goals

At the suggestion of her school guidance counselor, Alicia began solving her problem by writing down what she wants to accomplish

over the next five to ten years. She wrote down four goals:
- To graduate from a four-year college or university with a degree in art, fashion design, fashion merchandising, interior design, or textile design.
- To work full-time in business in my chosen career field.
- To be successful and maybe even famous in the career I choose.
- To incorporate a career with a family.

The resources

Alicia thought carefully about what she has that can help her make a career decision. She made this list of resources:
- Well developed abilities in art and design.
- An excellent scholastic record.
- Participation in extracurricular school activities, including those in art, design, and sewing construction.
- Money to pay for a college education.
- A helpful guidance counselor who can put me in touch with professionals in career areas in which I am interested.

The alternatives

Alicia began thinking about the career areas in which she was interested. She realized that the one thing that could help her make a career decision was to talk with people who are working in the careers in which she is interested. With the help of her guidance counselor, Alicia made appointments to talk with a number of

INGALLS MEMORIAL HOSPITAL

11-4 The satisfaction you get from your job will influence the satisfaction you get out of life.

professionals, 11-5. She talked with a clothes buyer at a large department store, two interior designers (one who specializes in home design and the other in commercial design), a yarn designer for a textile manufacturer, and an art director at an advertising agency. Alicia was unable to locate a fashion designer in her city, but the clothes buyer was able to tell her a great deal about designers from her buying experiences.

Alicia gained a wealth of knowledge from her "information" interviews. They helped her narrow her career choices to fashion design, fashion merchandising, and textile design.

The decision

When Alicia began researching her three career interests at colleges and universities, she realized just how closely the three areas are related. All three careers would require many of the same college courses. So Alicia decided that trying to choose one specific career right now was not necessary. She could make that decision after she had taken the basic courses in clothing and textiles. Alicia also decided the next step was to apply to schools that had a strong clothing and textiles department with an emphasis in design.

Implementing the decision

Alicia immediately applied to two colleges that had strong and reputable clothing and textile departments. One college was a private school and the other was a state university. She was accepted at both. She choose to attend the state university since it was a larger school with more educational and cultural opportunities available to students.

Evaluating the results

After two years of basic college courses and a few courses in clothing and textiles, Alicia realized that a career in fashion design, fashion merchandising, or textile design was not for her. She wanted a career in which she could use more of her painting and drawing skills. She heard about a visual arts program at a neighboring college that sounded perfect for her. So Alicia decided to transfer to that school. Lucky for Alicia, most of the courses she had taken up to now fulfilled most of the general requirements for a degree in visual arts. Alicia would be able to graduate in two more years and one summer school session.

Questions to discuss

1. How do you think the decision-making process helped Alicia make her decisions?
2. How did research play an important role in Alicia's decision making?
3. Why is "evaluating the results" such an important step in the decision-making process, especially in Alicia's situation?
4. What have you learned from Alicia's career planning experience that may help you make wise career decisions?

TO SCHOOL OR WORK?

Jerry will graduate from high school at the end of the year. He has already decided that he wants a career in food service. He became interested in the food service field when he began his cooperative education work experience as a cook's helper in a local restaurant. After four months of work, he is now helping the chef develop new recipes.

The problem

Jerry's problem is to decide what type of career he wants in food service. He thinks he wants to be a chef. However, he knows that to be a chef requires further training. Right now, Jerry is tired of school and classrooms, and he thinks he needs a break from school. And yet, Jerry doesn't want to spend the rest of his life being a cook's helper. Jerry just wishes be could start being a chef right away.

The goals

Jerry talked to his school counselor about the decision he's trying to make. The counselor suggested he write down the main things he wants most in a food service career. He made the following list:

- To become a successful chef in a large city restaurant.
- To work with agreeable and creative co-workers and superiors.
- To earn a good salary and have job security.
- To eventually own and manage a fine restaurant.

The resources

The counselor also suggested that Jerry write down the resources he can use to reach his career goals. Here's his list:

- A high school degree with good grades.
- Classes in food service.
- Cooperative education work experience as a cook's helper at a local restaurant.
- A strong desire to succeed in the food service business—willing to work long hours, weekends, and evenings.
- Money available to pay for training.

The alternatives

Jerry began researching food service careers a little more closely. He looked through all the information available in the school career center and the library on food service careers, especially chefs, 11-6. He also talked with one food service manager at a fast food restaurant, two restaurant owners, and a noted chef in a large restaurant. He realized he had three major alternatives if he wanted to pursue a career as a chef. He should do one of the following:

- Earn a two-year culinary arts degree at a college or culinary institute.
- Continue working as a cook's helper and begin taking food service courses at a community college.
- Enter into a three-year chef apprenticeship program.

GENERAL ELECTRIC

11-6 Researching careers at the library or school career center can help you identify the job you want.

SCOTTSDALE VOCATIONAL TECHNICAL CENTER

11-5 Talking with people who are working in careers that interest you will help you learn more about specific jobs.

The decision

Jerry decided an apprenticeship would be ideal for him. It would allow him to train to be a chef while he was on the job earning pay. There would be some classroom instruction, but most of his training would be learned in the commercial kitchen from highly qualified food service professionals. Jerry had not been aware of the apprenticeship program until he read about it at the career center. Now he could hardly wait to apply for the program.

Implementing the decision

Jerry immediately sent for an application and applied for an apprenticeship. He knew it was important to apply early because entry into the apprenticeship program is very competitive. If he didn't get into the program, he would have to make other career plans.

Evaluating the results

Due to Jerry's good grades, food service experience, and enthusiasm, he was accepted into the apprenticeship program. He began the program in the fall in Chicago, which was only three hours from his parents home. From day one, he knew he had made the right decision. He was learning so much every day and enjoying every minute of it. He also adjusted to living in a large city. He had been a little concerned about this before moving.

Now Jerry was looking forward to completing the apprenticeship and working as a professional chef.

Questions to discuss

1. How did Jerry's list of career goals help him make a decision?
2. How did Jerry's list of resources help him move closer to his career goals?
3. In Jerry's situation, how did research play an important role in his decision making?
4. What might have been the consequences if Jerry had not taken the time to plan his career through careful decision making?
5. What have you learned from Jerry's career planning experience that may help you make wise career decisions?

WHAT NEXT FOR VIC?

Vic worked as a welder's helper during his cooperative work experience in high school. He worked for a small family-owned company whose business was rebuilding heavy vehicle equipment. Not long after Vic began his work experience, his boss, the owner of the company, could see that Vic was a good worker. He gave Vic special instruction and showed him many tricks of the trade.

After Vic graduated, his boss offered him a full-time job with the company. Vic accepted the position. Within five years, Vic became shop supervisor and was practically running the place. Then some changes took place. The boss' son joined the business, the boss retired, and the son became head of the company.

Vic was surprised and discouraged when this happened. He was close to his boss. He had even thought there might be a chance for him to buy into the business and become part owner. With these unexpected changes, there seemed little chance for that.

With the new boss in charge, a lot of changes occurred. Three employees were fired. New work policies were posted. Then two new employees were hired. One was a friend of the boss who had six years of welding experience.

Now Vic is not only disappointed about not being able to buy into the business, he's concerned about his future with the company. He no longer feels secure about his job. He is wondering if he needs to look for another job. He's also wondering if he'll ever be able to have his own welding business. Vic feels he's at a turning point in his career, but he doesn't know where to turn next.

The problem

Vic's problem is to decide what he wants to do about his career. Until now, he'd been happy with his job. He had felt secure about his position and his future with the company and excited about the prospect of buying into the company.

Now, he's concerned that the new boss may be planning to replace him with the new employee with welding experience. Vic is also concerned about reaching his lifetime goals of owning and operating his own business. For the last three years, he had assumed he would be able to buy into this company. Now that doesn't seem possible. He needs to figure out a new way to reach this goal.

The goals

To help solve his problem, Vic wrote down a list of the things he wants to achieve from his career:

- To learn as much as he can about rebuilding heavy vehicle equipment and how to operate a rebuilding business.
- To feel secure about his job.
- To make a large enough salary to support a family comfortably.
- To own his own rebuilding business.

The resources

Vic also wrote down the resources he has to help him be successful in his career. Here is Vic's list:

- Seven years of welding experience.
- Six years of heavy equipment experience.
- Two years of supervisory experience.
- Eagerness to learn the ins and outs of the heavy equipment rebuilding business.
- Willingness to work hard to succeed.
- Married to a supportive wife.
- A steadily increasing savings account.

The alternatives

After outlining his goals and resources, Vic made another list—a list of alternatives concerning his career.

- Continue working for the company as if nothing has changed and hope that the new boss will get tired of running the company and sell it.
- Talk with the new boss about my future with the company and my interest in becoming a part owner.
- Go to college part-time to work on a degree in business, and continue saving money to start my own rebuilding business, 11-7.
- Borrow money to begin or buy my own rebuilding business.
- Take a job with another company.

11-7 Continuing your education can help you broaden your knowledge and advance in your career.

The decision

After careful thought, Vic chose two alternatives. He decided to talk with his new boss about his future with the company and his interest in becoming a part owner. By doing this, he would be able to find out for sure what the boss' plans are for him at the company. He would also find out if there's any possibility of buying into the company. Vic also decided to go to college part-time to work on a degree in business and to continue saving money to start his own business. He realized it would be wise to get more business experience before he invested or borrowed money to begin his own business.

Implementing the decision

The following week Vic talked to his boss about his future with the company and the possibility of buying into the business. Vic also signed up to take two business courses at the community college. And Vic began saving more money each month for the business he plans to establish.

Evaluating the results

Talking to his boss was one of the best decisions Vic could have made. Vic found out that his boss was very pleased with his work and that he was planning to give him more responsibility for running the business. His boss even said he might be interested in selling the entire company in four or five years. His boss also offered to pay half of Vic's school expenses since the courses should help him do a better job for the company.

Vic also gained a great deal of information from the two courses he took at the community college. This convinced him to take more courses and work on an associate degree in business.

The only problem Vic ran into was saving more money each month. Although he wasn't able to save as much as he had originally planned, he did transfer his account to a money market account where he began earning a higher interest rate.

Questions to discuss

1. How do you think the decision-making process helped Vic make his decisions?
2. How did Vic's goals help him make his decisions?
3. Do you think Vic made the right decisions at this point in his career? Why?
4. What is the most important thing you think Vic learned when he evaluated the results of his decisions?

to Review

1. Why is it important to be extra careful when making major decisions about your career and personal life?

2. What are the seven steps to logical decision-making?

3. What is the purpose of step three in the decision-making process?

4. What questions can you ask yourself to test alternatives for solving a problem or making a decision?

5. What is the purpose of the last step in the decision-making process?

6. The work you choose can largely determine what four factors?

7. Name ways some people make career decisions other than using the decision-making process.

to Discuss

1. Give examples of routine decisions people make everyday. Give examples of major decisions people must make in their lives.

2. What are the advantages of using the decision-making process to solve a problem or make a decision?

3. Explain how making the wrong decision about something that is important can affect a person's life?

4. Why do you think career decisions are some of the hardest decisions to make?

5. How might the decision-making process work for making family or group decisions, establishing government policies, or solving business problems?

to Do

1. Apply the decision-making process to an important decision (other than a career decision) you might face within a year or two. Write down the problem, your goals, your resources for reaching the goals, your alternatives, and the decision you would make. What are the pros and cons of using the decision-making process to solve problems and make decisions? Discuss your opinions with the class.

2. Use the decision-making process to help you narrow your career choices or choose a specific career. Write down the problem, your goals, your resources for reaching the goals, your alternatives, and the decision you would make. Share your results with the class.

part
four

The job hunt

Most employers will ask you to fill out an
application form when you apply for jobs.

12

Applying for jobs

After studying this chapter, you will be able to:

☐ Explain how to find job openings.
☐ Prepare job resumes and letters of application.
☐ Fill out job application forms correctly.

Once you know what kind of job you want, you are ready for the job hunt. The challenge now is finding a job that will fit into your career plans. Half the battle of job hunting is finding job openings. The other half is getting interviews with employers.

To be successful on the job hunt, you need to have a plan. First, you need to make a list of all the companies where you can apply for jobs. Second, you need to prepare a resume summarizing your education, work experience, and other qualifications for the job you want. And third, you need to contact the person in each company who has the ability to hire you.

FINDING JOB OPENINGS

Job hunting takes work. Jobs won't come to you, you have to go to the jobs. To find job openings you will need to find employers who are looking for a worker with your qualifications. How do your find these employers? You can find them through a variety of sources. Friends and relatives, school placement services, direct employer contact, want ads, trade and professional journals, and state and private employment services are all sources of job leads. Try using many or all of these sources in your job hunt. The more sources you use, the more job openings you are likely to find. Then you'll have a better chance of finding a job you really like instead of taking the first job that comes along.

Friends and relatives

Friends and relatives can be one of your best sources of job leads. They may know of employers who need a person with your skills. Or they may know other people who do the kind of work you're interested in, and these people may know of job openings.

When you mention your job search to friends and relatives, be sure to explain the type of job you want. Also give them copies of your resume. (Resumes are discussed later in this chapter.) A resume will help them become familiar with your educational background and work experiences. The more they know about you, the better able they will be to talk about your skills and abilities to possible employers.

Although you should not be bashful about asking friends and relatives for job leads, you should not expect them to find you a job. It's your responsibility to follow up on job leads, set up interviews, and sell yourself to a potential employer.

School placement services

Many schools have a placement office or a school or vocational counselor to help students find jobs in the community. Students are usually asked to register with the placement office. Then when a job comes available, the placement office contacts qualified students to interview for the job.

Although your school placement office can be a good source for jobs, remember you may be one of many selected to interview for available jobs. Competition is often stiff. Therefore, don't depend on your school as your only source of job leads. Investigate and use the many other sources available to you.

Direct employer contact

One of the best ways to find job openings is to contact employers directly. About half the people who use this method of job hunting are successful in finding a job.

To help you make a list of possible employers, look through the Yellow Pages in your phone book. Visit your chamber of commerce and public library. Ask your friends and relatives for contacts. Be sure to write down the names, addresses, and phone numbers of all the businesses that might have the job you want. Also, don't overlook the job possibilities where you work now or where you have worked in the past.

Once you have your list of employers, begin contacting the person in each company who has the ability to hire you. This may be the personnel director, the department manager, or the president of the company. If you do not know the name of this person, call the company and ask the receptionist. When you know the person to contact, write the person a letter, make a phone call, or visit the company in person. Sometimes it's best to use a combination of methods. For example, you may want to write a letter of application, then about a week later, call the person to try and arrange an interview.

Want ads

Newspaper advertisements are another source of job leads, 12-1. They are listed in newspapers under the section called the "Classified Ads" or the "Want Ads." Reading ads can teach you a lot about the job market as well as furnish you with job leads. You can learn what types of jobs are most available, what skills are needed for certain jobs, and what salaries are being paid for jobs. This information can help you when applying for any job.

One of the best days to read the want ads is Sunday. The Sunday paper tends to have more ads than any other daily paper. When reading the ads, look through all the jobs listed. Often, an interesting job might appear under the most unlikely heading. As you read, you may come across abbreviated words that are unfamiliar to you. Chart 12-2 lists some of the most commonly used abbreviations in want ads and the words they represent.

After reading all the ads, circle the ones that match your job interests. Then answer them as soon as possible. The longer you wait to apply, the more likely the jobs will become filled by other applicants.

Unfortunately, only 15 percent of all job openings are advertised. Therefore, don't rely on the want ads alone to help you find a job.

Trade and professional journals

Most trades and professions publish their own magazines and journals. Sometimes job ads are listed in these publications. Most of the ads advertise for experienced workers, and the jobs may be located anywhere in the United States or abroad. Therefore, trade and professional journals may be a weak source for job leads, but they can help you in other ways.

Trade and professional journals contain the latest information about the latest developments and trends in a trade or profession. This information can help you learn more about your occupational area and help you be more knowledgeable on job interviews.

State employment services

The federal government has established public employment offices in every state. These offices are available to help job seekers find job openings in and out of government. This service is provided free by the government.

BOOKKEEPER
Expd. bookkeeper req. for expanding Loop law firm. Require full charge person w/typing. Previous law office exp. a plus. Resumes to: Ms. Moen, 135 S. LaSalle, Suite 2610, Chicago, Ill. 60603

CARPENTER
Position open for experienced wood shop worker, laminator, furniture maker. Good opportunity for advancement. Call Mike, 528-8066.

CLERK/SECRETARY
Purchasing-Materials dept. of near North suburban mfr. needs versatile clerk. Some secretarial duties No shorthand, salary low teens. Excellent benefits. Good phone skills. Industrious, able to work independently. EOE. Send resume to: MHX 408 Tribune 60611.

COMPUTER OPERATOR
Hours 10 P.M.-6 A.M.
Candidates must have 1-2 years experience on System 3 or UNIVAC 9030. Experience with COBOL-RPG is desirable. This shift offers a 15% shift premium. Chicago Specialty 674-7500

COOK
Seeking full time cook, male or female. Call 832-1433 bet. 12-1 p.m.

DENTAL HYGIENIST
Full time, experienced, Loop practice with 2 doctors. Call 726-1901 for interview.

DRAFTSPERSON
Electrical contractor in NW suburbs needs experienced draftsperson. Non-smoker preferred. Send resume to: MDM 437 TRIBUNE 60611

DRIVER/WAREHOUSEMAN
West Chicago electrical contractor has opening for experienced driver/warehouseman. must be able to do minor tool and vehicle repairs and be able to secure class C drivers license. Some overnight travel required. Full co. benefits. EOE   Submit resume MSW 288 Chicago Tribune 60611

MACHINISTS
First shift openings for experienced machinists to repair and rebuild all plant equipment. A steady position with a well established cold. heading company. Good salary and comprehensive benefits including pension and dental plans. Apply at:
PHEOLL MFG. CO.
5716 W. Roosevelt Rd.
EOE M/F

MAINTENANCE ENGINEER
Needed for a 200 unit apt. complex in Chicago. Electrical experience required. Heating/a/c, refrigeration, plumbing experience desired. Salary + an apt. Available immediately. Send resumes to: MHX 592 Tribune 60611

MANICURIST
Sculpture nail experience necessary. For busy salon. 679-4730

MECHANICS
AUTOMATIC TRANSMISSION
If you have exp rebuilding &/or installing transmissions & desire to manage, call us. Good working cond. We are a major company w/oppts. thru-out Chicago & suburbs. Twin post lifts, uniforms, part time will be considered. Call Mr. Carter at 561-7402. Call now, this is a great opportunity.

Medical Opportunities
NURSE ASSISTANT
Nurse assistant to work for home health care agency to cover NW Chicago & NW suburbs. Must. have car. Must be certified by state of Illinois. Flexible hours. Call Mon-Fri., 9-4, 825-8480.

TYPIST
FOSTER & WESTERN
Our well known medical clinic is seeking an exc. Typist to assist us with reports & letters. Exc. salary, pleasant working cond. & flexible part time hours. Medical exp. a plus. Call our Rep, 878-5558.

WORD PROCESSING
Immediate opening for a mag card II operator with at least 2 to 3 years experience. Qualified individual will also perform the duty of switchboard relief. For additional information and a personal interview, please call: Ms. Ham, 431-5508 between 9-4 .

12-1 Reading the classified ads in your local newspaper can help you find job openings.

ABBREVIATIONS USED IN WANT ADS

ABBREVIATIONS	WORDS
appt	appointment
ass't	assistant
avail	available
ben or bene	benefits
co	company
EOE	Equal Opportunity Employer
exc	excellent
exp	experience
hrs	hours
hs grad	high school graduate
med	medical
mfg	manufacturing
morn/aft/eve	morning/afternoon/evening
nego	negotiable
ofc	office
p/t or PT	part-time
pos	position
pref	preferred
ref	references
req	required
sal	salary
temp	temporary
w/	with
wpm	words per minute

12-2 To understand the information given in want ads, you will need to become familiar with the abbreviations used in them.

State employment offices are located in most large cities and towns. The offices may have different names in different states. To locate your nearest state employment office, look in your local telephone directory under the name of your state. For example, in Chicago, Illinois, the state employment office is listed under Illinois (State of), Employment Service.

To be considered for a job at a state employment office, you must fill out an application at your local state employment office. Then an employment counselor will interview you to determine your skills and interests. If a job comes available for which you qualify, the office will arrange an interview for you. Keep in mind, however, that only five percent of all job seekers find a job through state employment services. Therefore, register for work at a state office, but use other job sources to find job leads.

Private employment agencies

Private employment agencies are in the business of helping employers locate workers and job seekers locate jobs. To stay in business, agencies must charge fees for their services. They either charge the job seeker or the employer. For most entry-level jobs, the job seeker can expect to pay the fee. For most high-paying professional jobs, the fee is usually paid by the employer. When employment agencies advertise job openings in the want ads, the ads will usually say "Fee paid" if the employer is paying the fee.

If you apply to a private agency, you may be asked to sign a contract concerning the payment of fees. Be sure to read any contract carefully. Make sure you know exactly what you're agreeing to pay if you take a job that the agency locates for you.

Before registering with a private agency, ask your school coordinator or counselor if they recommend any particular agency to contact. Some agencies specialize in placing people in certain jobs, such as sales, office, or professional jobs.

With only five to six percent of all job hunters finding jobs through private agencies, you should not spend a great deal of time at private agencies. Concentrate your efforts on other job-finding methods.

BEFORE YOU APPLY

By now you may have a long list of employers to contact. But before you begin applying for jobs, you need to write down all the important facts about yourself. You can call this your personal fact sheet. You need a personal fact sheet to help you write letters of application, prepare job resumes, and fill out application forms, 12-3.

Begin your personal fact sheet by identifying yourself. Write down your name, address, phone number, and social security number. Also list your date of birth, place of birth, and your height and weight. (Since some jobs may require certain heights and weights, you need to know this information.)

Then write down the facts related to your education. Include where you went to primary school, junior high, high school, and any other schools such as colleges or training schools. List the dates you attended these schools and the year you graduated from high school. Also write down your grade average by letter such as "A average," "B average," or "C average," or by grade point average such as "3.0 on a 4.0 scale."

Next, list any work experiences you have had. Write down the job title, your job duties, the name, address, and telephone number of the employer, and your job supervisor. Also write down the dates you were employed and the salary you earned. Be sure to list part-time jobs and volunteer work such as baby-sitting, delivering papers, mowing lawns, or being a candy striper at a hospital.

Other types of information you need to record include your skills, honors, activities, hobbies, and interests. Under skills, list the things you can do well that relate to the jobs for which you will be applying. For example, if you will be applying for secretarial jobs and you're a good typist, list typing as a skill. Under honors and activities, list the school and community organizations in which you

PERSONAL FACT SHEET

Name _____

Address _____

Telephone _____ Social security number _____

Date of birth _____ Place of birth _____

Height _____ Weight _____

EDUCATION

	Name	Location	Dates Attended	Date Graduated	Grade Average
Primary school					
Junior high school					
High school					
College					
Training school					
Other					

WORK EXPERIENCE

Name of employer _____

Address _____
         (street address)   (city)   (state)   (zip)

Telephone _____ Employed from _____ to _____
                                                        (mo./yr.)   (mo./yr.)

Job title _____ Supervisor _____

Starting salary _____ Final salary _____

Job duties _____

_____

Name of employer _____

Address _____
         (street address)   (city)   (state)   (zip)

Telephone _____ Employed from _____ to _____
                                                        (mo./yr.)   (mo./yr.)

Job title _____ Supervisor _____

Starting salary _____ Final salary _____

Job duties _____

_____

SKILLS _____

_____

HONORS AND ACTIVITIES _____

_____

HOBBIES AND INTERESTS _____

_____

REFERENCES

Name _____

Address _____

Home telephone _____ Work telephone _____

Name _____

Address _____

Home telephone _____ Work telephone _____

Name _____

Address _____

Home telephone _____ Work telephone _____

12-3 Having a personal fact sheet can help you fill out job application forms thoroughly and accurately.

have participated. Also list any awards you have received, any club offices you have held, and any other important accomplishments. Under hobbies and interests, list the activities you enjoy doing, especially the ones that relate to your job interests.

The last information you need for your records is a list of three or four references. A reference is a person who knows you well and who would be able to discuss your personal and job qualifications with employers. Most people ask former teachers, employers, and club advisors to be their references. Make sure you record the name, address, and home and work telephone numbers of each reference. You will be asked to list this information on application forms.

JOB RESUMES

A *resume* is a brief history of a person's education, work experience, and other qualifications for employment. A resume is usually sent to an employer in a letter of application or given to an employer with a completed application form. Reading a resume is a quick and easy way for an employer to learn about an applicant. A well prepared resume can help draw an employer's attention to your qualifications. It can help you get a job interview. And it can help give the employer a starting point for conducting the job interview.

An example of a well written resume is shown in 12-4. It includes all the information a company needs to know about the applicant. At the top of the resume is the information an employer needs to know first: your name, address, and telephone number. You should be sure to include the zip code in your address and the area code in your telephone number. You want to make sure the employer can contact you if he or she wants to hire you.

Beneath the name, address, and telephone number, the resume is organized into headings. This makes it easy to read. You may want to use the same headings used in 12-4 or similar ones when preparing your own resume. The order in which you list the headings may also vary. If you think your work experience will be more important to your employer than your education, list work experiences before education. Do a little experimenting to come up with a resume that will work best for you. The headings most often used in resumes are described below.

Job objective. The first heading in a resume is usually the "Job objective." Sometimes this heading is called "Job wanted," "Position wanted," or "Career objective." The purpose of a job objective is to give the employer some idea of the type of job for which you are applying.

Sometimes it may be best to list the area in which you want to work instead of writing a specific job objective. For example, suppose you want to be a company sales representative. However, you would be interested in other jobs in sales. Therefore, it might be best to state your job objective as "A challenging position in sales" instead of "Position as a sales representative." This way your job objective would be flexible enough to allow you to be considered for related jobs instead of just one job.

If you are interested in more than one type of job, you may need to write different job objectives. For example, suppose you're interested in applying for jobs as a secretary and an airline reservations clerk. Most likely you would need to write a different job objective for these two jobs. Therefore, you would need to prepare different resumes for these jobs. To avoid retyping resumes, some people choose not to include job objectives at all in their resumes. However, objectives are recommended.

Education. Under education, list the names of all the high schools, vocational schools, colleges, and other schools you have attended. (Primary and junior high schools do not need to be listed.) List the last school you attended, first. For example, suppose you attended a community college for two years after high school. Then you should list the name of the community college first and the name of your high school second. In your listing, include the name of each school, the location, and the dates attended. Tell when you

MARY R. POSTON
1036 Spring Street
Milwaukee, Wisconsin 53172
(414) 555-3214

JOB OBJECTIVE

Entry-level job as a receptionist or typist leading to a position as an executive secretary.

EDUCATION

1981-1984

Washington High School, Milwaukee, WI
Majored in business training. Graduated June, 1984. Skilled in typing, shorthand, and bookkeeping. Can operate dictaphone, calculator, and mimeograph machine.

WORK EXPERIENCE

1983-1984

Secretarial Assistant, Watkins Insurance Agency, Milwaukee, WI
As a cooperative education student employee, I typed, filed, and operated the telephone and office machines. I also handled some correspondence for the office manager.

Summer 1983

Grill Crewperson, McDonald's Restaurant, Milwaukee, WI
Responsible for cooking and preparing the food and keeping the work area clean.

HONORS AND ACTIVITIES

Member of the Office Education Association for two years. Secretary during senior year.
Member of the Student Council during junior year.
Member of the high school marching band for four years.
4-H member for eight years.

PERSONAL

Age 18. Single. 5'4'', 120 lbs. Excellent health.

REFERENCES

Mr. James Mitchell, Cooperative Education Coordinator
Washington High School, 3300 W. Glendale Avenue, Milwaukee, WI 53180

Ms. Donna Roberts, Office Manager
Watkins Insurance Company, 1122 Market Street, Milwaukee, WI 53177

Mrs. Jane Schilling, Business Teacher
Ames Business College, 1616 Lakewood Boulevard, Milwaukee, WI 53170

12-4 A well written resume will help you make a good impression on potential employers.

graduated or when you expect to graduate, what diploma or degree you earned, and what major programs you studied. If you received good grades, you also may want to mention your grade average.

Work experience. Under work experience, list the jobs you've held, listing your most recent job first. Include your cooperative work experience, part-time jobs, summer jobs, and any other significant work experience. Your work experience is very important to employers because it shows that you can assume responsibility. If you have never held a paying job, list any volunteer work you have done. If you have held regular jobs, it may not be important to list work experience like baby-sitting or volunteer work.

For each job you list, include the title of the job, the employer's name, and the location. Also include a brief description of the work you did on the job.

Honors and activities. Other names for this heading could be "Honors and organizations," or just "Activities," or "Organizations." Under this heading, list the organizations and activities you have participated in at school and in the community. These experiences will help the employer get a better picture of your interests and abilities. Include any offices you have held and any honors you have received. If you did not include volunteer work as work experience, you can list it here.

Personal. Listing personal information is optional on a resume. None is required, but some employers like to know this information. By law, employers cannot ask you about some of your personal qualifications. But if you have certain personal qualifications you want the employer to know, you can list them here. They could help you get the job you want. However, don't list any personal facts you think the employer will dislike. Remember, you want your resume to help you look your best in every way.

References. When listing references, be sure to include their names, titles, and addresses. Some people choose not to list individual references. Instead, they type centered near the bottom of the page "References available upon request." If the employer is interested in seeing your references, he or she can contact you for them.

Preparing a resume

After writing your resume, set it aside for a day or two. Then read it again. Did you include all the important facts about yourself? Did you organize the information well? Is it easy to read and understand? Ask your coordinator or counselor to read it over also. Either teacher may be able to offer some constructive comments.

Once you're happy with the content, the resume is ready to be typed. You should be able to include all the information you have on one sheet of white, regular size typing paper, 8 1/2 inches by 11 inches. The information should be typed neatly with evenly spaced margins.

After the resume is typed, you'll need to have copies of it made. You can use a photocopying machine. Or you can take the resume to an offset printer and have copies printed. Printed resumes usually look more professional than photocopied ones. However, printed resumes are more expensive. Check printing costs in your area before you make your decision.

LETTER OF APPLICATION

Sometimes you may need to write a letter to an employer to apply for a job. This type of letter is called a *letter of application*. The purpose of an application letter is to get an employer interested in your qualifications so that she or he will ask you for an interview. You will need to write a letter of application in the following situations:

- When you answer a newspaper ad.
- When you mail a resume to a prospective employer.
- When an employer requests you to write an application letter.

A letter of application should be written to the person in the company or business who has the ability to hire you. This may be the personnel manager, the department manager, or the president of the company, 12-5. If you do not know the name of this person, call the company and ask the receptionist for the name and title you need. Ask the receptionist to spell the name for you to make sure you write it down correctly. Some smaller companies may not have a person called a personnel director. In this case, ask the receptionist for the name and title of the person to whom a letter of application should be written. Every company has someone in charge of employment.

When writing the letter, keep it short and to the point. You want to attract the employer's attention but not overload him or her with too many facts. Three carefully worded paragraphs should be all you need to write a convincing letter of application.

In the opening paragraph, tell why you are writing. Mention the job or type of work for which you are applying. If you know there's a job opening, explain how you found out about it. For example, if you read about the job in the want ads or one of your teachers told you about the job, mention this to the employer.

In the middle paragraph, tell why you think you are right for the job. Briefly explain how your qualifications have prepared you for this line of work. If you are enclosing a resume, mention it here. Encourage the employer to refer to it for further information about your qualifications.

In the last paragraph, ask the employer for an interview. Make sure you mention where and when you can be reached by telephone.

BERNIE NOVIA

12-5 Send your letter of application to the person in the company who has the ability to hire you.

Although the content of a letter of application is very important, so is the appearance of the letter. A letter of application looks best typed on standard white typing paper, 8 1/2 by 11. A handwritten letter can be sent if you write neatly and legibly in black or blue ink. Remember, you are writing a business letter, and you should follow a standard business style. Your letter should include a return address, date, inside address, salutation, body, and complimentary close. A sample letter of application is shown in 12-6. To review the proper way to prepare a business letter, turn to pages 50 and 55 in Chapter Four.

After typing or writing the letter, read it over one more time. Make sure you have written complete sentences and have spelled every word correctly. By preparing a good first letter of application, you can use it to help you prepare others.

JOB APPLICATION FORMS

When you are applying for jobs, most employers will ask you to fill out an application form. Employers use application forms to screen job applicants. Therefore, the information you give on a form is very important. An application that is incomplete, difficult to read, or smudged with dirt may not make it beyond the first screening. Don't be one of those people who is not considered for a job because you didn't take time to fill out the application form correctly, 12-7.

Now is the time to rely on the personal fact sheet you prepared earlier in the chapter. With this information, you will have all your personal facts at your fingertips. You won't have to guess at your social security number. You'll have that written down on your fact sheet. If the application asks you to list your references and their phone numbers, you won't have to fumble through a telephone book. You'll have the information in front of you. Your personal fact sheet will help you fill out application forms accurately and completely. Always remember to carry this sheet with you when you go to apply for jobs.

When filling out an application form,

follow these tips:
- Read over the entire application before you begin writing in any information. Make sure you understand all the questions.
- Follow the instructions carefully for filling out the form. If you are asked to print, type, or use black ink, be sure to do so. Be careful not to write in the sections marked "for employer use only."
- Complete every question on the front and back sides of the form. If some questions do not apply to you, draw a dash through the space or write "does not apply." This will let the employer know you read the question and did not overlook it.
- In the section concerning the job you desire, there may be a question asking you what wages or salary you expect. The best answer for this question is usually the word "open" or "negotiable." Then you're not committing yourself to a figure too high or too low. If you were to write down a high salary, the employer might not consider you for employment. If you were to write down a low salary, the employer may think you're selling yourself short.
- In the section marked "employment history," remember to include part-time jobs like baby-sitting and mowing lawns. For each job, there may be a question asking your reasons for leaving the job. If it's a summer job you've listed, your reason for leaving will probably be that the job was a "summer job only." If you left a job for some other reason, word your reason carefully. Avoid writing any negative comments about yourself or a former employer.
- Be as neat as possible. Don't let the form get dirty or marked with stains. If you have to erase something, do it carefully.

As soon as you finish the application, hand it in or mail it in to the correct person. If you mail it, be sure to enclose a letter of application with it. You may also want to include a copy of your resume. But never expect to be able to skip filling out an application by handing in a resume. A resume can be optional, but a completed application form is a must to be considered for most jobs.

1036 Spring St.
Milwaukee, WI 53172
April 25, 19___

Mr. Robert Drake
Personnel Manager
Whitaker Publishing Company
1822 W. Meridian St.
Milwaukee, WI 53172

Dear Mr. Drake:

Through Mrs. Shirley Allen, Office Education Coordinator at Apollo High School in Milwaukee, I learned that your company plans to hire a full-time typist in June. I would like to apply for this position.

To prepare for a typist position, I have taken a number of business courses in high school. As mentioned in my resume, I am now skilled in typing, shorthand, and bookkeeping. As a cooperative education student at Apollo, I am presently gaining on-the-job experience as a Secretarial Assistant with Watkins Insurance Agency. With my education and work experience, I feel confident I could perform well as a typist for your company.

May I have an interview to discuss the job and my qualifications in greater detail? I can be reached at 555-3214 after 4:30. I will appreciate the opportunity to talk with you.

Sincerely,

Mary Poston

Mary Poston

12-6 A letter of application should attract attention to your qualifications.

GENERAL ⚙ ELECTRIC

AN EQUAL OPPORTUNITY EMPLOYER

APPLICATION
FOR EMPLOYMENT

It is the policy of the General Electric Company to provide employment, training, compensation, promotion and other conditions of employment based on qualifications, without regard to race, color, religion, national origin, sex, age, veteran status, or handicap.

PRINT
NAME _____
           LAST   FIRST   MIDDLE

ADDRESS _____
           NO. & STREET

           CITY   STATE   ZIP CODE

TELEPHONE _____ SOCIAL SECURITY NO. _____
           AREA CODE / NO.

IS YOUR AGE: UNDER 18? ☐   OVER 70? ☐

CITIZEN OF U.S.A.? ☐ YES ☐ NO*   *If you are not a U.S. citizen have you a legal } ☐ YES
                                    right to remain permanently in the U.S.? } ☐ NO

☐ PLEASE CHECK if you have a handicap and wish to be considered under our affirmative action program. Submission of this information is voluntary.

JOB INTEREST

POSITION DESIRED	WAGES OR SALARY EXPECTED $	PER ☐ HR. ☐ WK. ☐ MO. CHECK ONE
OTHER POSITIONS FOR WHICH YOU ARE QUALIFIED	DATE AVAILABLE	

WERE YOU EVER EMPLOYED BY GE? ☐ YES ☐ NO   IF YES, WHERE: _____ WHEN: _____

TRAINING

CIRCLE HIGHEST GRADE *COMPLETED* IN *EACH* SCHOOL CATEGORY	GRADE SCHOOL 1 2 3 4 5 6 7 8	HIGH SCHOOL 9 10 11 12	TECH. SCH. 1 2	COLLEGE 1 2 3 4	GRAD. SCH. 1 2 3 4
	NAME	LOCATION		COURSE–DEGREE	CLASS STANDING
GRADE SCHOOL					
HIGH SCHOOL					
COLLEGE					
GRADUATE SCHOOL					
APPRENTICE, BUSINESS, TECHNICAL OR VOCATIONAL SCHOOL					
OTHER TRAINING OR SKILLS (Factory or Office Machines Operated, Special Courses, etc.)					

MILITARY

BRANCH OF U.S. SERVICE	DATE ENTERED	DATE DISCHARGED	FINAL RANK	TYPE DISCHARGE *
SERVICE SCHOOLS OR SPECIAL EXPERIENCE				

*☐ Please check if you were discharged or released for a service-connected disability and wish to be considered under our affirmative action program. Submission of this information is voluntary.

This portion of the application form (below the perforation) will be shown only to members of the personnel or hiring office staff.

HAVE YOU EVER BEEN CONVICTED OF A MISDEMEANOR* OR A FELONY? ☐ YES ☐ NO IF YES, EXPLAIN FULLY.	
	* List information concerning convictions for any misdemeanor committed within the past five years, but do not list information on a misdemeanor which occurred more than five years ago, unless you were imprisoned for that offense.

FF-75A (6-79) REV.   *PLEASE COMPLETE OTHER SIDE*

12-7 Complete application forms accurately and neatly.

EMPLOYMENT HISTORY

Please list all employment starting with present or most recent employer.
Account for all periods, including unemployment and service with U.S. Armed Forces. Also include relevant voluntary and/or part-time work experience.
Use additional sheet if necessary.

DATE	NAME & ADDRESS – EMPLOYER	1 JOB TITLE / 2 DEPARTMENT / 3 NAME OF SUPERVISOR	DESCRIBE MAJOR DUTIES	WAGES	REASON FOR LEAVING
FROM MONTH YEAR / TO MONTH YEAR		1 / 2 / 3		STARTING $ per / FINAL $ per	
FROM MONTH YEAR / TO MONTH YEAR		1 / 2 / 3		STARTING $ per / FINAL $ per	
FROM MONTH YEAR / TO MONTH YEAR		1 / 2 / 3		STARTING $ per / FINAL $ per	
FROM MONTH YEAR / TO MONTH YEAR		1 / 2 / 3		STARTING $ per / FINAL $ per	
FROM MONTH YEAR / TO MONTH YEAR		1 / 2 / 3		STARTING $ per / FINAL $ per	
FROM MONTH YEAR / TO MONTH YEAR		1 / 2 / 3		STARTING $ per / FINAL $ per	

INTERVIEWER'S COMMENTS:

EMPLOYEE RELEASE AND PRIVACY STATEMENT

I understand that the General Electric Company requires certain information about me to evaluate my qualifications for employment and to conduct its business if I become an employee. Therefore, I authorize the Company to investigate my past employment and employment-related activities. I agree to cooperate in such investigations, and release those parties supplying such information to the Company from all liability or responsibility with respect to information supplied

I agree that the Company may use the information it obtains concerning me in the conduct of its business. I understand that such use may include disclosure outside the Company in those cases where its agents and contractors need such information to perform their functions, where the Company's legal interests and/or obligations are involved, or where there is a medical emergency involving me. I understand, however, that the Company intends to protect the confidentiality of personal information in Company record-keeping systems, other than the fact and location of past or present Company employment, the dates of employment, or the job name or description of general duties, will not otherwise be disclosed outside the Company with a personal identifier without my consent. Further, the Company will require its agents and contractors to safeguard personal information disclosed to them by the Company.

I understand that any false answers or statements made by me on this application or any supplement thereto, or in connection with the above-mentioned investigations will be sufficient grounds for immediate discharge, if I am employed.

APPLICANT'S SIGNATURE _____ DATE _____

INTERVIEWED BY _____ DATE _____

PRINT NAME _____ LAST _____ FIRST _____ MIDDLE _____

12-7 (continued)

to Review

1. What three things do you need to do to be successful on the job hunt?

2. Name six sources of job leads.

3. How should you go about contacting employers directly to find job openings?

4. What can you learn about the job market from reading the want ads?

5. Why should you not rely on the want ads alone to help you find a job?

6. What do the words "Fee paid" mean in an employment agency want ad?

7. Why is it helpful to prepare a personal fact sheet before you begin applying for jobs?

8. What is a resume? How might a well prepared resume help you in your job search?

9. List the headings most often used in resumes.

10. For each job you list under work experience on a resume, what information do you need to include about it?

11. What is a letter of application and what is its purpose? In what situations do you need to write a letter of application?

12. What points should you cover in a letter of application?

13. If a question on an application form does not apply to you, what should you do?

14. What is a good way to respond to an application question that asks you what wages or salary you expect? Why?

to Discuss

1. Why should you try using many sources of job leads to find a job instead of just one or two?

2. When you mention your job search to friends and family members, what should you tell them? Why would it be a good idea to give them copies of your resume?

3. Does your school have a placement office or a school or vocational counselor to help students find jobs in the community? How does a student go about using the placement services that are available?

4. What may be some disadvantages of using a private employment agency to help you find a job?

5. Who would you ask to be your references? Explain why you would choose these particular people for your references.

6. Why is it a good idea to include a job objective in your resume?

7. Why is it important to check and double-check your resume carefully before typing it?

8. How would you go about getting a resume typed and printed?

9. Describe the proper way to prepare a letter of application.

10. Discuss the tips you should follow when filling out an application form.

to Do

1. Go to your school or public library. Explain to the librarian the career area in which you are interested and ask to see the trade or professional journal that relates to that career. As you look through the journal, note the latest developments or trends in the trade or profession. Also check to see if the journal lists job ads.

2. Visit the state employment office nearest you. Find out how to register with their employment service. Also find out the procedure for applying and qualifying for state and federal government jobs.

3. Prepare a resume. Ask someone to review it and offer suggestions.

4. Write a sample letter of application for a job you would like to have. Follow the guidelines given on pages 176–178.

5. Collect several different application forms. Display them in class so all class members can study them. Then choose one form and complete it neatly and correctly.

HOMEWOOD-FLOSSMOOR HIGH SCHOOL, FLOSSMOOR, IL

When preparing your resume or filling out a job application, be sure to include any important school or community awards you have received.

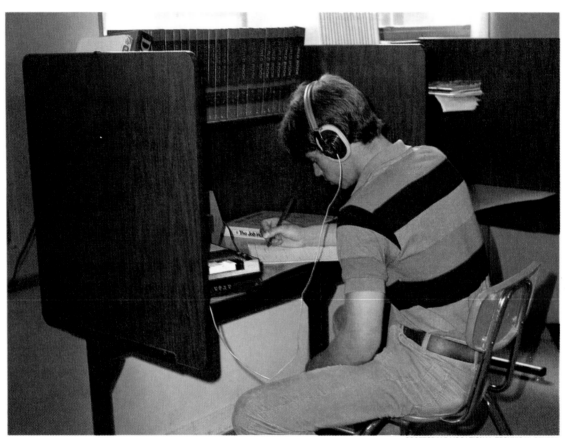

Being asked to take pre-employment tests
is often part of the job selection process.

13

Taking pre-employment tests

After studying this chapter, you will be able to:

☐ Explain why employers give pre-employment tests.
☐ Describe the types of pre-employment tests commonly given to prospective employees.
☐ Prepare for pre-employment tests.

Debbie had just returned from applying for three jobs. "I was surprised that I had to take so many tests," she said.

"Tests!" Dave said alarmingly. "You mean you have to take tests to get a job?"

"That's right," said Debbie. "You thought teachers were the only people that gave tests. Well, employers do too. When I was being interviewed at one company, the personnel manager told me that most large companies and about seventy-five percent of small companies give pre-employment tests to prospective employees. Almost all government employees, like mail carriers and civil service workers, have to take one or more pre-employment tests."

Why do employers give tests? Many employers give pre-employment tests to screen prospective employees. When hiring, companies want to choose the best people for the jobs available. They try to gather enough data about a job applicant to help them make their selections.

Another reason employers give pre-employment tests is to find out if a person will be suited to a given job. Employers give skill tests to evaluate a person's physical or mental skills. Psychological tests are given to evaluate a person's personality, character, and attitudes. Governments give exams to help them place people fairly in government jobs. Polygraph tests are given to help companies judge a person's honesty. Medical exams are given to determine a person's physical condition for the job.

Pre-employment tests can help you as well as the employer. Taking a pre-employment test may reinforce your interest in your chosen career. Or the results of a test might show that you are seeking a job for which you are not suited. You may find you need more training to meet an employer's requirements or that your skills and interests would be better matched to another career field. Pre-employment tests are only one part of the job selection process, but they can be an important part.

SKILL TESTS

Skill tests are used to test the physical or mental abilities of a job applicant. An employer will give these tests to decide if an applicant has the skills to do a job.

Skill tests are usually classified as hands-on tests or hands-off tests. Hands-on tests test your ability to operate tools and machines with your hands. Hands-off tests are usually written or oral tests that test your knowledge of how to perform certain skills.

A typing test is a good example of a hands-on test, 13-1. When a person applies for a job that involves typing, he or she may be asked to type a one-page sample or a letter. From the typing sample, the employer will rate the person's speed and accuracy. The applicant who types the fastest with the fewest amount of errors will probably be the person who will be offered the job. A hands-on skill test might also be required of word processors, drafters, welders, X-ray technicians, machine operators, and instrument technicians.

If you apply for a job as a bank teller, clerk, or computer operator, you may be asked to take a math test. A math test is an example of a hands-off test. A basic math test would test your ability to add, subtract, multiply, divide, find percentages, and work with fractions.

Clerical skill tests are another example of a hands-off test. These tests are often given to applicants seeking employment as file or accounting clerks. They are given to measure such things as a person's ability to perform simple math operations, to copy numbers and names correctly, and to place names in alphabetical order, 13-2.

Do not be afraid to take a skills test. If you have the skills to perform the job for which you are being tested, you will not have any problems. If you do poorly on a skills test, it's not

13-1 This job applicant is taking a typing test to try and qualify for an office job.

SPEED & ACCURACY TASKS
FILING

This task measures your ability to quickly and correctly file records alphabetically or to find names in an alphabetical list. You will find two lists of names. List A consists of names to be filed. List B is a list of names in alphabetical order as you would find them in. a telephone directory. The names in List A are to be filed in their proper alphabetical order with the names in List B. You will do this by placing the number corresponding to the name in List A in the appropriate space provided either above or below the names in List B. For example:

LIST A (To be filed)   **LIST B (Already filed)**

1. Lockport, H.A.
2. Logan, K.L.

( )
Lober, D.F.   Logan, J.G.
(1)   (2)
Lockwood, R.E.   Long, C.F.
( )   ( )
Lodge, H.A.   Lopez, J.M.
( )   ( )
Loffredo, S.A.   Loren, L.P.
( )   ( )

The first name in List A is Lockport, H.A., spelled L-O-C-K-P-O-R-T. It is number 1. Since L-O-C-K-P would follow L-O-B and come before L-O-C-K-W it should be filed between Lober, D.F. and Lockwood, R.E.

The number 1 is inserted in the parentheses after Lober, D.F. and before Lockwood, R.E. in List B.

The second name in List A is Logan, K.L. spelled L-O-G-A-N. It is number 2. Since the name Logan is in both lists, the initials would determine where the name would be filed. K.L. comes after J.G. and should therefore be filed between the names Logan, J.G. and Long, C.F. in List B.

The number 2 is inserted in the parentheses between the names Logan, J.G. and Long, C.F. in List B.

MOUNTAIN BELL

13-2 This is a hands-off clerical test to measure a person's ability to quickly and correctly file records alphabetically and to find names in an alphabetical list.

the end of the world. Instead, it's an opportunity to find out how you can improve your skills. Or the employer may offer to teach you the skills you need for the job.

Whatever you do, don't tell an employer that you have skills that you don't have. Eventually, the employer will find out that you were not honest about your skills. You could then be fired for being dishonest or for not being able to perform the duties of the job. Read what happened to Bob.

THE MISSING SKILL

Bob saw in the Sunday newspaper that a small company that repairs and rebuilds heavy diesel equipment was looking for an equipment operator. Since Bob has had some experience in auto and diesel mechanics and equipment operation, he applied for the job and was granted an interview.

At the interview, the shop supervisor explained to Bob the type of person he needed for the job. "I need a person who can do four things: drive a truck, operate a forklift, operate a crane, and keep our equipment in good working order."

Bob quickly thought about what the supervisor said before responding. Driving a truck and operating a forklift would be no problem because he had had experience doing both. He had also had experience repairing and maintaining heavy equipment. But the crane might be a problem because he has never operated one. He glanced at the crane that was parked nearby. It didn't look like it would be difficult to operate. So he said to the supervisor, "I can do all four, but I might need some help running the crane."

"Oh, you have never operated a crane?" the supervisor asked.

Bob made the mistake of saying, "Oh no, I have. It's been a while though. I'm just a little rusty."

The supervisor then said, "Well, let's find out how well you can operate it."

Bob climbed into the crane, and the supervisor explained the control levers. Bob was about to say he couldn't do it when the supervisor said, "Back it up about 10 feet and pick up that track to your right. Then set it down on the concrete pad to your left. Be careful, that track weighs over 1,000 pounds."

The supervisor climbed down from the crane leaving Bob all alone. Bob looked at the controls. Then he started the engine. He shifted the crane into reverse. The gears engaged and the crane moved backward. "Hey," he thought, "I'm driving a crane. I'm going to get this job after all."

Bob moved slowly, but he carefully got the crane into position. "That's far enough," the supervisor yelled to him. "Pick up the track."

Bob looked at the levers. "Here it is," he said to himself, "the lever to lower and raise the boom." He moved the lever and the boom slowly lowered. However, it wasn't directly over the track. The boom was just a few feet out of reach.

"You'll need to go forward about three feet," yelled the supervisor.

Bob shifted into gear, and the crane moved forward. And it kept going and going. "How do I stop it?" he yelled.

Bob finally got the crane stopped, but not before driving the boom into the wall of the office building.

Questions to discuss

1. Do you think Bob was hired for the job? Why?
2. Instead of lying to the supervisor that he had operated a crane, what positive things could Bob have told the supervisor about himself and his ability to do the job?
3. Do you think the supervisor would have still considered Bob for the job even if Bob had told him he had never driven a crane before? Why?
4. What would you have done if you had been in Bob's situation?

PSYCHOLOGICAL TESTS

Psychological tests are given to find out more about a person's personality, character, and interests. These tests do not measure a person's knowledge or aptitudes. They measure factors such as cooperation, assertiveness, adaptiveness, loyalty, honesty, and personal likes and dislikes. Some employers give these tests to determine how well an applicant will adjust to his or her job and will get along with others on the job, 13-3.

Most psychological tests are written tests such as multiple choice questions or short essay questions. An essay question might be: "Describe yourself in a paragraph."

Some psychological tests are given orally by a psychologist. The psychologist may ask you questions about yourself or your opinions on certain issues.

If you are asked to take a psychological test, don't be concerned. There are no right or wrong answers for these tests, so you should not feel any pressure in taking them. You should just answer the questions as best as you can. The best way is to be positive and truthful.

ALAN AND HAL

Alan just graduated from Central High School, and Hal just graduated from East High. They don't know each other, but they are alike in many ways. Both have studied vocational electronics in high school and both have similar cooperative education work experiences. And both saw the following job notice in the morning paper.

ELECTRONICS

Ground floor opportunities with growing national computer firm. Must be HS grad exp'd in electronics, microcomputer assembly & repair, digital electronics, data communications. Will be trained to work for a team of experts.
Contact:
    P.O. Box 1354
    Chicago, IL 60606

Both Alan and Hal applied for the job. After completing application forms, each was given an interview date. Alan and Hal were scheduled for interviews on the same day—Alan in the morning and Hal in the afternoon.

When Alan and Hal arrived for their interviews, each was asked to take a written test. It wasn't an electronics test; it was a

13-3 Some employers give psychological tests to determine how well an applicant will get along with others on the job.

psychological test. Here are some of the questions they were asked and their responses.

Why do you want to work in electronics?

Alan: I like electronics and feel it has good future opportunities.

Hal: I like to work in electronics, and I want to make a lot of money.

Would you enter a nine-month training program at a lower salary?

Alan: Yes, if it meant I would learn the business.

Hal: No. I'm prepared to go to work right now. I don't need much more training.

Do you prefer to work alone or with a group?

Alan: Either. At times I like to work alone, and at times I like to work with others.

Hal: In a group. I like to be with people.

Answer Yes or no. I always control my temper.

Alan: No. I try, but sometimes I get mad and lose my temper.

Hal: Yes. No matter how unreasonable others are, I control my temper.

The company interviewing Alan and Hal was looking for young people who have had some knowledge and training in electronics, but who are willing to be trained according to the company's system. After training, trainees would be in line for promotions.

Who do you think was hired—Alan, Hal, or both? Alan was offered a position, but Hal was not. The main reason for Hal not being hired was his answer to the last question about controlling his temper. Very few people, if any, are able to control their temper all the time. Therefore, Hal's answer sounded very unrealistic. His answer also gave the impression that he thinks he's always in the right and incapable of making mistakes. Therefore, the interviewer decided if Hal had this type of attitude that he would probably have problems getting along with group members and accepting constructive criticism.

Questions to discuss

1. Do you think the test questions were fair?
2. Do you agree with the interviewer's interpretation of Hal's answer? Why?

3. Who would you have hired if you were the interviewer? Why?
4. Would you have felt uncomfortable taking a test like the one Alan and Hal took? Why?

GOVERNMENT TESTS

The United States is our nation's largest employer. It hires many people for civilian jobs as well as military jobs. Discussed here are two types of tests you may encounter if you apply for a federal or state government job or choose to pursue a military career.

Civil service test

A civil service test is an examination a person may have to take before he or she will be considered for a government job. The Civil Service Commission is the federal government agency which administers the civil service tests and hires employees for federal government jobs. The Employment Service in each state administers tests and hires workers for state jobs. State and federal governments test job applicants to help them select the best qualified person for the job without regard to sex, race, religion, or political influence. The testing system attempts to give all U.S. citizens a fair chance at government jobs.

To find out federal job openings and which jobs require testing, call your nearest Federal Job Information Center. You can get the number by looking in a telephone directory under "United States Government—Job Information Center."

To find out about state job openings and which of these jobs require testing, call your nearest State Employment Service. You can get the number by looking under your state's name. For example, in Illinois, look under "Illinois, State of—Employment Service."

Armed Services Vocational Aptitude Battery

The Armed Services Vocational Aptitude Battery or ASVAB is a group of tests used by the military to help predict a person's success in military training schools. The ASVAB consists of twelve tests that measure verbal, math, perceptual speed, and mechanical aptitudes in five military career areas. Although the test was developed to help place people in the military, it can help people identify their aptitudes for vocational careers outside the military.

You do not have to join any branch of the military to take the ASVAB. You can arrange to take the test at a military recruitment office, or you may be able to take it at your school. Many people have found the test useful in their career planning.

POLYGRAPH TESTS

One fifth of the nation's largest companies and many other employers administer hundreds of thousands of polygraph tests each year. A polygraph test is used to determine if a person is telling the truth. Employers give polygraph tests to screen applicants for their "general honesty."

Polygraph tests, also called lie-detector tests, are given with a polygraph machine, 13-14. To give a polygraph test, an examiner places an inflated blood-pressure cuff around the subject's arm, a rubber tube around the chest, and small electrodes on one hand. Then the examiner asks the subject a series of questions. When the examiner asks each question, the machine measures changes in the subject's blood pressure, perspiration, and pulse rate and records these physical stress changes on graph paper.

A specific series of questions are asked in a specific sequence. The questions asked usually fall into two broad categories: relevant and control. A relevant question is very specific. For example, "Did you ever steal from your last

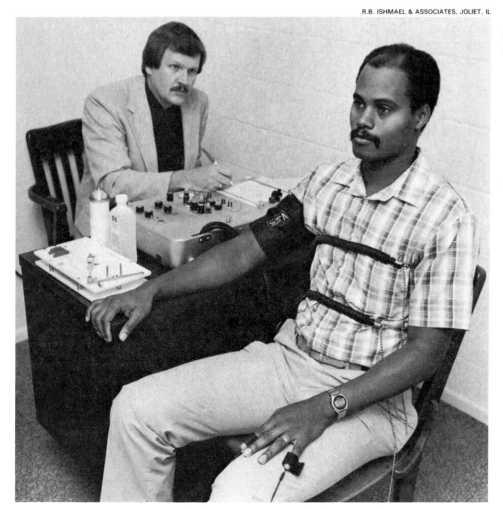

R.B. ISHMAEL & ASSOCIATES, JOLIET, IL

13-4 This job applicant is taking a polygraph test.

employer?" A control question is less precise such as "In the last 10 years, have you ever stolen anything?" Examiners say that a person who is lying will usually react more strongly to the relevant questions.

After a polygraph test, the examiner analyzes the graph and decides if the subject is lying or telling the truth. The machine by itself cannot do this; it only measures levels of stress. The examiner examines the stress levels and determines if the stress was caused by lying or by some other emotion such as anger or fear.

The use of polygraph tests is a controversial subject. Polygraph supporters argue that polygraph tests can be helpful tools to the employer when they are administered by a qualified, competent examiner. Others argue that lie-detector tests are not accurate indicators of a person's honesty or dishonesty and should not be given to job applicants and employees. Presently, employers in 29 states have the right to give polygraph tests when hiring. A person also has the right to refuse to take the test. However, if a person refuses, he or she will probably not be chosen for the job.

WRITTEN HONESTY TESTS

Written honesty tests are another type of test designed to measure a person's honesty in the workplace. These pencil and paper tests are supposed to help employers identify job applicants who are likely to be dishonest employees. Unlike polygraph tests, pencil and paper honesty tests can be given in every state. Also, job applicants feel more comfortable taking written honesty tests and less threatened by them.

The *Phase II Profile* is the name of one pencil and paper honesty test that is widely given. The test includes 116 multiple choice and true/false questions, and it only takes 20 to 30 minutes to complete.

MEDICAL EXAMINATIONS

Don't be surprised if you are asked to take a medical or physical examination before you are hired for a job. Some large companies even have their own clinics and doctors. One of the purposes of giving medical exams is to identify health problems that might prevent a person from performing his or her job safely and successfully. Another purpose is to screen those applicants with health problems that would become expensive insurance liabilities for the employer.

Certain jobs, such as airline pilots and professional athletes, require employees to be in top physical condition, 13-5. Some hospitals, medical clinics, and restaurants require workers to have medical exams for health reasons. It is also common practice for workers in management or stress-related jobs to have a complete medical exam prior to employment and periodically during employment.

PHOENIX SUNS

13-5 Professional basketball players must pass thorough medical examinations before they are hired by a pro team.

HOW TO TAKE PRE-EMPLOYMENT TESTS

Unlike most tests you have taken in school, there are few pre-employment tests for which you can study. However, there are some things you can do to prepare yourself for any test. To help you feel calm and collected at test time, follow these suggestions:

1. Try to find out ahead of time the tests you will be asked to take. If it is a skill test, such as typing, you can practice. But don't practice too much. You don't want to tire yourself just before test time.
2. Get plenty of rest the night before the test so you will feel fresh and alert.
3. If you're taking a written test, take along an extra pencil just in case you need it.
4. Arrive at the test site early. Select a seat where you can see and hear the examiner well.
5. Follow directions exactly. Know how and where your answers are to be made. You may know the answer, but it will be marked wrong if you write it in the wrong place on the answer sheet.
6. When taking a written test, try not to spend too long on one question. Answer the easiest questions first. Then go back and try to answer the harder questions.
7. Have confidence in your ability.

to Review

1. Give two reasons why employers give pre-employment tests.
2. In what ways might your taking a pre-employment test help you as well as an employer?
3. Explain the difference between a hands-on skill test and a hands-off skill test. Give an example of each.
4. What do psychological tests measure? Why do some employers give these tests to job applicants?
5. Who administers federal civil service tests and who administers state civil service tests?
6. Why do state and federal governments test job applicants?
7. Why might a person want to take the ASVAB even though that person does not plan to pursue a career in the military?
8. Explain how a polygraph test is given.
9. Who determines if the person taking a polygraph test is lying or telling the truth?
10. Give two purposes for companies giving prospective employees medical examinations before hiring.

to Discuss

1. Discuss the different pre-employment tests you may be asked to take when you apply for jobs.
2. What is the harm of telling an employer you have skills that you don't have?
3. How well do you think you would score on a psychological test? What do you think the test would reveal about you?
4. Would you feel uncomfortable taking a polygraph test? Why?
5. Do you think employers should use polygraph tests to screen job applicants? Why?
6. Discuss the things you can do to prepare yourself to take a pre-employment test.

to Do

1. Find out the types of pre-employment tests you may be asked to take when applying for jobs in your career area.
2. Obtain sample questions from pre-employment tests and answer them in class.
3. Assume the role of an employer. Make a list of the skills a job applicant would need to qualify for a specific job in your company. Then describe a hands-on or hands-off skill test you could give applicants to evaluate their skill levels.
4. Invite a polygraph examiner to demonstrate to the class how polygraph tests are given. Prepare a list of questions to ask the examiner about polygraph testing, following the demonstration.

A job interview is your chance to sell yourself to an employer.

14

Interviewing for jobs

After studying this chapter, you will be able to:

☐ Prepare yourself for an interview.
☐ Explain how to make a good impression on the interviewer during an interview.
☐ Write a follow-up letter after an interview.
☐ Describe the factors you need to consider before accepting a job offer.

The interview is usually the most important step in getting a job. Your application form, resume, letter of application, or telephone call may have caught the employer's attention. But it's the personal interview that will determine if you are offered the job.

For the employer, the purpose of an interview is to evaluate the job seeker in person. The interviewer wants to find out if you have the skills to do the job and if you will work well with the other employees in the company.

For you the job seeker, the purpose of the interview is to convince the employer that you're the right person to hire for the job. The interview also gives you a chance to find out more about the job and the company.

PREPARING FOR AN INTERVIEW

An interview can be a very important twenty or thirty minutes in your life. You should never expect to just walk into an interview without preparing yourself ahead of time. The better prepared you are for an interview, the better the impression you will make on the interviewer. To prepare for an interview, follow these tips:
• Learn about the employer.
• Make a list of questions to ask the employer.

- List the materials to take with you.
- Decide what to wear.
- Think about the questions you might be asked.
- Practice for the interview.
- Know where to go for the interview.

Learn about the employer

Become familiar with the employer before you go on your interview. You should know more about the company than the position for which you are applying. Find out about the company's products or services, the size of the company, and its possibilities for growth and expansion. Some companies publish annual reports that include this information.

You will probably be able to get some information about employers at your local or school library, 14-1. Descriptions of most corporations can be found in library references such as Dunn and Bradstreet's Directory, Moody's Industrial Manual, Standard and Poor's Register of Corporations, and state-published business directories. Ask the librarian to help you locate these sources and obtain the information you need. Also ask your cooperative education coordinator and guidance counselor if they can provide you with any information about the company. Having some knowledge of the company will help you talk intelligently with the interviewer. It will also show the interviewer that you were interested enough in the company to do some outside research.

Make a list of questions to ask the employer

As you prepare for the interview, write down a few questions you would like to ask the interviewer about the job and the company. Asking questions, like researching the company, shows the employer that you have a serious interest in the company. The questions you ask can also help you decide if you really want to work for the company.

You may want to ask some of the following questions. "How would I be trained for this job?" "What hours would I be working?" "Would there be opportunities for advancement?" "May I see the area where I would be working?" "Is there anything I should read or study to get a head start on learning this job?" Avoid asking questions about the salary and benefits of the job. You will have plenty of time to ask these questions after you are offered the job.

List the materials to take with you

When you go to an interview, there are a few items you will need to take with you. You will need a pen and your personal fact sheet for filling out an application, your resume, and the list of questions you plan to ask the interviewer. To keep your papers neat and clean, it's a good idea to carry them in a file folder or large envelope.

If you are applying for a job as a drafter, photographer, writer, or artist, you may also need to take samples of your work. A collection of work samples is called a *portfolio*. Only put your best samples in a portfolio. It would be best to only have three good samples than ten samples that are not very good.

Decide what to wear

Be sure to think carefully about what to wear to the interview before the morning of the interview. Your clothes and appearance will influence the employer's impression of you. To make a good impression you should strive to look your very best, 14-2.

A guideline you may want to follow when making your selection is: Dress one step above what you would wear on the job. For example, if you are interviewing for a job as an auto mechanic, nice, casual clothes would be appropriate to wear. Avoid wearing work clothes, jeans, t-shirts, and tennis shoes. These clothes would probably appear too casual. If you are still in doubt about what to wear, ask your coordinator or counselor for advice.

In addition to choosing clothes that are appropriate, the clothes should also be clean, neat, and in good condition. Don't wear a torn shirt, a wrinkled coat, or muddy shoes. Have the shirt mended or choose a different one, get your coat pressed ahead of time, and have your shoes cleaned.

14-1 Take the time to research an employer before you go on an interview.

14-2 Strive to look your very best for every job interview.

Remember, however, nice, clean clothes will not be impressive if you are not neat and clean yourself. Hair should be neatly styled. A beard should be neatly shaven or trimmed. And makeup should be applied sparingly.

Think about the questions you might be asked

During an interview, the interviewer will be asking you many questions to find out if you're the right person for the job. There are some questions that almost every job seeker is asked when interviewed, 14-3. You need to become familiar with these questions and think about how you would answer them. In fact, it's a good idea to write your answers down on paper. Then you can read them over and decide if you phrased your thoughts clearly and positively.

One of the first things the interviewer is likely to say to you is, "Tell me about yourself." What do you think the interviewer wants to find out by asking you this? He or she wants to learn about your education and job skills. The interviewer also wants to see how well you express yourself. Answer this question and all other questions as they relate to the skills you need for the job.

Practice for the interview

Take some time to rehearse your interview. Ask a friend or family member to interview you or interview yourself in front of a mirror. Practice answering questions that you are likely to be asked. Try to make your answers sound natural and positive.

Most people usually get nervous about being interviewed. That's why it's important for you to practice ahead of time. Practicing will give you more self-confidence and help you feel more relaxed for the actual interview.

Know where to go for the interview

What a waste of time and energy it would be to get prepared for an interview and then miss it because you went to the wrong place. This has happened. One job seeker just assumed his interview would be at the company's manufacturing plant. When he arrived

for the interview, he found out all interviews are held at the company's corporate headquarters across town. Another job seeker missed her interview because she wrote down the wrong time of the interview. She didn't double-check the time like she should have. For these reasons, it's important to keep an accurate record of each interview you schedule.

One easy way to keep a record of your interviews is to prepare a note card for every interview, 14-4. On the card, write down the date and time of the interview, the name of the employer, and the exact location of the interview. Also write down the name of the person you are to see and the job title for which you are applying. Be sure to double-check all the information you write down to make sure you have recorded it correctly.

On the bottom and back of the card, leave space for comments. Then, after each interview, make notes about the questions you

INTERVIEW QUESTIONS

"Won't you tell me about yourself?"

"What do you know about our company?"

"Why do you want to work for this company?"

"Why do you think you will like this kind of work?"

"What were your best subjects in school?"

"What were your poorest subjects in school?"

"What other jobs have you had?"

"Have you ever been fired from a job? If so, why?"

"What is your major weakness?"

"What do you expect to be paid?"

"Are you willing to work overtime?"

"What are your future plans?"

"Why should I hire you?"

"When can you start work?"

14-3 Be prepared to answer these questions completely before you go on your first interview.

were asked and how well you answered them. Evaluating yourself can help you do even better on your next interview.

When arranging the interview, remember to ask where to park. Some companies have special areas for visitor parking. If you are interviewing in a city, you may need to park in a parking garage or a parking lot. Knowing where to park can save you valuable time.

THE INTERVIEW

Once you've prepared yourself for an interview, you're ready to meet your interviewer face to face. However, there are a few other details you need to consider. For example, what time should you arrive at the interviewer's office? How should you greet the interviewer? How should you behave during the interview? How should you end the interview? Knowing the answers to these questions will help you handle yourself with confidence and help you make a good impression on the interviewer.

Arrive five to ten minutes early for the interview. Tell the receptionist or person in charge who you are and who you've come to see. Do not take anyone with you to the interview. Taking a friend or family member may give the interviewer the impression that you're not used to doing things on your own. You certainly don't want to give this impression.

Greet the interviewer with a firm handshake and a friendly greeting. When you are offered a seat, sit down in a comfortable position. However, don't slouch. Sit up straight and look alert. Avoid doing anything that might be distracting such as smoking, chewing gum, or cracking your knuckles. It's natural to be nervous, but do your best to be relaxed.

As the interviewer asks you questions, listen very carefully. Then respond positively and honestly about yourself and your experiences. Keep your answers brief and to the point.

```
                        JOB INTERVIEW

Date of interview _____

Time of interview _____

Employer _____

Location_____

_____

Job title_____

Comments_____

_____

_____

_____
```

14-4 Filling out a note card for every interview you have can help you keep track of your interviews and the results of each.

Don't brag about your qualifications, but don't be bashful to tell the interviewer about your accomplishments.

All through the interview, act interested in what the interviewer is saying. Don't look out the window, around the room, or stare at the floor. Look pleasantly at the interviewer and make eye contact! Show you are enthusiastic about the job and the company.

When the interviewer asks you if you have any questions, that's usually a signal that he or she has all the information needed about you. This is the time to ask the questions you have about the job and the company. After your questions are answered, the interview is just about over. At this time, thank the interviewer for seeing you and tell him or her you would like the job.

Seldom will you be offered the job at the end of the interview. Most likely, the interviewer will want time to consider you for the job. The interviewer will probably promise to contact you on a certain date to let you know if you have the job. Or the interviewer may ask you to call him or her at a later date. If no mention is made of "what's to happen next," it is appropriate to ask when a decision is to be made about the job. You should leave an interview with a clear idea of what is to happen in the future.

AFTER THE INTERVIEW

After an interview, you don't just sit back and hope you'll be offered a job. You follow up the interview with a *follow-up letter*. This is a brief letter written in business form to thank the interviewer for the interview. A follow-up letter reminds the employer of your interview and your interest in the job. See 14-5. In some cases, sending a follow-up letter can make a difference in who the interviewer chooses for the job.

If the interviewer promised to contact you by a certain date and doesn't, also follow up with a telephone call. Be as pleasant and as positive as you were during your interview. You may want to say something like this. "Mr. Roberts, this is Terry Brooks. I filled out an application and interviewed with you two weeks ago. You mentioned that you would probably be making a decision about the job by yesterday. I'm still interested in the job and was wondering if you have made your decision." You may learn that the job has been filled. Or you may find out that you're still in the running but that a decision will not be made for another two weeks. Whatever the response, you will know where you stand on the job.

Don't be discouraged if you don't get a job offer right away. Very few job seekers land a job after just one or two interviews. You may need to interview with a number of employers to find the best job for you. However, if you have missed out on several jobs, try to figure out why. Check the comments you have written down on your interview cards. Have you had any problems on your interviews? To help you evaluate yourself on the job hunt, ask yourself the following questions. You may discover there's a specific reason why you aren't getting job offers.

Are you qualified for the jobs for which you are applying? Perhaps you are applying for jobs that require more training and experience than you have. Be willing to start at the bottom if necessary.

Are you applying to the wrong places? Apply where there are likely to be job openings. Consider applying for jobs in neighboring towns or moving to an area where there are more job opportunities.

Are you filling out job application forms properly? If you are not filling out applications correctly and neatly, employers may think you will not be able to perform a job properly. Read the directions carefully on all applications and answer all the questions completely.

Do you lack interest and energy? Not asking questions about the job or seeming enthusiastic could convince the interviewer you don't really care if you are hired or not.

Do you lack confidence? Appearing very nervous and ill at ease may make it difficult for the interviewer to talk with you.

Are you being discourteous? Arriving late

1036 Spring St.
Milwaukee, WI 53172
May 15, 19____

Mr. Robert Drake
Personnel Manager
Whitaker Publishing Company
1822 W. Meridian St.
Milwaukee, WI 53172

Dear Mr. Drake:

Thank you for taking time yesterday to interview me for the typist position that will come available in June.

After talking with you, I am very excited about the possibility of joining your company. I am confident I could do a good job for you.

I look forward to hearing your decision and hope it will be a favorable one.

Sincerely,

Mary Poston

Mary Poston

14-5 It is a good idea to send a follow-up letter after a job interview.

for the interview or not thanking the interviewer for seeing you may cause the interviewer to form a bad impression of you.

ACCEPTING A JOB OFFER

Ask questions about the pay and fringe benefits before accepting a job offer. The salary for a job should be in line with the salaries paid for similar jobs at other companies. If the salary is a lot lower, you should probably consider a job with an employer that pays a more reasonable salary. However, sometimes you may find that a lower salary is balanced with very good fringe benefits.

Fringe benefits are the financial extras in addition to the regular paycheck. Check to see if your employer provides any of the following benefits.

Insurance. Does the company offer group health, dental, and/or life insurance? If so, how much coverage do the policies provide? Does the employer pay all the coverage or do you have to pay a share of the cost?

Paid vacation. Will you receive paid vacation? If so, how many days? Will you receive more paid vacation days after you've worked at the company a certain number of years?

Sick pay. Will the company pay for any days you are sick and unable to come to work? How many sick days will they pay you per year?

Retirement plan or profit sharing plan. Does the company contribute a set amount of money to a retirement plan or a percentage of its profits to a profit sharing plan for you? Will a portion of your income also be contributed to one of these plans? If so, how much? Do you have to work for the employer a certain number of years before you can collect any of the benefits or profits?

Bonuses. Does the company give yearly or Christmas bonuses? How are the amounts of bonuses determined?

As discussed in Chapter 10, the pay and fringe benefits are just two factors to consider about a job. Also consider the location of the job, the working conditions, the working hours, and the opportunities for advancement before you make a final decision about a job.

to Review

1. What is the purpose of the interview for the employer? For the job seeker?
2. What can you do to prepare for an interview?
3. What information is good to know about an employer before you interview?
4. Why is it important to have some knowledge of a company before you interview?
5. Why is it important to prepare a list of questions to ask the interviewer?
6. What items do you need to take with you on an interview?
7. What is the guideline you may want to follow to help you decide what to wear to an interview?
8. Why is it a good idea to keep an accurate record of each interview you schedule?
9. Why should you go alone to an interview?
10. If the interviewer makes no mention about what is to happen next, what should you do?
11. What is a follow-up letter? Why is it important to send one after an interview?
12. If the interviewer promises to contact you by a certain date and doesn't, what should you do?
13. How can you evaluate yourself on the job hunt?
14. What questions should you ask the employer after you've been offered a job?
15. What are fringe benefits? Give examples.

to Discuss

1. What questions do you think are important to ask during an interview?
2. Why is it so important to be well groomed and dressed for an interview?
3. What clothes would you recommend a person wear if he or she was interviewing for a job as a(n):
    a. Typist?
    b. Auto mechanic?
    c. Waiter or waitress?
    d. Salesperson?
4. What are some of the questions you will probably be asked during an interview? How will you answer them?
5. Why is it important to practice for an interview? What are some good ways to practice?
6. What impression do you want the interviewer to form of you during the interview?
7. How should you behave during an interview?
8. Do you have a firm handshake or one like a dead fish? Why is this important?
9. How can you tell when an interview is coming to a close?
10. Why is it important to make notes after each interview about the questions you were asked and how well you answered them?

to Do

1. Assume you have been asked to interview for a job you would really like to have. Prepare for the interview by doing the following:
    a. On a note card, record all the important information about the interview.
    b. List three questions to ask the interviewer.
    c. List five questions that the interviewer is likely to ask you.
    d. Decide what would be appropriate to wear.
2. Role play the interview above. Have a classmate interview you for the job as if it was an actual interview. Be sure to give the interviewer a copy of your resume. Discuss the interview in class.
3. Write a follow-up letter for the interview above.

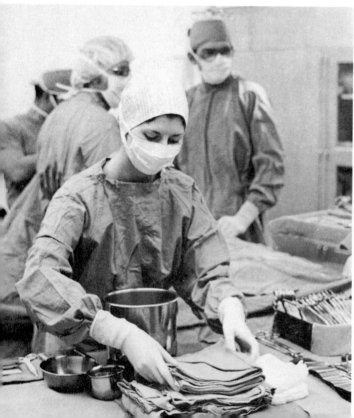

Job satisfaction

The more you can learn and accomplish on the job,
the faster you will succeed on the job.

15

Succeeding on the job

After studying this chapter, you will be able to:

☐ Evaluate your job performance and the job itself.
☐ Explain the purpose of job performance ratings.
☐ Describe the best way to go about changing jobs.
☐ Cite reasons most employees are fired from their jobs.
☐ Explain the pros and cons of union membership.

What does it mean to succeed on the job? To many people, being successful on the job means doing their jobs well and not getting fired. To others, job success is being given a promotion, more responsibilities, and/or a pay raise.

To succeed at any job, you must stick with it. Don't be surprised if it takes a number of weeks for you to get adjusted to your job and to learn all your responsibilities. You will need to work hard to learn all your duties, but you shouldn't try to get too far ahead of yourself. You can't expect to accomplish everything in only a few weeks time.

After working at a job for several weeks, then you can begin to evaluate your job performance and the job itself. To help you find out if you are having success with your job, ask yourself the following questions.

Do you seem to be making progress in your job? Have you learned how to perform all your duties and to perform them well? If you're having a problem learning how to do a task, ask your supervisor for assistance. If you're accomplishing your work with time to spare, let your supervisor know you are capable of taking on more responsibility. The more you can learn and accomplish on the job, the faster you will succeed on the job, as Marla well knows.

Marla learned her job duties quickly and became a very productive worker in a matter of weeks. When she accomplished her regular assigned work, she asked the assistant supervisor or the supervisor what other work she could do in the office. Marla was a responsible and cooperative employee who was always willing to help others with tasks when asked to do so. When the assistant supervisor was promoted to a new position, Marla was asked to assume this position. She accepted the promotion and continued to work just as conscientiously at her new job. Marla's hard work paid off, and it helped earn her other promotions in the future.

Do you get personal satisfaction from your job? Do you enjoy the work you do? You can't expect a job to be all fun and games, but it shouldn't be all drudgery either. Job success depends a lot on the way you feel about your job. To be successful, you must feel your job is useful and of service to others. If you feel you are making important contributions on the job, you will probably feel pleased about your life and the work you accomplish, 15-1.

Do you feel you're getting paid adequately for the work you do? Although salary is only one aspect of job success, it is an important one. Check to see what other people with similar jobs are making at other companies. Your wages should be in that range. However, don't expect to begin an entry-level job at a high salary. Normally, a worker can expect to start at the lower end of the wage scale and move up as he or she becomes more productive. If you don't get a salary review or pay increase after six months on the job, you should find out why.

Do you foresee opportunities for advancement? If you do well in the job you're in now, will you be able to move into a higher-paying job with more responsibilities? If you find you're in a job that leads to nowhere, it's doubtful that you'll find much success in your work. Having a goal to work toward—a job promotion—can motivate you to succeed at your present job, 15-2.

Keep in mind that no job is perfect. Every job is going to have its good points and bad

points. It's when the bad points outweigh the good that you may find you need to change jobs.

JOB PROBATION

Sometimes new workers are hired on a probationary basis. This means a worker is hired for a trial period of time to see how well he or she can do the job. A probationary period can be as short as a few days or as long as a few months. During this period, a supervisor helps train the new worker and oversees his or her work. The supervisor also evaluates the

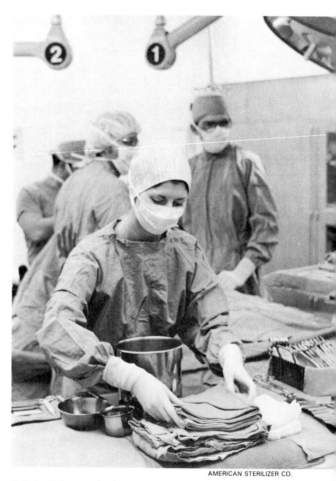

AMERICAN STERILIZER CO.

15-1 This surgical nurse gets satisfaction from her work because she feels that what she accomplishes on the job is important and of service to others.

worker's job skills, work habits, and ability to get along with co-workers.

Most workers complete their probationary period with very little trouble. With the help of their supervisors, they learn how to be productive at their jobs and how to avoid making mistakes.

If a worker does not pass probation, he or she is simply not hired. If this should ever happen to you, be sure to find out why you did not pass. You don't want to make the same mistakes again at your next job.

Cooperative education students who have had work experience are less likely to have problems during their probationary period. This is because their work experiences tend to help them adjust to new jobs more easily.

PERFORMANCE RATINGS

Job success depends a great deal on how your supervisor rates your performance on the job. At most companies, employees are reviewed every six months or once a year. During these reviews, employees are rated on their work and social skills as well as their attitudes toward work.

Check sheets are often used by companies to rate employee performance, 15-3. Employees are rated on job factors such as accuracy of work, ability to work with others, ability to think problems through, and willingness to accept responsibility. The supervisor evaluates an employee's performance according to a rating scale such as excellent, good, fair, or poor.

15-2 This employee knows she can advance to assistant office manager if she does a good job as a cashier.

EMPLOYEE APPRAISAL FORM

EMPLOYEE NAME:_____ HIRE DATE:_____

JOB CLASSIFICATION:_____ APPRAISAL DATE:_____

SUPERVISOR:_____ LAST APPRAISAL DATE:_____

PRODUCTIVITY - Employee's performance (is)

( ) Must Improve   ( ) Meets Expectations   ( ) Exceptional
    in meeting company productivity standards.

Explain: _____

_____

QUALITY - Employee's performance (is)

( ) Must Improve   ( ) Meets Expectations   ( ) Exceptional
    in meeting company quality standards.

Explain: _____

_____

TEAMWORK - Employee's ability to work with/for others (is)

( ) Must Improve   ( ) Meets Expectations   ( ) Exceptional

Explain: _____

_____

DEPENDABILITY - Employee's attendance and promptness (are)

( ) Must Improve   ( ) Meets Expectations   ( ) Exceptional

Explain:_____

_____

SAFETY - Employee's judgement, actions and attention to safety in the work environment (are)

( ) Must Improve   ( ) Meets Expectations   ( ) Exceptional

Explain: _____

_____

Performance Appraisal continued:

OVERALL SUMMARY: _____

_____

_____

_____

_____

_____

_____

EMPLOYEE COMMENTS: _____

_____

_____

_____

_____

_____

_____

_____

_____

SIGNATURES:

_____   _____
APPRAISING SUPERVISOR   PERSONNEL

_____   _____
DEPARTMENT MANAGER   EMPLOYEE

15-3 Employers consider many factors when
evaluating a worker's job performance.

The purpose of performance ratings is to help supervisors identify the weaknesses and strengths of their employees. After a performance rating, a supervisor may decide that an employee's skills would be better used for a different job. Therefore, the supervisor may promote the employee to another position or transfer him or her to another department. For example, after a performance rating, a supervisor may decide to promote a receptionist, who has shown excellent typing skills, to the position of secretary. A receptionist who has been especially skilled at working with the public may be promoted to the customer service department.

If the employee is having problems doing certain tasks, the supervisor can work with the employer to help him or her improve his or her weaker skills. Or the supervisor may assign the worker to another job.

As a result of the performance ratings, employees also become aware of their strengths and weaknesses. Most supervisors show workers their evaluations or talk to them about their past performance and future with the company, 15-4. This gives employees a chance

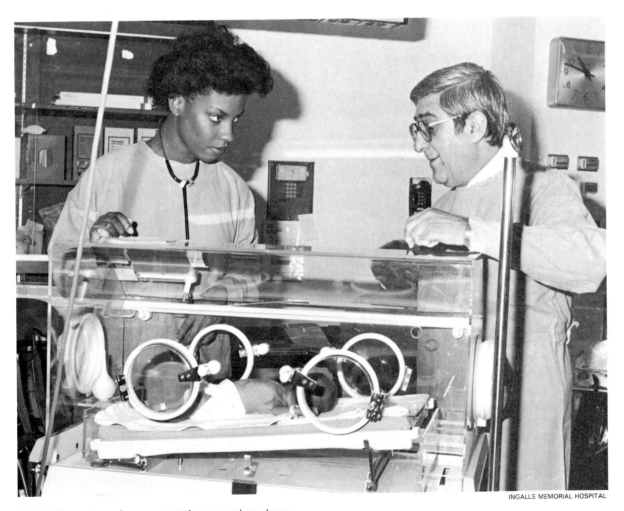

INGALLS MEMORIAL HOSPITAL

15-4 Through performance ratings, workers learn how they can become better professionals.

to learn how they can improve their work and become more productive employees. By improving their job performance, they will have an opportunity to get more pay raises and be considered for possible promotions.

CHANGING JOBS

In the United States, people tend to change jobs often, especially in their early years of employment. People give many reasons for wanting to change jobs.

"I'm in a dead-end job. There are no opportunities to advance with this company."

"The work is boring; it just doesn't interest me anymore."

"I have a hard time getting along with my boss, and I don't care much for my co-workers either."

"I found another job that I'll like doing better, and it pays more too."

Any of these reasons may be good ones to change jobs. Whatever the reason, if you decide to change jobs, you should plan the change carefully. Avoid making a quick decision. Think about your career and future plans. Think about the reasons you want to leave your present job and the type of job you want to move into next. What do you plan to accomplish by making a change? You don't want to just walk off the job where you are now. You want to make sure you have another job lined up before leaving the one you have.

If you decide to leave a job, you should try to leave on good terms. Quitting on the spur of the moment is not fair to your employer nor will it leave your employer with a good impression of you. As a general rule, notify your supervisor at least two weeks before you plan to leave. This will give your employer a chance to find another worker to replace you. If your job involves a great deal of responsibility and training, you may want to notify your employer even earlier.

Although hopping from job to job is something you should avoid, changing jobs can be a very positive move to make. In fact, all too often, many people stay in a job they dislike because they don't have the courage or ambi-

tion to look for another job. It does take courage and drive to look for a new job and make a change, but the rewards can be well worth it. Feeling satisfied with your job will make you feel happier about your life and the work you accomplish.

Of course, changing jobs is not always the employee's idea, but the employer's. This is called getting fired. Here are the most common reasons employers give for firing employees:

- Absenteeism—not showing up for work on a regular basis.
- Loafing—daydreaming on the job, taking long coffee breaks, wandering away from assigned work stations for no good reasons.
- Personality conflicts—not getting along with the person in charge or with co-workers.
- Violating company rules—fighting, drinking, smoking in non-smoking areas, ignoring safety regulations.
- Incompetence—not having the knowledge, skills, experience, or attitude to perform the job responsibilities as requested.

Being dismissed from a job can come as a great surprise, and it may take a few days to recover from such a shock. If you should ever find yourself out of a job unexpectedly, give yourself a couple of days to recover. Then, try to figure out why you were fired. Did you do or say something to contribute to the situation? Was your employer fair to you? Were there financial reasons that made the action necessary?

Be honest with yourself. If you made a mistake or did something you weren't supposed to do, admit it. Don't lie about it or try to blame someone else. If you care about your future and career, you will not make the same mistake again.

A JOB PROMOTION

Being offered a job promotion is a sign that your employer thinks you are succeeding at your job. A promotion is not something an employer just gives an employee. A promotion is an advancement that employees must earn by being productive, cooperative, dependable, and responsible on the job, 15-5.

If you are promoted, you will probably be given a new job title, an increase in pay, and more responsibility. With increased responsibility, you may be asked to supervise the work of others. This means your role as a co-worker would change to that of a supervisor. Not only would you have the responsibility of your work, you would also be responsible for the work of those under your authority.

Becoming a supervisor will mean you will develop new relationships with the employees you will be supervising. You will no longer be working as a follower, you'll be working as a leader. Your success as a supervisor will depend on your success as a leader and communicator.

To get started on the right foot with your employees, do not brag about your promotion to supervisor. Be happy about your promotion, but don't look down on your former co-workers. Stay on friendly terms with them and continue to work with them as a team. Remember, you can't do all the work yourself. You will need to delegate responsibility and help your workers accomplish their tasks correctly. For you to be successful, your employees will need to be successful at their jobs as well.

A good leader can supervise effectively without having to be bossy. If you give directions clearly, treat workers fairly, and perform your work duties properly, you will be respected by your workers. They will know you are the boss without you having to tell them.

The idea of becoming a supervisor may sound like a lot of work. In fact, you may be wondering if you can handle the responsibility. Chances are, if you've been asked to become a supervisor, you are capable of handling the job. Many companies have training classes to help new supervisors adjust to their new responsibilities and learn how to be successful at their jobs. If you are given the opportunity to advance to a supervisory position, consider the offer carefully. Review your occupational plans and think about how this promotion can help you further your career. The opportunity to become a supervisor doesn't come along every day. If you turn down a promotion, it may be a long time before you're offered another one.

Not all promotions, however, lead to supervisory positions. Some are simply a matter of

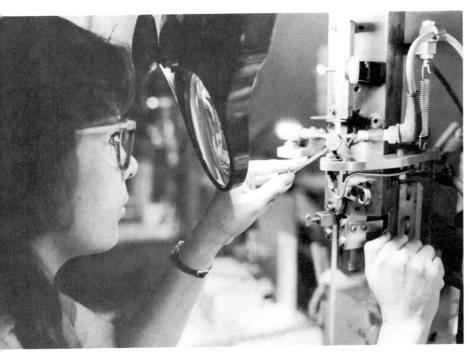

15-5 Employees who are productive, cooperative, dependable, and responsible are most likely to be promoted on the job.

reclassification. For example, Maria was hired as a secretary at a number three classification. After working six months and receiving good performance ratings, Maria was advanced to a number two classification. Although her duties stayed the same, Maria's salary increased 10 percent. When Maria advances to a number one classification, she will have advanced as far as she can go as a secretary in that company. She'll continue to receive small pay increases as long as her work remains good, but she will not be given any new responsibilities.

Would you be happy with a job like Maria's? Or would you want the challenge of working toward a promotion of supervisor? Which type of job will make you feel successful and satisfied about your work?

UNIONS

In order to work in some occupations, workers are required to join a labor union. A union is a group of workers who have formed together to voice their opinions to their employer or the employer's representatives (management). Ideally, the purpose of a union is to help workers be successful and secure on the job by bargaining with management for better wages, working hours, working conditions, and benefits.

Labor unions came about in the early days of industry because of poor working conditions, low wages, child labor, and unfair treatment of employees. By banning together, workers found that they gained strength and power to discuss these problems with management.

As a result of unions and changes in corporate attitudes, many of the problems that faced workers in the early 1900s have been solved. Workers are no longer faced with terrible working conditions. Laws have been passed to protect workers' rights and safety. Management has learned over the years that satisfied workers are more productive workers, 15-6. And more productive workers yield higher profits. For these reasons, many workers have found that they no longer need

to be part of a union to be treated and paid fairly. They no longer want to pay expensive union dues to support their local and national union organizations when they hear how some union officials have misused union money. Some people feel that unions have accomplished their original purposes and are no longer needed.

On the other hand, some people feel that unions can still do many things for its workers. They can continue to campaign for increased wages and benefits. They can help retrain workers whose jobs are assumed by automation. And they can influence the legislation of labor and fair trade laws.

Must you join a union?

The answer to this question depends on the state in which you work and the kind of job you have. Some occupations do not have union affiliations. However, others require union membership.

If a workplace has a *union shop agreement,* all of its workers must join the union as a condition of employment. In such cases, you might be hired by a company, but you would not be able to work more than a certain period of time unless you joined the union.

If a workplace has an *open shop agreement,* its workers are free to join or not to join the union. Most unions oppose this type of agreement because they represent all workers in their negotiations. Therefore, they feel every worker should be required to join the union.

To find out what type of shop agreement a company has, call the company or check with your state department of labor. If you have a choice about whether to join a union or not, do a little investigating first. Find out the following information to help you decide if joining a union will help you be more successful at your job.

● Track record of the union. Find out what the union has accomplished and what it plans to accomplish in the future.
● The size of the workplace. The larger the company you work for, the greater the need may be for workers to negotiate terms

through the help of a union.

- Cost of union membership. Find out what the initial fee is to join and the amount of monthly or weekly dues withheld from your paycheck.

Keep in mind that if you join a union, you will have to abide by union rules. You must be willing to give up some of your independence. If you have a complaint about work, you will have to follow a specific procedure for getting the problem solved. It's possible that you and your manager could solve the problem yourselves, but you will have to follow union rules. If the union votes to go on strike, whether you want to or not, you will have to go along with it and manage without pay.

Organization of unions

Today, two major types of labor unions exist in the United States: craft unions and industrial unions.

Craft unions are formed by workers who have the same craft or trade. There are craft unions for carpenters, painters, plumbers, electricians, and machinists. For example, the union for carpenters is called the United Brotherhood of Carpenters and Joiners. The union for electricians is called the International Brotherhood of Electrical Workers (IBEW).

Industrial unions are formed by workers who belong to the same industry. Most industrial union members work in factories

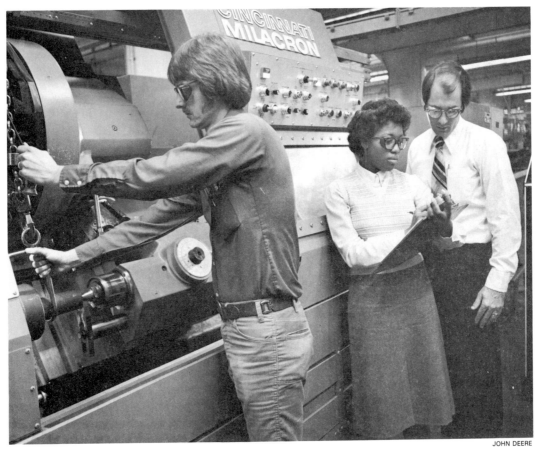

JOHN DEERE

15-6 Safe working conditions, fair wages, and good management yield more productive and satisfied workers.

where cars, clothing, steel, and other products are made. The industrial union for auto workers is called the United Automobile Workers (UAW). The union for garment workers is the United Garment Workers of America (UGW).

Some national unions are large with over a million workers such as the United Automobile Workers. National unions consist of many local unions. For example, the UAW has local unions wherever cars are being manufactured in the United States.

The basic work of unions is done in the locals. A local union has its own constitution, bylaws, and set of officers. The local union also elects shop stewards to handle members' complaints about management.

Collective bargaining

Collective bargaining is the process that labor and management use to discuss what they expect from each other in the workplace. In a way, collective bargaining is like a buyer and a seller debating the price of something to be sold. Labor may first demand much more than they expect to get. Management will offer much less than they intend to give. Through debate, discussion, and possibly, arguments, a compromise is finally reached in the form of a labor contract. A *labor contract* is an agreement which spells out the conditions for wages, benefits, job security, work hours, working conditions, and grievance procedures (the way a complaint is handled).

Bargaining for a new contract can be a long process. It usually begins weeks before the date that the existing contract expires. Representatives from management and labor each present things they want to go into the contract. When an agreement is reached for a new work contract, then the union members vote to accept or reject the agreement. If the union members reject the contract, their representatives go back to the bargaining table and bargain for different terms.

If no agreement can be reached and the existing contract expires, there may be trouble. Sometimes union members will vote to strike until the company meets their demands or comes closer to their demands, 15-7. On the other hand, management can threaten to close down the company unless an agreement is reached. Obviously, either action can be a loss to both labor and management. This is why it's important for both labor and management to be reasonable in their expectations.

15-7 Workers on strike usually picket in front of the company that has not met their contract demands.

to Review

1. What questions can you ask yourself to help you determine if you are having success with your job?

2. What does it mean for a worker to be hired on a probationary basis? What happens if a worker does not pass probation?

3. What is the purpose of performance ratings for the employer and the employee?

4. How much notice should you give your supervisor before leaving a job?

5. List the reasons most employers give for firing employees.

6. What should you do if you are fired from your job?

7. Succeeding as a supervisor depends on what two factors?

8. Why were labor unions originally formed?

9. Why has the growth of unions practically stopped?

10. Explain the difference between a union shop agreement and an open shop agreement.

11. What should you consider before joining a union if you have a choice?

12. Describe the two major types of labor unions that exist in the United States.

to Discuss

1. How would you describe job success?

2. Discuss the job factors upon which a supervisor evaluates an employee's job preformance.

3. What may happen after a supervisor rates an employee's performance on the job?

4. For what reasons do you think most people change jobs? Under what circumstances would you change jobs?

5. Explain how you would go about changing jobs.

6. For what reasons do you think most employees are given promotions?

7. How can you be an effective supervisor without being bossy?

8. Do you think unions are needed in today's society? Explain your answer.

9. If you had the choice between joining a union and not joining a union, what would you do?

10. What are the laws in your state concerning union membership?

to Do

1. List five reasons why you think you are succeeding at your cooperative work experience. Also list five things you can do to improve your job performance. Then divide into groups of four. Share your lists with each other, and discuss ways each person in the group can improve his or her job performance.

2. Ask a local employer or an employee in a supervisory position to talk with the class about two topics:
   a. The problems of new employees and how these problems can be avoided.
   b. How a person should prepare for and work toward a supervisory position.

3. Talk to three people who recently changed jobs. Find out why and how each person changed jobs and what each one hopes to accomplish in their new job. Are there any similarities in the answers given by the three workers? Does it sound as if each person made the right decision by changing jobs? Discuss your findings in class.

Mass production of goods helped our
nation develop a strong business economy.

16

Succeeding in our economic system

After studying this chapter, you will be able to:

☐ Describe our economic system.
☐ Compare the three forms of business ownership.
☐ Describe the responsibilities involved in managing a business.
☐ Explain the advantages and disadvantages of starting your own business.

For years, the United States has been recognized as a highly industrialized nation that developed through a strong business economy. This was not always the case. In the early years of our nation, agriculture was the main industry. Land was available to farmers and ranchers who moved freely across the country. The land was developed, and thousands of communities sprang up. The United States did not develop into a great producer of world goods until the 1800s.

With the industrial revolution, American industries were born. Machines were invented to mass produce goods. The production of goods grew and grew which made more goods available to more people. Manufacturers worked hard to produce more and better goods at lower and lower prices.

Along with a good production system, the United States had great supplies of natural resources such as lumber, coal, iron ore, and copper. The rivers were used to supply power and energy and provide easy transportation of goods.

Through the United States patent system, inventions of all kinds were encouraged. The patent system helped protect the inventor because it required all inventions to be registered with the federal government and issued a patent number. Once an invention was patented, it was illegal for someone else to copy the invention and assume it as his or her own. As a result, many foreign inventors came to the United States. With the invention of new products and processes, industries grew and grew. Everyone seemed to benefit.

The working people who immigrated to the United States brought their training and skills with them. What tools they could not bring, they made. With their skill and desire to succeed, these workers provided a very productive labor force which industries needed to manufacture goods.

To pull the entire industrial system together required organization. Business leaders gave the needed direction as they built their companies and produced their goods and services for the world market. As businesses continued to grow and expand, more emphasis was placed on management. The owners of many companies continued to provide money (capital) for business. However, they came to depend on highly trained persons to manage their businesses and to keep them profitable.

Why, then, did the United States develop into such a strong industrial nation? It became strong economically because it had natural resources, a patent system, skilled labor, good management, and capital for investments. The United States also had another very important asset. That was a system of government which permitted industry to operate as a free enterprise. It was the free enterprise system that allowed individuals and groups the right to start businesses and earn profits from them.

OUR FREE ENTERPRISE SYSTEM

Free enterprise is only one of many names used to describe our economic system. It has also been called a consumer economy, a market economy, a profit system, and capitalism. Although all these words have slightly different meanings, they all represent the same basic economic system. This system is based on six major factors: private ownership and control of productive resources, the profit motive, supply and demand, competition, a free market, and limited government involvement.

Private ownership and control of productive resources. The government does not own or control business and industry. Private citizens do. Individuals and businesses decide how to use their productive resources to produce and provide goods and services. *Productive resources* are all the resources such as labor, land, capital, and equipment that can be used to produce and provide goods and services. See 16-1.

Free market. People have the right to decide how and where to earn, spend, save, and invest their money. They also have the freedom to produce whatever they think they can sell.

Profit motive. The desire to earn profits (money) motivates individuals and businesses to use their resources to produce goods and services. Without the opportunity to earn profits, people would not be motivated to work or invest their money. Then there would be no labor or money to produce goods and services.

Supply and demand. The products and services businesses produce are determined by the products and services consumers demand. Consumers express their demand through their spending choices in the marketplace. Whatever consumers are willing to buy, there are businesses willing to supply it.

Competition. Any individual or business has the right to enter into the same business as any other company and compete for consumer dollars. Competition encourages businesses to produce quality goods and services at low prices. If a company charges too high a price for a product or service, consumers can go to a competitor who sells the same product or service and buy it for less. The company that produces the best products and services at the lowest prices will earn the most profits.

Limited government involvement. To keep the free enterprise system free and fair requires some government involvement. Federal, state, and local governments establish and enforce economic laws and policies to promote economic growth and stability. For example, to promote fair competition, government

FORD MOTOR CO.

SOUTHWEST FOREST INDUSTRIES

16-1 Labor, land, equipment, and capital (money) are all productive resources.

enforces laws that prevent monopolies. A *monopoly* is a single company that controls the entire supply of a product or service. If a monopoly was allowed to exist, it could charge consumers unfair prices for goods and services and limit their production and availability. Then the economy would not be operating on a free enterprise basis.

HOW BUSINESSES ARE ORGANIZED

As a result of our free enterprise system, the United States has thousands of businesses that produce a variety of products and services. Businesses range from only one person as the owner-worker to thousands of employees in a large company. However, they all operate on the same basic principle. They must earn a profit to stay in business. This means all businesses depend on consumers to buy their goods and services to create a demand for more goods and services.

To understand more about the way businesses operate in our economic system, it helps to understand the three forms of business ownership. These are a proprietorship, a partnership, and a corporation.

Proprietorship

A *proprietorship* is a business that has only one owner. It is the simplest form of business organization because usually only one person makes the decisions and manages the business. There are no business partners or board of directors to consult. For these reasons, there are many single-owner businesses.

In a proprietorship, the owner or proprietor supplies all of the money to start and operate the business. As a result, the owner receives all the profits that are made and assumes all the debts and losses.

Most proprietorships are small companies in which the owner does much of the work. Many retail and service shops such as the corner grocery store, barbershop, hair salon, dry cleaner, auto repair shop, and restaurants are proprietorships, 16-2. However, a proprietorship can be a multi-million dollar business with hundreds of employees.

Partnership

A *partnership* is a form of business organization where two or more people go into business together, 16-3. Have you ever seen or heard of a company that has two names in its title? The title Wagner and Son would suggest a father and son in partnership. Smith and Jones Plumbing could be a company formed by two friends owning and operating a business as equal partners.

In a partnership, all the partners pool their money to establish and operate the business. The partners share the work responsibilities as well as the profits and debts.

One of the advantages of a partnership over a proprietorship is that more money is available to finance the business. A partnership also brings together the skills and experiences of two or more people. This often makes it easier for a partnership to solve problems and make wise business decisions. It is the idea that "two heads are better than one."

16-2 Gino's Pizza & Subs is a proprietorship because it is a business that has only one owner.

Partnerships may have their disadvantages as well. Problems can arise when partners do not agree on business decisions. Or there can be problems when one partner feels he or she is assuming more of the work and responsibility than the other partner(s).

In addition to regular partnerships, there are limited partnerships. *Limited partners,* sometimes called silent partners, invest money or property into a business but do not work in the business. As the business makes a profit from the sale of its goods or services, limited partners receive a percentage of those profits. If the business fails, limited partners are only responsible for any debts of the business up to the amount of their investments.

Corporation

A *corporation* is a business owned by many people. A corporation is formed by selling portions or shares of a business which are called *stocks.* The people who buy the stocks become part owners of the business and are called *stockholders.* See 16-4.

16-3 Sal and Tony's Pizza Restaurant is a partnership because it is a business that has more than one owner.

16-4 Pizza Hut is a corporation because it is a business owned by many people.

Unlike the other two forms of ownership, (with the exception of limited partners) a stockholder is only responsible for any debts of the business up to the amount of his or her investment. Therefore, if a stockholder invests $500 in a corporation, the most the stockholder can lose if the business fails is $500. This is called limited liablity. Stockholders are only liable for the amounts they have invested. If the corporation makes a profit, the stockholder receives a share of those profits according to the amount he or she has invested.

Limited liability is one of the major advantages of forming a corporation. The other major advantage of corporate ownership is the fact that large amounts of money can be raised to expand a business and produce more goods or services.

Although stockholders are part owners in a corporation, they have very little input in the decision making. A board of directors, elected by stockholders, make most of the business decisions along with the top level managers hired to run the corporation. The president and vice presidents of a corporation are the top level managers. These officials give leadership and direction to the entire corporation. They work together to see that the corporation makes a profit.

In 16-5 is an example of the levels of management that exist in some corporations. The president oversees all corporate activities and hands down decisions to the vice presidents. The vice presidents delegate responsiblities to managers (in this example, plant managers). The plant managers oversee the department heads. The department heads oversee the supervisors. The supervisors, the lowest level of management, oversee the workers. Each person reports to the person in the next highest position and, in turn, receives direction from that person. The larger the corporation, the more specialized the levels of management become.

BUSINESS MANAGEMENT

For a business to be successful, it must be well managed. This is true for a proprietorship, a partnership, and a corporation. Managing a business involves many responsibilities. It requires careful planning, staffing, directing, marketing, and financing.

The purpose of planning is to set goals for the business by deciding which goods or services to produce or provide and how to market those goods or services. Planning includes researching the competition and determining the amount of profits to be made. It also includes organizing the business so it can operate efficiently and reach its goals.

Staffing involves hiring workers to help produce, market, and distribute goods and services. The larger the business, the larger this function will be. In large corporations, the staffing and training of employees is usually handled by a personnel manager.

Directing the production of goods is another job for management. Production managers and supervisors oversee the manufacture of goods.

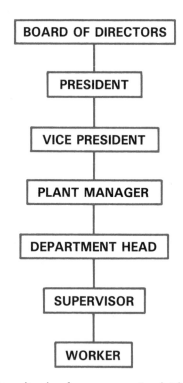

16-5 Many levels of management exist in some corporations. Most of the important business decisions are made by the board of directors and top level managers.

Managers of stores, restaurants, health clubs, and other businesses that provide services see that services are being provided efficiently and satisfactorily. Production and service managers are both responsible for the quality of goods and services their businesses provide.

Marketing includes the promotion, selling, and distribution of goods and services. The purpose of marketing is to get customers and consumers to use the products or services.

Financing involves keeping records of accounts, paying debts, collecting payments from customers, making out the payroll, and paying taxes.

As managers plan, staff, direct, market, and finance their businesses, they must constantly make decisions. A personnel manager must decide who to hire. A production manager must decide how goods will be manufactured. A marketing manager must decide how products or services will be promoted. A business manager must decide how to keep accurate financial records. Since decision-making is such an important part of management, workers with the most training and experience are most often promoted to management positions. The more knowledge and experience people have, the more likely they are to make wise business decisions.

A BUSINESS OF YOUR OWN

Do you ever have thoughts of starting your own business? This is the dream of many people. They may say, "I want to be self-employed," "I want to be my own boss," or "I want to be independent." There are many reasons why people want to go into business for themselves. Being self-employed can be very exciting and rewarding. You may be able to look around your commuunity and name a number of people who are successful with their own businesses. Your list may include the florist, cafe owner, photograper, furniture storeowner, barber, or the auto mechanic who has her own repair shop. Unfortunately, many attempts to start a business never succeed. Some people invest a lifetime of their savings into a business only to see it all lost.

Owning your own business requires many hours of hard work. The self-employed person will usually work hours beyond the normal working day of a wage earner. There is also the emotional strain of owning your own business. Most small business owners worry about making a profit and with good reason. It is estimated that the average small business must operate three years before it shows a profit. Not having enough money to manage through the first few years is why most small businesses run into problems.

Making the decision to open a small business should be done only after careful study and thought. If you decide to "take the plunge," here are some helpful guidelines to follow.

- Make a careful plan before starting. Don't rush into any business. Investigate the potential for such a business in your community, and identify your competition. Find out if similar businesses have had difficulties succeeding and why.
- Get the skills and experience necessary for the business. Work for someone who is already in the business, 16-6. Learn everything you can about financing the business and buying and pricing the goods or services you want to sell.
- Talk to others who are in similar businesses. Also, read all you can about starting a business of your own.
- Have enough funds (money) to carry you through the first months of little or no income.
- Start small, then add and build on to the business as you begin to make profits. Acquire tools and equipment as you can afford them.
- Hire trained, well qualified, honest workers.
- Keep records of all business transactions and inventories to evaluate the progress of the business and to prepare tax returns.
- Make all business decisions based on facts and not wishful thinking.
- Be willing to sell if you do not make a profit.

One way to get into business for yourself is to buy one that is already doing well. Small businesses often come available for sale because the owner retires, dies, or just wants to be free of the responsibilities of operating a business. However, buying an established business would probably be more expensive than starting your own. This is because you would be paying for the good reputation of the business.

Another way to begin your own business is by franchise. A *franchise* is the right to market a product or service owned by a large company. A company may have a product or service it wants to market in several communities. They will allow someone else to sell the product or service for a specified amount of money. Some fast food restaurants, convenience stores, dry cleaners, and retail stores are examples of businesses sold through franchises. It's best to buy a franchise with exclusive selling rights in a community. This means that no one else can buy into the franchise and sell the same product or service in your specific geographic area. If you ever consider investing in a franchised business, be sure to investigate it carefully.

Sometimes a new business can be started at home. It may be the only way you can afford to start out on your own. Using your garage, basement, or a room in your home reduces the cost of getting started. However, there can be drawbacks. A home business may interfere with the activities of other family members. Local zoning laws may not permit some businesses if it changes the appearance of the property. And a home business could increase your home insurance rates.

Keep in mind that the desire to go into business for yourself is not enough. It requires a very dedicated worker, a self-starter, and a wise decision maker. Even then, there are no guaranteed formulas for success. For more information about starting a small business, contact the Small Business Administration office nearest you. It will be listed in the telephone directory under "United States Government."

BERNIE NOVIA

16-6 Before attempting to go into business on your own, get the skills and experience necessary for the business.

to Review

1. Why did the United States develop into a strong industrial nation?
2. What are the six basic factors on which our free enterprise system is based?
3. What are productive resources?
4. Why is limited government involvement necessary in a free enterprise system?
5. What is a monopoly? What would happen if monopolies were allowed to exist?
6. Describe the three forms of business ownership.
7. Name two advantages of a partnership over a proprietorship. What are the disadvantages of a partnership.
8. What are limited partners? For what are limited partners responsible if a business fails?
9. What are the two major advantages of corporate ownership?
10. Who makes most of the business decisions in a corporation?
11. What are the disadvantages of starting your own business?
12. Name at least five guidelines to follow when opening a small business.
13. What is a franchise? If buying a franchise, why is it best to buy one with exclusive selling rights in a community?

to Discuss

1. How would you describe our economic system?
2. Why is competition so important in a free enterprise system?
3. What is the one principle on which all businesses operate? Give examples of this principle in action.
4. Name at least five proprietorships that exist in your community or surrounding area.
5. How would you go about selecting a business partner?
6. What does the concept "limited liability" mean?
7. Explain the levels of management that exist in many corporations.
8. Describe the responsibilities involved in managing a business.
9. Why do you think people go into business for themselves?
10. Would you ever want to own your own business? Why?
11. What does it take to be successful in a business of your own?
12. Discuss different ways you could go about starting your own business.

to Do

1. Ask someone who has lived under an economic system different from our free enterprise system to speak to the class about life under that system. Then discuss the differences that exist between a free enterprise system and the other economic system.
2. Prepare a chart showing the levels of management that exist in your school system. Begin with the school board and work down to the teaching and non-teaching positions.
3. Invite the president of a proprietorship, a partnership, and a small corporation to your class to discuss their responsibilities as a company president. After hearing them speak, discuss the similarities and differences in their responsibilities.

The
Valley National
Banking Machin

Consumer responsibilities

Most people use the services of financial institutions
to help them manage their money effectively.

17

Banking services

After studying this chapter, you will be able to:

☐ Select the banking services and financial institutions that will best meet your financial needs.
☐ Endorse, deposit, and write checks correctly.
☐ Balance a checkbook.
☐ Describe the special types of checks that can be used in place of personal checks and cash.
☐ Explain the two basic types of savings plans.

As you work and earn income, you are likely to need the services of financial institutions. Commercial banks, savings and loan associations, and credit unions are all financial institutions that can help you manage your money effectively.

Commercial banks are often called full-service banks because they offer a variety of services. At a commercial bank you can open a checking or savings account, buy special types of checks, and buy certificates of deposit. You can also buy U.S. Savings Bonds, take out a loan, and rent safe-deposit boxes. In most commercial banks the money you deposit is safe because it is insured by the *Federal Deposit Insurance Corporation* (FDIC). The FDIC is the U.S. government agency that insures bank deposits up to $100,000. Therefore, at an FDIC-insured bank, you will not lose your money if the bank is robbed or goes bankrupt.

A *savings and loan association* offers many of the same services offered by commercial banks. Although savings and loan associations are limited by law in the kinds of services they can provide, they can offer higher interest rates for savings accounts and time deposits than banks offer. Like most commercial banks, deposits in savings and loan associations are insured up to $100,000 by the *Federal Savings and Loan Insurance Corporation* (FSLIC).

A *credit union* differs from a commercial bank and a savings and loan association in that its services are for its members only. Members of credit unions are people who share a common bond such as members of a union, employees of a company, or members of a professional organization. Since credit unions are nonprofit organizations run by its members, operation costs are usually low. Therefore, credit unions usually charge lower interest rates on loans and offer higher interest rates on savings than commercial banks and savings and loan associations. Most credit unions are insured by the *National Credit Union Association* (NCUA).

Whether you bank at a commercial bank, a savings and loan association, a credit union, or all three, you need to become familiar with banking services.

The first banking service you are likely to need is a checking account. You also need to learn about special types of checks, savings plans, and safe-deposit boxes.

CHECKING ACCOUNTS

Most people do not like to carry a large amount of cash around with them or leave it laying around their homes. Cash is too easy to spend, lose, have stolen, or even destroyed by fire. To avoid these problems, many people put their money in a checking account. Although you may have to pay a small fee to have a checking account, this service has many advantages:

- Provides a safe place to keep cash and an easy way to withdraw it.
- Provides a convenient way to buy goods and services and pay bills by mail.
- Provides a record of spending and receipts of payment.
- Helps you establish a credit rating.

Types of accounts

Basically, there are three types of checking accounts: the budget account, the minimum-balance account, and the interest-bearing checking account. The type of checking account you need will depend on the amount you can afford to leave on deposit. It will also depend on the number of checks you plan to write each month.

With a *budget account,* you are charged a fee for every check you write and/or a monthly service charge. However, you are not required to keep a minimum balance. If you plan to write a few checks and keep a small amount of cash in your account, a budget account would be a good choice. It works very well for people with small earnings and few financial obligations.

A *minimum-balance account* requires you to keep a minimum amount of money in the account at all times to avoid paying a service charge. If you fall below the minimum, there is a charge. A minimum-balance account is good to have if you write a large number of checks and can maintain the minimum balance.

The *interest-bearing checking account* allows you to earn interest and write checks on the same account. It's a savings and checking account all in one. In credit unions, these accounts are called *share drafts.* In banks and savings and loan associations, they are called *negotiable orders of withdrawal* or *NOW accounts.*

Since checking accounts may vary from one financial institution to another, compare plans carefully. Make sure you find out what the service charges, check fees, and/or minimum-balance requirements are for each account. Then choose the account that best meets your needs.

Opening a checking account

Opening a checking account is very easy once you decide what type of account to open and where to open it. All you need to do is talk to the person in charge of opening new accounts, fill out a signature card, and make a deposit.

On the signature card, you will be asked to sign your name as you plan to sign it on all the checks you write. This will then be the only signature the financial institution will honor on checks and withdrawal slips that have your name and account number. Therefore, you should sign the card with the signature you intend to use for all of your financial transactions. Then remember to sign all your checks this way.

If you want another person to be able to write checks on your account, you will need to have that person sign the signature card also. When two or more people share an account, it is called a *joint account*. Joint accounts are often shared by husbands and wives. If you choose to have a joint account, make sure you and your partner(s) decide how records of checks and deposits will be recorded.

After you open your account you will receive a checkbook with personalized checks and a register. Each check will have your name, address, and account number on it. The register will be for keeping track of all the deposits you make and checks you write. To help you handle your checks and account successfully, follow the tips in 17-1.

Making deposits

To put money into your checking account, you will need to fill out a deposit ticket (sometimes called a deposit slip) so there will be a record of the transaction, 17-2. A deposit ticket states what is being deposited—currency, coins, or checks—and the amount of each. When filling out a ticket, follow these steps:

1. Write in the date.
2. Enter the amount of money being deposited. Write the amount of cash being deposited beside the word "Currency." Write the amount of coins being deposited beside the word "Coin." Write the amount of checks being deposited beside the word "Checks," listing each check singly.
3. Enter the amount of cash you want to receive, if any, after the words "Less cash received."
4. Subtract the "Less cash received" from the "Total" of deposits.
5. Enter the actual amount of the deposit

TIPS FOR SUCCESSFUL CHECKING

1. Treat your checks as you would cash. Keep them as safe and secure as possible.

2. Don't make changes on the face of a check that's issued to you. Don't take a check that looks as if it has been altered. The bank may refuse to honor such checks.

3. Avoid carrying checks made out to "Cash." If they're lost or stolen, you have no control over who can cash them.

4. For the same reason, never sign your personal check until you have filled in the amount and the payee.

5. Check all deposit slips to make sure they are legible and correct. If you're taking cash back from the deposit, count your money carefully to see that it's the correct amount. Do both of these things before you leave the bank.

6. Always inspect new check orders for accuracy. Check the spelling of your name, your address, and phone number. Also make sure your account number is properly encoded. Any errors should be reported to the bank.

7. If you don't understand a checking procedure, ask an officer at your bank to explain it to you.

17-1 These guidelines can help you manage your checks and checking account successfully.

after "Net deposit."

6. Then sign your name on the line below the date, using the signature you signed on your bank signature card.

Every time you make a deposit, you will be given a receipt. At that time you should enter the amount of the deposit in your checkbook register.

Endorsing checks

In order to deposit a check, cash a check, or use a check to pay someone else, you must endorse it first. This means you must sign your name on the back of the check at the left end. Checks may be endorsed by using a blank endorsement or a restrictive endorsement, 17-3.

A *blank endorsement* only requires your signature (the payee's signature). A check with this type of endorsement can be cashed by anyone who possesses it. Therefore, a blank endorsement should only be used at the time and place the check is being cashed or deposited in case the check is lost or stolen.

A *restrictive endorsement* states what is to be done with the check. "For deposit only" is a common restrictive endorsement. You write "For deposit only" and then sign your name underneath. This means the check can only be credited to your account. It cannot be cashed by someone else. This type of endorsement is best to use if you're banking by mail.

"Pay to the order of" is another restrictive endorsement. This is used to transfer a check to another person or party. For this endorsement, you write "Pay to the order of," the name of the person or party to receive the check, and your signature.

Writing checks

Have you ever looked at a blank check and wondered why it has so many numbers on it? The numbers and the words on checks are important information. This information helps banks, savings and loan associations, and credit unions process checks, 17-4.

In order for a check to be processed, it must be written correctly. When writing a check, you need to enter the following items in the correct spaces, 17-5.

1. The date, including the month, day, and year.
2. The name of the payee or the person, business, or organization receiving the check.
3. The amount of the check in numbers. Write as close to the dollar sign as possible to prevent anyone from adding or changing the amount.
4. The amount of the check in words. Write as far to the left as possible. After the amount of dollars, write the word "and." Then write the amount of cents in one of

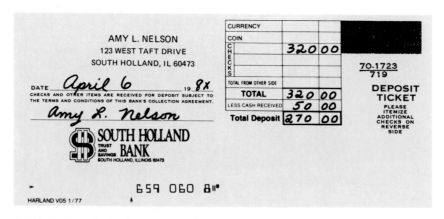

17-2 A deposit slip is a record of the money you deposit into your account.

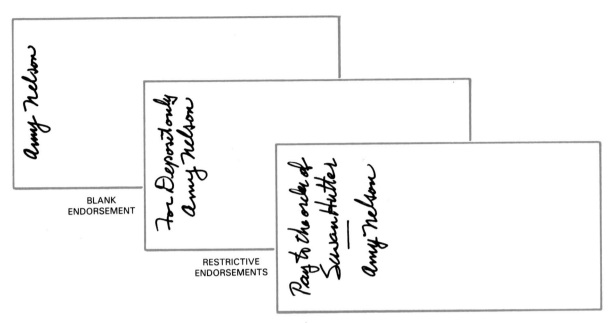

BLANK
ENDORSEMENT

RESTRICTIVE
ENDORSEMENTS

17-3 You must endorse a check before you can cash or
deposit it. A blank or restrictive endorsement may be used.

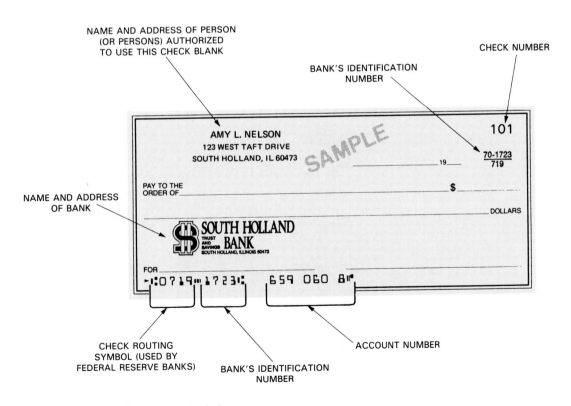

NAME AND ADDRESS OF PERSON
(OR PERSONS) AUTHORIZED
TO USE THIS CHECK BLANK

BANK'S IDENTIFICATION
NUMBER

CHECK NUMBER

NAME AND ADDRESS
OF BANK

CHECK ROUTING
SYMBOL (USED BY
FEDERAL RESERVE BANKS)

BANK'S IDENTIFICATION
NUMBER

ACCOUNT NUMBER

17-4 The information on checks helps
financial institutions process them correctly.

the following ways: 45/100, 00/100, or no/100. Draw a line through the remaining space.

5. The purpose of the check.
6. Your signature. Sign your name the same way each time, using the signature you used on the bank signature card.

Each time you write a check, you will need to record the check number, the date, the payee, the purpose of the check, and the amount of the check in your checkbook register. Then you should subtract the amount of the check from your existing balance. If you keep an up-to-date record of all checks and deposits, you will always know how much you have in your account, 17-6. This is important to know so you won't write a check for an amount you do not have in your account. If this should happen, your account is said to be *overdrawn*. Accounts that are overdrawn are charged a fee. If you overdraw your account a number of times, your financial institution may report your poor banking record to the local credit reporting agency. This may cause you to have a low credit rating and make it

harder for you to get credit cards or borrow money.

Balancing a checkbook

After you open a checking account, you will start receiving bank statements monthly, bimonthly, or quarterly. A *bank statement* is a record of the checks, deposits, and charges on your account for a specific length of time, 17-7. It also includes your *canceled checks*. These are the checks you have written and your bank has paid.

Each time you receive a bank statement, you will need to make sure your record of deposits and withdrawals (checks) agrees with the bank's record. This is called balancing your checkbook.

The first step in balancing your checkbook is to mark off, in your checkbook register, the canceled checks the bank returned to you. These checks should correspond exactly to the checks listed on your statement. In your register you also need to mark off the deposits that are shown on the statement. If there are any service charges listed on the bank statement, be

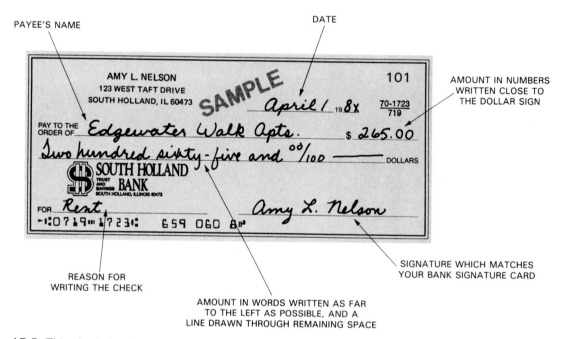

17-5 This check has been written correctly.

sure to subtract them from your checkbook balance. If you have an interest-bearing account and have earned interest, be sure to add that amount to your checkbook balance.

The next step is to account for the checks and deposits that do not appear on the statement. On the back of most bank statements is a worksheet provided for this, 17-8. On the worksheet follow these steps:

1. On line 1, write the closing balance shown on the bank statement.
2. List any of the deposits you have made which are not included on the statement.
3. Add the amounts from steps 1 and 2 and write down the total.
4. List by number and amount any checks you have written that are not included on the statement. Add these amounts together and enter the total where it says, "Checks outstanding."
5. Subtract the amount in step 4 from the amount in step 3.

The balance on your worksheet and the balance in your checkbook should now read the same. If these figures do not agree, go through the above steps again and recheck your arithmetic. Also check your addition and subtraction in your checkbook register. You may have made a mistake subtracting a check or adding a deposit. If your figures still do not agree with each other after checking for errors, take your statement, canceled checks, and checkbook to your bank for assistance.

SPECIAL TYPES OF CHECKS

Paying by personal check instead of cash is a safe and convenient way to make a payment. Other types of checks are used for the same reason. These include traveler's checks, cashier's checks, certified checks, and money orders. They are available at most banks, savings and loan associations, and credit unions for a small fee.

NUMBER	DATE	DESCRIPTION OF TRANSACTION	PAYMENT/DEBIT (-)	√ T	FEE (IF ANY) (-)	DEPOSIT/CREDIT (+)	BALANCE	
		RECORD ALL CHARGES OR CREDITS THAT AFFECT YOUR ACCOUNT					$336	27
101	4/1	Edgewater Walk Apts. Rent	$265 00		$	$	265 00	
							71	27
102	4/3	Jewel Food Stores groceries	18 35				18	35
							52	92
103	4/4	K-mart exercise mat	13 49				13	49
							39	43
	4/6	Deposit				270 00	270	00
							309	43
104	4/9	Commonwealth Edison electricity bill	15 60				15	60
							293	83
105	4/15	Jewel Food Stores Groceries	20 02				20	02
							273	81
	4/20	Deposit				270 00	270	00
							543	81
106	4/23	Martin's Shoe Store black shoes	23 58				23	58
							520	23
107	5/1	Edgewater walk apts. Rent	265 00				265	00
							255	23
108	5/2	Jewel Food Stores groceries	16 98				16	98
							238	25

REMEMBER TO RECORD AUTOMATIC PAYMENTS / DEPOSITS ON DATE AUTHORIZED.

17-6 After writing a check or making a deposit, always record the transaction in your checkbook register.

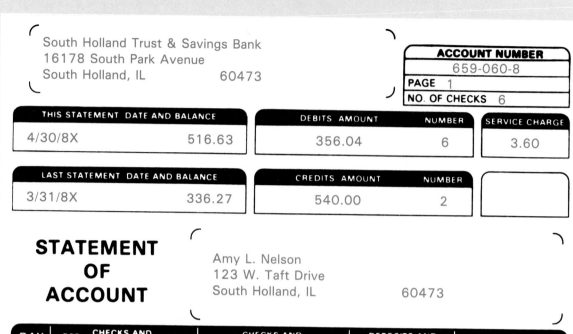

South Holland Trust & Savings Bank
16178 South Park Avenue
South Holland, IL 60473

ACCOUNT NUMBER
659-060-8
PAGE 1
NO. OF CHECKS 6

THIS STATEMENT DATE AND BALANCE		DEBITS AMOUNT	NUMBER	SERVICE CHARGE
4/30/8X	516.63	356.04	6	3.60

LAST STATEMENT DATE AND BALANCE		CREDITS AMOUNT	NUMBER	
3/31/8X	336.27	540.00	2	

STATEMENT OF ACCOUNT

Amy L. Nelson
123 W. Taft Drive
South Holland, IL 60473

DAY	REF	CHECKS AND OTHER DEBITS	AMT	REF	CHECKS AND OTHER DEBITS	AMT	DEPOSITS AND OTHER CREDITS	DAILY BALANCE
4 5	101		265.00					71.27
4 5	102		18.35					52.92
4 6		CHECK DEPOSIT					270.00	322.92
4 8	103		13.49					309.43
413	104		15.60					293.83
419	105		20.02					273.81
420		CHECK DEPOSIT					270.00	543.81
429	106		23.58					520.23
			3.60		SERVICE CHARGE			516.63

17-7 A bank statement is a summary of your checking account for a specific length of time.

MONTH _April 1-30_ 19 _8X_

THIS FORM IS PROVIDED TO HELP YOU BALANCE YOUR ACCOUNT STATEMENT

CHECKS OUTSTANDING
NOT CHARGED TO YOUR ACCOUNT

NO.	$	
107	265	00
108	16	98
TOTAL	$ 281	98

ENDING BALANCE SHOWN
ON THIS STATEMENT $ _516.63_

ADD +

DEPOSITS NOT CREDITED
IN THIS STATEMENT

(IF ANY) $ _____

_____

_____

TOTAL $ _____.00_

SUBTRACT -

CHECKS OUTSTANDING $ _281.98_

BALANCE $ _234.65_

CURRENT CHECK
BOOK BALANCE $ _238.25_

ADD +

INTEREST PAID
(IF ANY) AS SHOWN
ON THIS STATEMENT $ _____

SUBTRACT -

SERVICE CHARGES AND
OTHER CHARGES (IF ANY)
AS SHOWN ON THIS
STATEMENT $ _3.60_

NEW CHECK BOOK
BALANCE
should agree with $ _234.65_

NOTE Be certain to add to your register any interest paid and subtract from your register any
miscellaneous charges (service charge, check
printing charge, NSF charge, etc.) applied in the
current statement period.

17-8 A balancing worksheet and directions for balancing a
checkbook can be found on the back of most bank statements.

If you're going to be traveling, *traveler's checks* are the checks to use. Personal checks may only be accepted in your community or state, but traveler's checks can be cashed most places around the world. Traveler's checks can also be replaced if lost or stolen.

If you are paying a large sum of money, a *cashier's check* may be a more acceptable form of payment than a personal check. The person receiving the check may feel more secure being paid with a cashier's check because it is drawn on a bank's own funds and signed by a bank officer. The receiver doesn't have to worry if there are sufficient funds in the payer's account to cover the check.

Another way to make a payment to someone who does not want to accept a personal check is by *certified check*. A certified check is a personal check with a bank's guarantee that the check will be paid. When a bank certifies a check, the amount of the check is immediately subtracted from the payer's account. Therefore, the check receiver is assured of getting paid the amount of the check.

If you do not have a checking account, you can use a *money order* to make a payment safely by mail. A money order is an order for a specific amount of money payable to a specific payee. Money orders can be bought at a number of places such as post offices and drug stores as well as financial institutions.

SAVINGS

Instead of keeping all of your money in a checking account, you may want to put part of it into some form of savings. Saving money in a financial institution has two major advantages. It provides a safe place to keep your money, and it pays interest. A savings program can also help you save money for a specific purpose and help you establish a good credit rating. The two basic types of savings plans are passbook savings accounts and certificates of deposit (CD's).

A *passbook savings account* can be started with only a few dollars. It allows you to make deposits and withdrawals in varying amounts at any time. Although a passbook savings account is a convenient form of savings, it pays the lowest rate of interest.

If you have money to deposit for a set period of time, you can buy a *certificate of deposit*. A certificate of deposit pays a higher rate of interest because it requires you to commit your money for a set period of time such as six months, two and a half years, or five years. With a CD, you deposit money for a set period of time and earn a set annual rate of interest. (A minimum deposit is usually required.) The longer you agree to hold a CD, the higher the rate of interest you earn. If you cash in the certificate before the time period is over, you lose a significant amount of interest.

The more money you have to save, the more important it is for you to choose the right savings plan. For example, if you are just starting to put aside money for savings, a regular passbook savings account would be the account for you to open. However, suppose you already have a $1000 or more saved and don't intend to use the money for at least two years. It would then be better for you to buy a two-year certificate of deposit and earn a higher rate of interest than to leave all your money in a passbook savings account earning less interest. Once you have $2000 or more saved, you would want to consider other ways of using your money to earn interest such as some form of investments. Investments will be discussed in Chapter 18.

Once you choose a savings plan, then compare the same type of plan at various financial institutions. Find out what the interest rates are and how interest is paid. Also ask about the policies on making deposits and withdrawals. Look for a financial institution and a savings plan that will pay the highest rate of interest for the fewest number of restrictions.

SAFE-DEPOSIT BOXES

In addition to checking accounts and savings plans, banks and some other financial institutions rent safe-deposit boxes in their vaults, 17-9. Safe-deposit boxes are small metal containers that people rent to protect their valuables from fire and theft. Jewelry, wills, deeds, birth certificates, stocks and bonds, insurance policies, and other important items are often kept in safe-deposit boxes.

If you rent a box, you will be given a key for it. Each time you use the box, you will have to sign your name and present your key to the person guarding the vault. It takes two keys to open a safe-deposit box, yours and the guard's. Therefore, no one else can open your box unless you give him or her your key.

17-9 A safe-deposit box can be rented at many financial institutions to protect small valuables from fire and theft.

to Review

1. Name the three common financial institutions that can help you manage your money effectively.
2. What are the advantages of having a checking account?
3. Describe the three basic types of checking accounts.
4. What do you have to do to a check in order to deposit it, cash it, or use it to pay someone else?
5. What type of check endorsement would be best to use if you're banking by mail?
6. What should you do each time you write a check?
7. What happens if you overdraw your checking account?
8. What is a bank statement? How often are bank statements mailed?
9. What is a canceled check?
10. What checks, besides personal checks, can be used to make a safe payment?
11. What are the two major advantages of saving money in a financial institution?
12. How does a passbook savings account differ from a certificate of deposit?
13. For what purpose do people use safe-deposit boxes?

to Discuss

1. Why should you carefully compare checking accounts at a number of different financial institutions before opening an account?
2. Explain the procedure for opening a checking account.
3. What important information appears on a blank personal check? How is this information used by a financial institution?
4. Describe how to write a check correctly.
5. Explain how to balance a checkbook correctly.
6. What should you do if your checkbook doesn't balance?
7. How does a cashier's check differ from a certified check?
8. Explain why it is more important for you to choose the right savings plan when you have more money to save.
9. How would you go about choosing a savings plan?
10. What are current interest rates for passbook savings accounts at commercial banks and savings and loan associations?
11. What is the minimum deposit required for a certificate of deposit at commercial banks and savings and loan associations?

to Do

1. Visit at least three financial institutions in your area. Make a list of the services offered by each.
2. Demonstrate the correct way to endorse, deposit, and write checks.
3. Assume you have $1000 to save for three years. Then compare savings plans at three or more financial institutions to find out which institution will pay the highest rate of interest on $1000. In a short report, explain which savings plan you would choose and why.

Some financial institutions have available automatic teller machines so that you can cash checks, make deposits, and withdraw money at any time of the day.

Taking the time to prepare a budget can help
you manage your financial resources wisely.

18

Managing cash and credit

After studying this chapter, you will be able to:

☐ Prepare a budget to help you manage your money wisely.
☐ Compare different types of investments.
☐ Explain the advantages and disadvantages of using credit.
☐ Identify the different types of credit.
☐ Describe how to establish a credit rating.

Now that you are earning money, what are you going to do with it? Are you going to spend it, save it, invest it? What expenses do you have? What do you want to be able to buy in the future?

To make the most of the dollars you earn, you need to know how to budget your money. Managed and invested wisely, money can help you reach many goals. The same is true for credit. Used carefully and intelligently, credit can help you get more of the things you need when you need them.

BUDGETING YOUR MONEY

Bob and Larry have both been working for four years and have earned the same income from their jobs. They each pay the same amount for rent, food, and transportation. Bob has a nice, used car, a versatile wardrobe, and a few nice pieces of furniture. He has also been on two vacations since he's been working. On the other hand, Larry has a beat-up car, an "ailing" wardrobe, and no money to his name. For four years, Larry has been saying he wants to take a vacation, but he never comes up with enough money to do it. It seems he's constantly in debt or borrowing money.

Why is there such a difference between Bob's and Larry's finances? Bob has learned to manage his income and Larry has not. Bob's secret to good money management is a budget.

A *budget* is a plan to help you make the most of the money you have. A budget helps you:
- Control where your money goes.
- Work toward short-range and long-range goals.
- Keep from overspending.
- Reduce wasteful spending.

Developing a budget involves four major steps: establishing financial goals, keeping track of your income, keeping track of your expenses, and evaluating the budget. A sample monthly budget is shown in 18-1. This should help you organize a budget of your own.

Establish financial goals

As with any plan, the first step in developing a budget is to set goals. Decide what you need and want. Start with your short-range goals; then write down your long-range goals. Short-range goals may include money for a college education, a camera, or a new pair of shoes. Long-range goals may include buying

SAMPLE PLAN FOR A MONTHLY BUDGET

GOALS		Approximate cost	Date you want to attain the goal
Short-range _____		$_____	_____
	_____	_____	_____
Long-range _____		_____	_____
	_____	_____	_____

INCOME		EXPENSES	
		Fixed	
Salary	$_____	_____	$_____
Interest on savings	_____	_____	_____
Interest on investments	_____	_____	_____
Part-time work	_____	_____	_____
Other	_____	Flexible	
	_____	_____	_____
	_____	_____	_____
	_____	_____	_____
	_____	_____	_____
TOTAL INCOME	$_____	TOTAL EXPENSES	$_____

18-1 A budget should include a list of your financial goals, income, and expenses.

contact lenses, a car, or a stereo. Once you have your goals listed, estimate the cost of each and the date you want to attain each goal.

Keep track of income

The second step is to record the total amount of money available for spending. This includes your take-home pay and any other sources of income such as interest on savings and investments, part-time earnings, and allowances. When figuring your income, only count income that you are certain to receive. Don't include money that might be available from overtime work or gifts.

Keep track of expenses

The third step is to keep a record of expenses. This is a list of all the things you buy with your money and their costs. As you record expenses, list them under two headings: fixed expenses and flexible expenses.

Fixed expenses are the expenses that must be paid regularly such as rent or mortgage payments, installment payments, and insurance premiums. They are the expenses you have contracted to pay, and you must follow through on your commitments.

Flexible expenses are all the other expenses you have for which you pay varying amounts. Food, clothing, utilities, home furnishings and equipment, transportation, health care, recreation, education, and savings are some of the flexible expenses you may have, 18-2. You can adjust these expenses to fit your income. For example, you may decide to spend more on clothing and delay buying that new camera you've been eyeing. Or you may decide to buy a more expensive car and forgo a vacation.

18-2 Clothing accessories, such as handbags, are flexible expenses. You can adjust these expenses to fit your income.

Evaluate the budget

The final step is to evaluate the budget. Do you have enough income to cover your expenses? Is the budget flexible enough to handle unexpected expenses and emergencies? Is your money doing what you want it to do? Is your budget helping you reach important goals on schedule?

If you answered "no" to any of these questions, you will probably need to make some changes in your budget. It may be that you need to find ways to increase your income or reduce certain expenses. To increase your income, you may be able to get an increase in wages or take on a part-time job. To reduce spending, you may find there are some expenses you can omit entirely.

Keep in mind that your goals will change. As your goals change, your budget will need to change as well.

INVESTING YOUR MONEY

As you continue to work and earn money, you will have more money to spend. What will you do with the money you have left over after paying all your necessary expenses? What about the financial goals you established when you developed a budget? Will you be able to achieve these goals simply by depositing a little money each month into a savings account? There is another way to work toward important goals. You can invest some of your money.

Although most investments involve some degree of risk, there are many safe, low risk investments that can yield higher returns than regular savings accounts. Learning a few basic investment facts may help you reach your financial goals faster. Two types of investments are discussed here: securities and real estate.

SECURITIES

Stocks, bonds, mutual funds, and money market funds are all securities. *Securities* represent either ownership or indebtedness. Corporations and governments issue securities to get money to operate and expand. Many securities are sold and traded on security exchanges and markets, 18-3. Securities also can

be bought and sold at some banks and savings and loan associations.

Stocks

A *stock* is a share in the ownership of a corporation. When you buy stock in a corporation, you become part owner of that company. If the company is profitable, you and other stockholders share in the profits after debts and operating expenses are paid. Most corporations issue two types of stocks: preferred stock and common stock.

Preferred stock is a more conservative, less risky investment than common stock. Preferred stockholders are paid set dividends (profits) at stated rates, regardless of the amount of profits the company earns.

Common stock is a more risky investment because the amount and frequency of dividends depend on company earnings and economic conditions. When company earnings are good and the economy is expanding, a company's common stock tends to increase in value. When the economic outlook is poor, common stock tends to decline in value. Because of the higher degree of risk involved, common stocks offer greater opportunity for large gains.

Bonds

A *bond* is a certificate of debt or obligation issued by a corporation or a government. It's like an I.O.U. The issuing government or corporation promises to repay the bondholder the face value of the bond after a certain number of years. The bond issuer also promises to pay a fixed rate of interest on the face value of the bond during the loan period.

Bonds are among the safest investments you can make. However, the safety of the bond depends on the credit rating of the bond issuer. Rating agencies, such as Standard and Poor and Moody, rate bonds. Bonds with high ratings carry little risk. Bonds with low ratings tend to be risky, but they also provide greater returns.

The only drawbacks to investing in bonds are that a $1000 minimum is required, plus your money is tied up for a certain length of time. For these reasons, investors who have limited funds and who can't afford to make a long-term investment may choose other forms of investments.

The three types of bonds are corporate bonds, municipal bonds, and U.S. Government bonds. *Corporate bonds* are issued by corporations. *Municipal bonds* are issued by state, county, and city governments. *U.S. Government bonds* are issued by the federal government. Interest rates and yields on all three types of bonds depend on market interest rates and the financial soundness of the issuing corporation or government.

U.S. Government bonds are the safest bonds you can buy. *Treasury Bills, Treasury Notes,* and *Treasury Bonds* are all types of U.S. Government bonds. They vary with the minimum investment required and the length of maturity dates.

U.S. Savings Bonds are also government bonds. However, they are more a source of savings rather than an investment. They are issued for as little as $50 at a variable interest rate for a set length of time.

Mutual funds

A *mutual fund* is a company that collects money from a number of investors and invests that money in securities. If you buy shares in a mutual fund, you automatically become part

NEW YORK STOCK EXCHANGE

18-3 Many securities are sold through stock exchanges.

investor in all the securities included in the fund. A mutual fund pays dividends on shares just as any stock does.

Different mutual funds invest in different securities. A company may buy all balanced funds, specialized funds, or growth funds. *Balanced funds* are investments in a variety of securities such as preferred stock, common stock, and bonds. They provide a safe investment with dividend income. *Specialized funds* are investments in securities of certain industries, such as all utilities, or in certain types of securities, such as all government bonds or common stocks. *Growth funds* are investments in common stocks with growth potential. Emphasis is placed on growth of the principal instead of dividend income.

Investing in a mutual fund has many advantages. It allows you to invest in a variety of securities instead of just one or two you might only be able to afford as a single investor. This reduces the degree of loss. Mutual funds can be bought and sold at any time. And mutual funds are operated and managed by experienced investors who work hard to earn the highest rate of return for its shareholders.

Money market funds

A *money market fund* is a type of mutual fund that deals only in high interest, short-term investments such as U.S. Treasury Bills and certificates of deposit. Money market funds are managed and sold by mutual funds, investment firms, and some insurance companies, banks, and savings and loan associations. The rate of interest earned on these funds varies with money market rates.

Money market funds can be good investments because they have many advantages. They can provide small savers with high returns. They can be cashed in at any time since they have no term. And money market funds bought through a bank or savings and loan association are federally insured. This means you would be able to recover all or some of your investment if the issuer of the fund went bankrupt.

Money market funds have some disadvantages too. The rate of money market funds is not a set rate; it can change daily. If money market rates drop, so does the rate of return on the fund. Also, a minimum of $1000 or more is usually required to invest in a money market fund.

REAL ESTATE

An investment in real estate is an investment in land or building property, 18-4. Since most real estate involves a large sum of money, a large amount of money may be needed to make such an investment. Investing in real estate can yield big returns, but considerable risk may be involved.

MAKING INVESTMENTS

The key words to remember when you are considering making investments are "investigate before you invest." Below are four other pointers to help you get the most from the money you have to invest.

- Set an investment goal. Begin with a small investment and build from there.
- Do not invest money you cannot afford to lose. Very few investments are completely safe from loss.
- Evaluate the company, corporation, government, or real estate in which you will be investing. Look for an investment that is expected to increase in value.
- Find reliable professionals to help you make investments. Don't deal with any financial broker or real estate agent who's experience and knowledge are questionable.

USING CREDIT

Credit allows a buyer to make a purchase now and pay for it later. People who are good credit risks can buy almost anything on credit. They can buy expensive items like cars, vacations, and furniture. They can also charge smaller items such as clothes, meals, and gasoline.

Why should you establish credit? As you continue to assume more financial responsibility, you will probably need to buy expensive items like a car or a home. Unless you are very wealthy, you will not have enough money to buy an expensive item in one lump sum. It could take you years to save enough money to buy a car or house. However, credit allows you to buy and use goods and services as you pay for them. Being able to wear a new coat or drive a car as you pay for it is one of the major advantages of credit.

Convenience is another advantage of credit. Credit eliminates the need to carry large amounts of cash. It can also be a source of cash for emergency or unexpected expenses. Thanks to Jim's gasoline credit card, he was able to have his car fixed when the alternator unexpectedly had to be replaced. Without this immediate source of money, Jim would have had to have waited a month before he would have had the cash to pay for the repair.

Although credit can be a very successful buying tool, it can also cause many problems if misused. Credit usually costs money. The more credit you use and the longer you take to repay, the more you will pay in finance charges.

Another disadvantage of credit is the temptation. Credit makes it easy to spend money you don't have. Then if you are unable to pay your debts, the items you bought on credit can be repossessed. You could go bankrupt. You could also abuse your right to obtain credit from reputable creditors.

The cost of credit

Any time you use credit, it's important to find out how much it will cost you. Knowing the exact cost of credit can help you compare finance charges and find the best deal. It can help you decide how much credit you can afford. It can also help you decide if buying now and paying later is worth the extra price.

By law, creditors are required to state finance charges in credit contracts as a dollar amount and as an annual percentage rate. For example, suppose you plan to borrow $500 to repay in 12 monthly payments at a monthly rate of one percent. Then the creditor must state the

18-4 Some investors buy apartment complexes as an investment and lease them to renters to earn a return on their money.

dollar cost of credit as $33.16 and the annual percentage rate as 12 percent.

Types of credit

Various types of credit are available to consumers. Each type comes in different forms to meet different consumer needs. Some types are used to buy goods and services; others are used to borrow money.

Credit card accounts. Many department stores and companies issue credit cards so consumers can use credit to buy their goods and services, 18-5. Banks and credit card agencies also issue credit cards. These cards can be used wherever they are accepted by businesses. Bank credit cards may be used to obtain cash as well.

Most credit card accounts are *revolving charge accounts*. The cardholder has a choice of paying for purchases in full each month or spreading payments over a period of time.

Here's how a typical credit card account works. Donna opened a credit card account at a department store. In September, she used her credit card to charge $56 worth of clothes. In October, she got a statement showing the amount she owed. Then, Donna had a choice to make. She could either pay the amount in full or make a minimum payment of $20. If she paid in full within a month, she would avoid paying finance charges. If she only made a minimum payment, she would have to pay finance charges on the remaining balance of $36. Donna could continue to charge merchandise as long as she did not exceed her credit limit for that card. And each month she would receive a monthly statement showing the amount owed.

Donna knows she must be very careful not to lose her credit card. If her card is lost or stolen, she should immediately contact the company that issued the card. Then, by law, she will not be charged more than $50 if someone else uses her card.

Charge accounts. Some businesses, usually small local businesses, will allow customers to charge merchandise on a charge account card on file at the business. This is another way businesses can extend credit to customers without using credit cards. Once a month, the business will send the customer a bill. The customer is then expected to pay in full within 25 days of the billing date. If the customer pays on time there is no finance charge.

Installment accounts. This type of account is often used to charge expensive items like a stereo, major appliance, or a piece of furniture. The buyer pays for the merchandise according to a set schedule of payments. Finance charges are included in the payments. Buyers are usually asked to sign a contract for this type of credit purchase, and a cash down payment may be required. If the buyer fails to make payments, the seller can repossess the merchandise.

Cash loans. There are times when it may be necessary to borrow money to buy the things you need or want. This type of credit is called a cash loan. Commercial banks, savings and loan associations, credit unions, loan companies, and some life insurance companies make various types of cash loans.

In order to get most cash loans, a borrower is required to pledge some kind of property as *collateral*. For an auto loan, the car is collateral. For a mortgage, the house serves as collateral. If the borrower fails to pay as agreed, the creditor may take the property to settle the claim against the borrower.

Although a person may have nothing to pledge as collateral, it is still possible to get a loan if the person has a cosigner. A *cosigner* is a responsible person who signs the loan with the borrower. By signing the loan, the cosigner promises to pay the loan if the borrower fails to pay.

Most cash loans are repaid like an installment account. The borrower makes regular monthly payments which includes finance charges.

Establishing credit

The first time you try to establish credit, you may have a hard time. This is because creditors want evidence that you can and will pay your debts before they grant you credit. When you apply for credit, you will be asked to fill out a credit application form, 18-6. This form helps creditors evaluate your credit rating. A *credit rating* is the creditor's evaluation of a person's willingness and ability to pay debts.

If you have never bought anything on credit, you can begin establishing a favorable credit rating by taking some of the following steps.

- Open a checking account. A well managed checking account shows that you can handle money responsibly.
- Open a savings account. Saving regularly can help you establish a good banking record which can serve as a credit reference. Your savings may also be used as collateral for a loan.
- Buy an item on a lay-away plan. After paying for the purchase, the store will probably be willing to grant you a charge account.
- Apply to a gasoline company or a local department store for a credit card. Then make small purchases and pay for them promptly when the bills come.

Once you use credit, you automatically establish a credit record at the local credit reporting agency. If you pay your bills on time and meet all terms of credit agreements, you will have a good credit record. If you make late payments or fail to pay, you will have a poor rating. A poor credit record will make it difficult to get credit in the future, and it may cause you to have to pay higher finance charges.

If you should ever have a problem paying your bills on time, don't just ignore the problem. Notify your creditors promptly. They may let you delay payments to a later date. Or they may be willing to decrease the size of your monthly payments. Working out some type of payment with your creditors will help you keep your credit rating a good one.

18-5 A credit card is one of the most convenient types of credit.

SEARS, ROEBUCK AND CO. INDIVIDUAL CREDIT ACCOUNT APPLICATION

APPLICATION TO BE COMPLETED IN NAME OF PERSON IN WHICH THE ACCOUNT IS TO BE CARRIED.

COURTESY TITLES ARE OPTIONAL   PLEASE PRINT

☐ MR.   ☐ MRS.   ☐ MISS   ☐ MS. _____
                                    First Name   Initial   Last Name

Street Address _____ Apt. # _____ City _____ State _____ Zip Code _____

Phone No: Home _____   Phone No: Business _____   Soc. Sec. No. _____   Age _____   Number of Dependents _____ (Excluding Applicant)

Are you a United States citizen? ☐ Yes ☐ No   If NO, explain immigration status: _____

How Long at Present Address _____   Own ☐   Rent-Furnished ☐   Rent-Unfurnished ☐   Board ☐   Monthly Rent or Mortgage Payments $ _____

Name of Landlord or Mortgage Holder _____   Street Address _____   City and State _____

Former Address (If less than 2 years at present address) _____   How long _____

Employer _____   Street Address _____   City and State _____

How long _____   Occupation _____   Net Income $ _____ (Take Home Pay)   Monthly ☐ Weekly ☐

Former Employer (If less than 1 year with present employer) _____   How long _____

> ALIMONY, CHILD SUPPORT, OR SEPARATE MAINTENANCE INCOME NEED NOT BE REVEALED IF YOU DO NOT WISH TO HAVE IT CONSIDERED AS A BASIS FOR PAYING THIS OBLIGATION.

Alimony, child support, separate maintenance received under:
☐ Court order   ☐ Written agreement   ☐ Oral understanding   Amount $ _____   Monthly ☐ Weekly ☐

Other Income, if any: Amount $ _____   Monthly ☐ Weekly ☐   Source _____

Name and Address of Bank _____   Savings ☐ Checking ☐ Acc't No. _____

Name and Address of Bank _____   Savings ☐ Checking ☐ Acc't No. _____

Previous Sears Account ☐ Yes ☐ No _____   At What Sears Store do you usually shop? _____   Account No. _____   Is Account Paid in Full ☐ Yes ☐ No   Date Final Payment Made _____

Relative or Personal Reference not living at above address _____ (Name)   _____ (Street Address)   _____ (City and State)   _____ (Relationship)

CREDIT REFERENCES (Attach additional sheet if necessary.)   List all references   (Open or closed within past two years)

Charge Accounts Loan References Bank/Store/Company Address	Date Opened	Name Account Carried In	Account Number	Balance	Monthly Payments

Authorized buyer _____   First Name _____ Initial _____ Last Name _____ Relationship to applicant _____

Authorized buyer _____   First Name _____ Initial _____ Last Name _____ Relationship to applicant _____

THE INFORMATION BELOW IS REQUIRED IF: (1) YOUR SPOUSE IS AN AUTHORIZED BUYER OR (2) YOU RESIDE IN A COMMUNITY PROPERTY STATE (ARIZONA, CALIFORNIA, IDAHO, LOUISIANA, NEVADA, NEW MEXICO, TEXAS, WASHINGTON) OR (3) YOU ARE RELYING ON THE INCOME OR ASSETS OF ANOTHER PERSON, INCLUDING A SPOUSE OR FORMER SPOUSE, AS A BASIS FOR PAYMENT.

Name of spouse ☐
Name of former spouse ☐ _____   Address _____   City and State _____   Age _____
Name of other person ☐   Street Address _____

Employer _____   Street Address _____   City and State _____

How long _____   Occupation _____   Soc. Sec. No. _____   Net Income $ _____ (Take Home Pay)   Monthly ☐ Weekly ☐

Name and Address of Bank _____   Savings ☐ Checking ☐ Acc't No. _____

Name and Address of Bank _____   Savings ☐ Checking ☐ Acc't No. _____

THE PERSON ON WHOSE INCOME OR ASSETS YOU ARE RELYING AS A BASIS FOR PAYMENT MUST SIGN BELOW, HOWEVER, YOUR SPOUSE NEED NOT SIGN IF YOU RESIDE IN A COMMUNITY PROPERTY STATE OR IF YOUR SPOUSE IS AN AUTHORIZED BUYER.

SEARS IS AUTHORIZED TO INVESTIGATE MY CREDIT RECORD AND TO VERIFY MY CREDIT, EMPLOYMENT AND INCOME REFERENCES.   X _____ (Signature of person on whose income or assets applicant is relying.)   Date _____

18-6 A credit application form helps creditors decide if a person will be a good credit risk.

to Review

1. What is a budget?
2. What are the four steps involved in developing a budget?
3. Explain the difference between fixed expenses and flexible expenses. Give two examples of each.
4. What questions can you ask yourself to help you evaluate a budget?
5. What are securities?
6. What is the difference between a bond and a stock?
7. What is the difference between a mutual fund and a money market fund?
8. What are the advantages of investing in a mutual fund?
9. What key words should you remember if you are considering making any type of investment?
10. What are the advantages and disadvantages of using credit?
11. How are creditors required to state finance charges to consumers?
12. How can you begin establishing a favorable credit rating?

to Discuss

1. How can a budget help you manage your money?
2. What are some steps you can take to increase your income and to reduce unnecessary spending?
3. When during your life can you expect your financial goals to change?
4. If you were going to invest money in stocks, would you buy preferred stock or common stock? Why?
5. Explain the difference between the three major types of bonds. In which type of bond would you prefer to invest your money?
6. Explain the difference between balanced, specialized, and growth mutual funds.
7. What are the advantages of investing in a money market fund?
8. Discuss the guidelines you should follow to help you get the most from the money you have to invest.
9. Why is it important to establish credit?
10. Why is it important to find out how much credit will cost before you use it?
11. Describe the five types of credit available to consumers.
12. How can you maintain a high credit rating?

to Do

1. Prepare a monthly budget based on your short-range and long-range goals, income, and expenses. After following the budget for a month, evaluate it carefully. What are its strengths and weaknesses? Is it helping you reach your goals? How can you improve the budget?
2. Assume that you have $1000 to invest. Calculate the amount of return you would earn after one month if you invested the $1000 in one of three ways:
   - Passbook savings account at a savings and loan association.
   - Common stock in a company listed under the New York or American Stock Exchange
   - Money market fund.
   Compare the results. Which investment yielded the highest rate of return?
3. Suppose you want to buy a $300 video recorder on credit. Find out what the credit terms would be if you bought the recorder at a video shop, department store, or with a bank credit card. Find out about finance charges, annual percentage rate, and length of the repayment period. Where would you get the best deal?

Whenever you become financially responsible for yourself, a car, a home, and/or a family, you will need to consider insurance protection carefully.

19

Insurance

After studying this chapter, you will be able to:

☐ Determine the types of auto insurance coverage you need.
☐ Describe the three types of health insurance coverage.
☐ Summarize the two basic types of home insurance coverage.
☐ Describe the different types of life insurance and the purpose of each.

You may be wondering, "Why do I need insurance? Is it really worth the money you pay for it?" Insurance is a plan—a plan to help people protect themselves from unexpected financial losses. You and other people need insurance to help recover financially from accidents, serious illnesses, theft, fire, and other misfortunes.

Insurance works like this. When you buy an insurance policy, you become a policyholder. As a policyholder, you agree to pay a set amount of money, called a *premium,* to the insurance company on a regular basis. In return, the insurance company provides financial protection for you in the event a misfortune occurs that is covered by your policy. The premiums you and other policyholders pay are invested by the company to earn money. Part of these earnings is used to pay the claims made by policyholders, and part is used to cover the expenses of operating the company.

Some people tend to think insurance is something that only people with a lot of money or possessions should have. However, it is not. Whenever a person becomes financially responsible for him or herself and for such things as a car, a home, or a family, that person needs insurance protection for each. The amount of protection a person needs depends on his or her potential for financial loss. For example, a person with a new car would need more insurance coverage than a person with an older, used car. This is because the person with the new car has a higher potential for financial loss. More money would be needed to replace the new car than the older one.

The four types of insurance you are likely to need during your lifetime are automobile insurance, health insurance, home insurance, and life insurance. They are discussed in the following pages.

AUTOMOBILE INSURANCE

Anyone who drives or owns a car takes certain financial and personal risks. If you are involved in a car accident, you may have to pay thousands of dollars in damages. Very few people are able to afford such large expenses unexpectedly. Therefore, the possibility of being in a car accident makes auto insurance essential for all drivers, 19-1.

An auto insurance policy may include one or several types of coverage for an individual or a family. There are six types of insurance coverage: bodily injury liability, property damage liability, medical payments, uninsured motorists, comprehensive physical damage, and collision.

Bodily injury liability coverage protects you if you are legally liable for an accident in which others are injured or killed. It pays for the legal fees and the damages assessed against you, up to the limits of the policy. Liability insurance covers the car owner and anyone else who drives the car with the owner's permission. The amount of coverage is usually stated in two amounts. For example, suppose under liability coverage you see "$100,000-$300,000." This means that the insurance company will pay up to $100,000 for any one injury and $300,000 for any one accident.

Property damage liability coverage pays for damages your car causes to the property of others if you are responsible for the accident. More often than not, the property is another car. But it also covers damages to other properties such as lamp posts, telephone poles, or buildings. It does not cover damage to your car. Like bodily injury liability, it will also pay for legal fees up to the limits stated in the policy.

Medical payments coverage pays for the medical expenses resulting from an accident, regardless of who was at fault. It covers you, your family, and any guests in your car if your car is involved in an accident. It also covers you and your family if you are injured while riding in another car or while walking.

Uninsured motorist coverage pays for bodily injuries for which an uninsured motorist or hit-and-run driver is responsible. You and your family are covered as drivers, passengers, and pedestrians. Guests in your car are also covered.

Comprehensive physical damage coverage pays for damage to your car caused by something other than another vehicle. Some policies pay for damage caused by such things as fire, theft, vandalism, hail, water, and collision with animals.

Collision coverage pays for the damage to your car caused by a collision with another vehicle or object. Damages are paid regardless of who was at fault.

No-fault insurance is another form of auto insurance protection. It was designed to eliminate the legal process of proving who is at fault in an accident. This type of insurance is thought to lower insurance rates because it reduces costly court trials to determine who is at fault. No-fault insurance works like this. When an accident occurs, each policyholder makes a claim to his or her own insurance company for the actual financial losses and medical expenses caused by the accident. Each company pays its policyholder regardless of who is at fault. No-fault insurance does not exist in all states. In the states that it does exist, laws vary in the amount awarded for medical costs, funeral and burial expenses, loss of income, and other benefits.

When buying auto insurance, compare premiums carefully. Premiums can vary greatly because they are usually based on a number of factors. Some of these factors include your age, driving record, the year and model of your car, your residence, the distances you drive, and the amount of the deductible. The older you are, the better driving record you have, the older the year and model of your car (unless it's a classic model), the shorter the distances you drive, and the higher the deductible, the lower your premiums are likely to be. Some insurance companies also give premium discounts if you have completed a driver education course, if you were a good student, if you are a nonsmoker, and if you own more than one car. Be sure to find out what discounts you may be eligible to receive.

As you check several insurance companies for the lowest premium, don't forget the importance of having adequate coverage. Don't give up important coverage just to save a few dollars on premiums. Inadequate coverage will do you little good if you are involved in a serious auto accident.

HEALTH INSURANCE

With health care costs so high, major surgery or a long hospital stay would spell financial ruin for most people. That's why everyone needs to be covered by some form of health plan. There are three types of health insurance coverage which you should consider: basic medical, major medical, and disability.

Basic medical insurance covers the costs of hospitalization. This includes room, board, and nursing services, 19-2. It also pays for some other services such as laboratory tests, X rays,

19-1 If you are a car owner, you need insurance to cover your financial responsibility in case you are involved in an accident.

and medicine. Depending on the policy, it may pay some of the costs of doctor visits and surgical procedures.

Major medical insurance is sometimes called the catastrophic insurance because it protects individuals and families from huge, disastrous medical bills. Major medical coverage begins paying where basic coverage stops. It pays the largest share of expenses resulting from a major illness or serious injury.

Disability insurance provides regular income payments when a person is unable to work because of injury or illness. The maximum coverage of the insurance is two-thirds of a person's gross income.

Many people are able to get group health insurance coverage through employers, unions, or professional associations. If group health insurance is available to you, consider it carefully. Generally, group health insurance provides more coverage at a much lower cost than individual coverage. Also, some employers pay part or all of the costs of group health coverage.

If you have a group health insurance policy from an employer, union, or association, check to see how much coverage you have. You may have all the coverage you need. If not, you may need to purchase more insurance.

When buying health insurance, check policies for exclusions and limitations on coverage. Some companies may exclude certain illnesses and treatments from their policies. Also check the renewal conditions and cancellation clauses. Make sure you will be able to continue the policy even if you file certain claims.

Another factor to consider with health insurance is the amount of the deductible. A *deductible* is the amount you must pay before the insurance company will pay a claim. If a policy has a $100 deductible, the policyholder must pay the first $100 of medical expenses. Usually, the higher the deductible you have in your policy, the lower your premiums will be.

Although group health insurance is the most widely used health plan, there is another health plan available in some areas. This type of health plan is a membership into a *Health Maintenance Organization* (HMO). HMOs differ from health insurance companies because they provide health services rather than pay medical bills. As a member of an HMO, you or your employer pay a lump sum or a monthly fee. The fee usually covers the cost of many hospital and medical services. If you become ill, you go to a doctor who is associated with your HMO to receive the health care you need, usually at no additional cost.

Before choosing an HMO over a traditional health insurance plan, make sure you find out what services it offers and what facilities are associated with it. Also check the qualifications

19-2 When this young man was hospitalized for a leg injury, his family's basic medical insurance covered most of the costs.

of the health care professionals at the HMO, and ask about fees and what they include. Carefully compare the costs and services of HMO health care to the costs and services of health insurance. Then choose the plan that will be best for you.

HOME INSURANCE

If you own or rent a home, there is another type of insurance you should consider— homeowner's insurance or renter's insurance.

Homeowner's insurance provides two basic types of coverage: property protection and liability protection. Property coverage insures you against such dangers as fire and lightning,

burglary and theft, vandalism, and explosions. It covers the damage or loss of the dwelling and your personal property and possessions such as your clothes and furnishings. It also pays for your living expenses if you should have to move out of your home because of damages to the property.

Liability coverage protects you against financial loss if others are injured on or by your property or if you or your property accidentally damages the property of others, 19-3. It pays for the legal costs of defending you if you are sued because of injuries to others or damages to their property. It pays for damages assessed against you if you are held legally liable for injuries or property damage.

SENTRY INSURANCE

19-3 If a tree pruner was injured while working on your property, liability coverage in your homeowner's policy would cover the damages.

Renter's insurance provides similar protection for the home renter. However, property protection only covers damage or loss of personal property and possessions, not the dwelling itself.

When you need to buy home insurance, follow these guidelines provided by the Insurance Information Institute, a public information and educational organization:

- Make a complete inventory of household possessions with estimated values to help you determine how much coverage to buy and to help you make claims.
- Find out the current replacement value of your home and insure it at 80 percent of that value.
- Consider insuring your home for full value or more or securing a special endorsement if household belongings and personal possessions exceed 50 percent of the value of your home.
- Consider a larger deductible to reduce premiums. They can help you get maximum coverage at lowest rates for major losses if you are able to pay minor losses.

LIFE INSURANCE

Life insurance protects against the loss of income due to death. The main purpose of life insurance is to provide income for anyone who depends on your income such as a spouse, children, or elderly parents, 19-4. If you have no dependents, you really don't need life insurance.

When a life insurance policyholder dies, the insurance company pays the face value of the policy to the beneficiary. The *beneficiary* is the person named by the policyholder to receive the death benefit.

Whole life and term insurance are the two basic types of life insurance plans. Each type is available in different forms and combinations with different benefits.

Whole life insurance. Whole life insurance covers the policyholder for a lifetime. It is also a form of savings. As the policyholder pays premiums, the policy builds up a cash value. Cash value is the amount the policy is worth.

The policyholder can borrow against this cash value or collect the cash value if he or she decides to cancel the policy. Therefore, a whole life policy pays benefits when the policyholder dies or when the policyholder turns it in for its cash value.

When choosing whole life policies, policyholders have two basic options. They may choose a straight life policy or a limited payment policy. With a straight life policy, the policyholder pays premiums throughout his or her life. With a limited payment policy, the policyholder pays higher premiums, but for a limited number of years. By paying higher premiums, the policyholder can buy whole life protection in a certain number of years and still receive coverage for life.

A form of limited payments whole life insurance is endowment insurance. It is bought for a set period of time—usually 10, 20, or 30 years. At the end of that time period, the cash value of the policy is paid to the policyholder. If the policyholder should die before the end of the endowment period, the death benefit is paid to the beneficiary. Premiums are higher on endowment policies because the cash value builds up faster.

Term insurance. Term insurance covers the policyholder for a set period of time—5, 10, or 20 years or for whatever term specified in the policy. This type of life insurance is simply for protection; it builds no cash value. It pays benefits only if the policyholder dies during the term of the policy. That is why premiums for term insurance are lower than those for whole life insurance.

When choosing term insurance, policyholders should check to see if a term policy is renewable and if it's convertible. A renewable privilege allows the policyholder to renew the policy at standard rates, regardless of any changes in health. Without this privilege, the policyholder would not be able to renew the policy at regular rates if his or her health had declined. A term policy with a convertible option lets the policyholder switch from term insurance to whole life insurance at standard rates, regardless of the state of his or her health.

CHOOSING AN INSURANCE COMPANY, AGENT, AND POLICY

The company and agent from whom you choose to buy insurance are just as important to consider as the policy you select. Choosing the right company and agent can make a big difference in the coverage you receive and the premiums you pay.

Before choosing an insurance company, do a little research. Make sure a company has a reputation of settling its claims fairly and promptly before you buy any insurance from it. Also take a close look at the policies at various companies. Buy from a company that offers policies with the benefits and options that are most important to you.

Select an agent or broker just as you would select a doctor or lawyer. Find someone with good training and experience in insurance and financial planning. A good agent is one who will advise you honestly about the type and amount of coverage you need. A responsible agent will also help you evaluate your coverage periodically and will process policy revisions and claims promptly.

After you have chosen a company and agent, then concentrate on choosing a policy for your insurance needs. Before you agree to a policy, look it over carefully. Be sure to ask questions about any terms, provisions, options, or sections you do not understand. Also make sure the policy provides the coverage you and your agent discussed specifically for you.

19-4 Life insurance is especially important to have if you have children that depend on your income.

to Review

1. When does a person need insurance protection?
2. Name the four types of insurance you are likely to need during your lifetime.
3. Which auto insurance coverage pays for damages your car causes to the property of others if you are responsible for the accident?
4. What is no-fault auto insurance?
5. What seven factors determine auto insurance premiums?
6. For what reasons do some insurance companies give premium discounts on auto insurance?
7. Describe the three basic types of health insurance coverage.
8. Generally, what are the advantages of having group health insurance?
9. Define the word "deductible" as it pertains to insurance.
10. How do HMOs differ from health insurance companies?
11. Describe the two basic types of coverage provided by a homeowner's insurance policy.
12. What is the main difference between homeowner's insurance and renter's insurance?
13. What is the main reason for having life insurance?
14. Describe the two basic types of life insurance.

to Discuss

1. Why is it so important for most people to have insurance?
2. Explain how insurance works.
3. What kinds of auto insurance coverage do you or your family have?
4. If your employer gave you the choice between an HMO membership and a traditional health insurance plan, which health program would you choose? Explain why.
5. What factors should you consider before choosing an HMO membership over a traditional health plan?
6. What are the guidelines to follow when buying home insurance?
7. What happens to a life insurance policy when its policyholder dies?
8. Discuss the two options policyholders have when choosing a whole life policy.
9. Why should a policyholder check to see if a term insurance policy is renewable and convertible?
10. How would you go about selecting an insurance company, agent, and policy?

to Do

1. At three different insurance companies, compare insurance costs for a new car and a used car (five years old) of the same model based on the same coverage. Report to the class how insurance rates for a new and used car differed at each company.
2. Find out what type of health care protection you and your family have. Make a list of the protection included.
3. Prepare a complete inventory of your household possessions with estimated values for insurance purposes.
4. Obtain copies of life insurance policies from three or four different insurance companies. Compare coverage, benefits, options, premiums, and claim procedures.

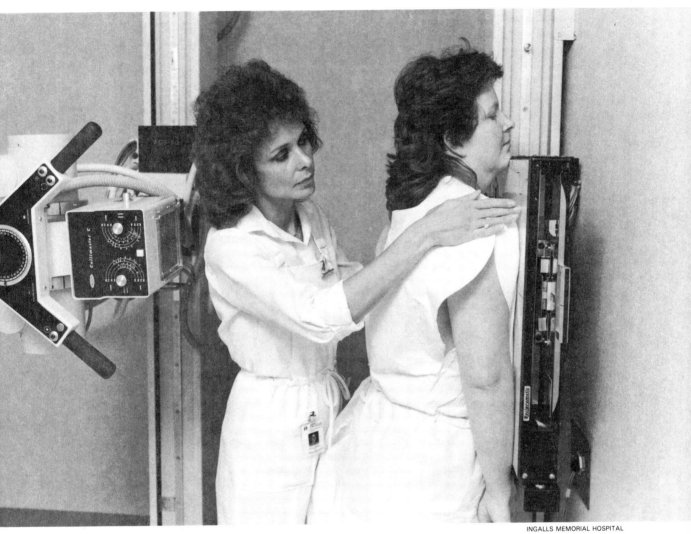

Most basic medical health insurance policies
cover the costs of X-ray services.

The White House in Washington, D.C., home of the President of the United States, was built and is maintained with federal tax dollars.

20

Taxes and social security

After studying this chapter, you will be able to:

☐ Identify the various services and facilities provided by tax dollars.
☐ Describe how consumers are taxed and the types of taxes they pay.
☐ Explain how to file a federal income tax return.
☐ Describe the purpose of the social security program and the benefits it provides.

Government plays a very important role in your life. It provides many things such as parks, highways, public schools, and police and fire protection. It also helps people financially when they retire, become disabled, or lose their income unexpectedly. Government can provide these services because of our tax system and social security program. This chapter examines these key areas of government activity.

TAXES

Taxes? What are they? And why do we have to pay them? Taxes are payments that citizens and businesses are required to pay to city, county, state, and federal governments. Very few people like or want to pay taxes. However, without taxes, governments would not be able to provide the variety of services and facilities they do. Chart 20-1 lists many of the services provided by the different levels of government.

Types of taxes

As you are probably aware, there are many types of taxes. The five most common taxes you probably will have to pay are personal income taxes, social security taxes, property taxes, sales taxes, and excise taxes.

The *personal income tax* is a tax on the amount of money a person earns. The *social security tax* is also a tax on a person's income. It is used to pay for the social security program administered by the federal government. Both of these taxes are deducted from your paychecks by your employer and sent to the federal government. Your state government may also tax your personal income.

As explained in Chapter 5, the amount of personal income tax and social security tax withheld depends on how much you earn and the number of exemptions you are allowed. An *exemption* is a source or an amount of income not subject to taxes. Every taxpayer can take a $1000 personal exemption. This means you do not have to pay taxes on $1000 of your income. Additional exemptions can be claimed for blindness, for people over 65, for a spouse, and for dependents.

As you may remember when you were hired for your work experience, your employer asked you to fill out a W-4 Form. This form is called the Employee's Withholding Allowance Certificate. From this form, your employer determines how much income tax and social security tax to withhold from your paychecks.

Property tax is a tax on the value of personal property and real estate a person owns. This may include houses, land, cars, boats, home furnishings, and expensive jewelry. Property taxes are assessed by city, county, and/or state governments.

Sales tax is a tax on goods and services. You pay this tax at the time of purchase, 20-2. Sales taxes may be charged by the state and/or city. In some states, food and drugs may be exempt from sales tax. In other states, all merchandise is subject to a sales tax.

An *excise tax* is a tax placed on certain products or services such as gasoline, cigarettes, liquor, and telephone service. Like the other taxes, city, state, and/or federal governments can place excise taxes on products and services.

In addition to the different types of taxes, taxes can be classified in different ways. Taxes

20-2 In many states, you must pay a sales tax on the food you purchase.

SERVICES AND FACILITIES FUNDED BY TAX DOLLARS

Police protection	Postal service
Fire protection	Scientific research
Garbage collection	National defense
Public schools	Airports
State universities	Hospitals
Community colleges	Medicare
Libraries	Public welfare
Parks and recreation	Social security benefits
Road maintenance	Unemployment
Public transportation	compensation

20-1 The primary purpose of taxes is to pay for government facilities and services.

can be direct or indirect, and they may be progressive or regressive.

Direct taxes are those charged directly to the taxpayer. Personal income taxes, property taxes, and sales taxes are examples of direct taxes.

Indirect taxes are taxes that are included in the price of taxed items. They are passed on to the buyer in the form of higher prices. Indirect taxes are sometimes referred to as "hidden taxes" because they are hidden within the total price of an item. Excise taxes on such products as cigarettes and gasoline are examples of indirect taxes.

Progressive taxes tax the rich at a higher percentage than they do the poor. For example, income tax is a progressive tax. As a person's income increases, the person's income is taxed at a higher rate.

Regressive taxes are the opposite of progressive taxes. *Regressive taxes* take a lower percentage of income from the rich and a higher percentage of income from the poor. Sales tax is an example of a regressive tax. People with high incomes pay a smaller percentage of their incomes for sales taxes than people with low incomes.

Preparing tax returns

Although your employer has been deducting federal income taxes and social security taxes all year from your paycheck, it's possible that too much or not enough tax was deducted. To determine how much federal tax you owe for a given year, you must file a federal income tax return each year. (State income taxes usually work this way too.) If too much tax was withheld during the year, you can receive a refund from the federal government. If too little tax was withheld, you will have to pay additional money to the federal government.

In January of each year, you will receive a Wage and Tax Statement which is called a *W-2 Form*. See 20-3. This form states the amount you were paid in the previous year. It also gives the amounts of income tax and social security tax that were withheld during the year. (Remember, social security tax is also called FICA tax.) You use the W-2 Form to help you prepare your federal income tax return.

1 Control number		OMB No. 1545-0008		
2 Employer's name, address, and ZIP code		3 Employer's identification number		4 Employer's State number
		5 Stat. employee / Deceased / Legal rep. / 942 emp. / Subtotal / Void ☐ ☐ ☐ ☐ ☐ ☐		
		6 Allocated tips		7 Advance EIC payment
8 Employee's social security number	9 Federal income tax withheld	10 Wages, tips, other compensation		11 Social security tax withheld
12 Employee's name, address, and ZIP code		13 Social security wages		14 Social security tips
		16		
		17 State income tax	18 State wages, tips, etc.	19 Name of State
		20 Local income tax	21 Local wages, tips, etc.	22 Name of locality

Form **W-2 Wage and Tax Statement**   **Copy B To be filed with employee's FEDERAL tax return** This information is being furnished to the Internal Revenue Service.   Department of the Treasury Internal Revenue Service

20-3 At the beginning of each year, employers will send each of their employees a W-2 Wage and Tax Statement. Copies of this form must be filed with all income tax returns.

Form 1040A US Individual Income Tax Return

Department of the Treasury—Internal Revenue Service

Form 1040A US Individual Income Tax Return (0)

OMB No. 1545-0085

Step 1
Name and address

Use the IRS mailing label. If you don't have a label, print or type:

Your first name and initial (if joint return, also give spouse's name and initial) | Last name | Your social security no.

Present home address (number and street) | Spouse's social security no.

City, town or post office, State, and ZIP code

Presidential Election Campaign Fund
Do you want $1 to go to this fund? .... ☐ Yes ☐ No
If joint return, does your spouse want $1 to go to this fund? ☐ Yes ☐ No

Step 2
Filing status
(Check only one)

1 ☐ Single (See if you can use Form 1040EZ.)
2 ☐ Married filing joint return (even if only one had income)
3 ☐ Married filing separate retur... full name here. _____
4 ☐ Head of household (with qual... your dependent, write this ch...

Exemptions

Always check the exemption box...
5a ☐ Yourself ☐ 65 or ...
  b ☐ Spouse ☐ 65 or ...
  c First names of your dependent c...

Attach Copy B of Form(s) W-2 here

  d Other dependents:
    1. Name   2. Relationship

  e Total number of exemptions clai...

Step 3
Total income

6 Wages, salaries, tips, etc. (Attac...

7 Interest income. (If line 7 is ove...

8a Dividends. (If line 8a is over $40(... Schedule 1, Part II.)

Attach check or money order here

  b Exclusion. See the instructions...
  c Subtract line 8b from line 8a. W...

9a Unemployment compensation (i... Form(s) 1099-G.
  b Taxable amount, if any, from the...

10 Add lines 6, 7, 8c, and 9b. Write...

Step 4
Adjusted gross income

11a IRA deduction, from the worksh...
  b Write IRA payments made in 19... you included on line 11a: ($
12 Deduction for a married couple... Complete Schedule 1, Part III.

13 Add lines 11a and 12. Write the...
14 Subtract line 13 from line 10. W... gross income.

Form 1040EZ Income Tax Return

Department of the Treasury - Internal Revenue Service

Form 1040EZ Income Tax Return for Single filers with no dependents (0)

OMB No. 1545-0675

Name & address

If you don't have a label, please print:

Write your name above (first, initial, last)

Present home address (number and street)

City, town, or post office, state, and ZIP code

Please write your numbers like this.

1234567890

Social security number

Presidential Election Campaign Fund
Check box if you want $1 of your tax to go to this fund. ▶

Figure your tax

Dollars | Cents

1 Wages, salaries, and tips. Attach your W-2 form(s). **1**

2 Interest income of $400 or less. If more than $400, you cannot use Form 1040EZ. **2**

Attach Copy B of Form(s) W-2 here

3 Add line 1 and line 2. This is your **adjusted gross income.** **3**

4 Allowable part of your charitable contributions. Complete the worksheet on page 19. Do not write more than $25. **4**

5 Subtract line 4 from line 3. **5**

6 Amount of your personal exemption. **6**   1,000.00

7 Subtract line 6 from line 5. This is your **taxable income.** **7**

8 Enter your Federal income tax withheld. This should be shown in Box 9 of your W-2 form(s). **8**

9 Use the tax table on pages 29-34 to find the **tax** on your taxable income on line 7. Write the amount of tax. **9**

Refund or amount you owe

10 If line 8 is larger than line 9, subtract line 9 from line 8. Enter the **amount of your refund.** **10**

11 If line 9 is larger than line 8, subtract line 8 from line 9. Enter the **amount you owe.** Attach check or money order for the full amount, payable to "Internal Revenue Service." **11**

Attach tax payment here

Sign your return

I have read this return. Under penalties of perjury, I declare that to the best of my knowledge and belief, the return is true, correct, and complete.

Your signature   Date

X

For IRS Use Only—Please do not write in boxes below.

For Privacy Act and Paperwork Reduction Act Notice, see page 38.

20-4 Many taxpayers can use Form 1040EZ or Form 1040A to file their taxes.

On a tax return you must list all the income you made from wages, salaries, tips, and bonuses. You must also include any interest or dividends earned from savings accounts, stocks, bonds, and any other investments.

The three common forms for filing a federal tax return are the 1040EZ, 1040A, and the 1040. *Form 1040EZ* and *Form 1040A* are called the short forms because they are easier to file, 20-4. Either of these two forms may be used by taxpayers whose income falls within certain limits and who do not choose to itemize deductions. However, the 1040EZ can only be filed by certain single taxpayers.

Form 1040 must be used by taxpayers whose income is more than a certain amount annual-ly. Others also may be required to use the long form because of their sources of income or because of deductions, adjustments to income, and tax credits they want to claim.

Deductions, adjustments to income, and *tax credits* are all expenses taxpayers can claim on Form 1040 to lower their tax bills. Charitable contributions, interest on loans, some medical and dental expenses, certain financial losses, and certain other expenses can be listed as deductions. (A percentage of charitable contributions can also be deducted on Forms 1040EZ and 1040A.) See 20-5. Moving expenses, employee business expenses, and alimony are some of the adjustments that can be made. Tax credits can be claimed for

20-5 Making a charitible contribution to an organization such as the American Cancer Society is an expense that you can claim on tax returns to lower your tax bill.

political contributions, home improvements for energy conservation, and child care. Tax credits are also available for the elderly.

Taxpayers should use Form 1040 when deductions, adjustments to income, and tax credits can reduce their taxes. When using this form, some taxpayers consult a tax specialist to help them determine what expenses they can claim. Reducing taxes by claiming legitimate deductions, adjustments, and credits is a legal way to avoid paying unnecessary taxes. Failing to declare all income and falsifying deductions, adjustments, and credits are forms of *tax evasion*. This is a criminal offense which can carry heavy penalties.

The form or forms you will need for filing taxes can be obtained from post offices and most banks and public libraries. Forms are also available from the *Internal Revenue Service* (IRS). This is the federal government agency that enforces federal tax laws and collects taxes. Once you file an income tax return, you will receive tax forms at the beginning of each year from the IRS. It will provide instructions for filing.

When preparing your federal income tax return, follow these helpful suggestions.

1. Get all your financial records together. For tax purposes you may need:
   - Records of income including wages, tips, and taxable benefits.
   - Records of interest earned and dividends received.
   - Canceled checks for expenses entered on tax returns as deductions.
   - Records of interest paid on charge accounts, home mortgages, and other loans.
   - Past tax returns.

   If your return is audited by the IRS, you may need these records to verify your deductions, adjustments, and credits.
2. Read all the instructions carefully before beginning.
3. Prepare the form in pencil first so any errors can be erased easily. Before writing the final copy in ink, check over all your figures or have someone else check them. If you make a mistake, you can always get another form.
4. Make a copy of the completed form, and keep it with other important papers.

The final date for filing taxes for the previous year is April 15. If that date falls on a Saturday, Sunday, or legal holiday, returns are due on the next business day. Returns must be postmarked no later than the due date. If you file late, you may have to pay penalties and interest. Mail the return to the Internal Revenue Service Center for your state.

SOCIAL SECURITY

You may be wondering exactly what social security is and why a portion of your paycheck is deducted for social security. Social security is the federal government's program for providing income when family earnings are reduced or stopped because of retirement, disability, or death. See 20-6. The purpose of social security is to provide a basic level of income that people can build on with savings, pensions, investments, or other insurance. It is not intended to replace all earnings lost. Social security taxes also help provide hospital insurance to the elderly and the disabled through the Medicare program.

Most workers, with the exception of federal government employees employed before 1984, railroad workers, and some state and local government employees, pay social security taxes and are eligible to receive benefits. Employees not covered by social security are covered by other forms of insurance.

Employees are not the only people who pay social security taxes. Employers do too. The social security tax is figured as a percentage of an employee's income. Whatever an employee pays in social security taxes, the employer must pay an equal amount. The employer deducts the tax from each employee's paycheck. Then the employer sends this amount and the employer's share to the Internal Revenue Service under the employee's name and social security number. The amount of social security tax deducted appears on an employee's paycheck under the letters FICA. This stands for the Federal Insurance Contributions Act.

Social security benefits

The social security taxes now being deducted from your paychecks pay for the benefits others receive. When you retire, become disabled, or die, the taxes of others will pay for the benefits you and your family will receive. Before a worker or a worker's family can receive benefits, the worker must have worked a certain amount of time under social security. The amount of the benefits received depends on the worker's average earnings over a period of years and the age of the worker. Here are the types of benefits the social security program provides.

Retirement benefits. Workers become eligible for full retirement benefits at age 65. Workers may retire as early as age 62, but they will receive lower retirement benefits. The amount of reduction depends on the number of months the worker gets checks before he or she reaches 65. If a worker choses to start getting checks early, the worker will get about the same value in total benefits over the years as the worker who retires at 65. However, the amounts will be smaller to take into account the longer period the worker will be getting checks. Monthly retirement benefits may also be made to a worker's:

- Unmarried children under 18 (or under 19 if full-time high school students).
- Unmarried children 18 or over who were severely disabled before 22 and who continue to be disabled.
- Wife or husband 62 or over.
- Wife or husband under 62 if she or he is caring for a child under 16 (or disabled) who's getting a benefit based on the retired worker's earnings.

Disability benefits. A worker who becomes severely disabled before 65 can receive disability checks. Under social security, a worker is considered disabled if he or she has a severe physical or mental condition which prevents him or her from working and is expected to last (or has lasted) for at least 12 months, or is expected to result in death. Disability benefits may also be paid to a disabled worker's:

- Unmarried children under 18 (or under 19 if full-time high school students).
- Unmarried children 18 or over who were

severely disabled before 22 and who continue to be disabled.
- Wife or husband 62 or over.
- Wife or husband under 62 if she or he is caring for a child under 16 (or disabled) who's

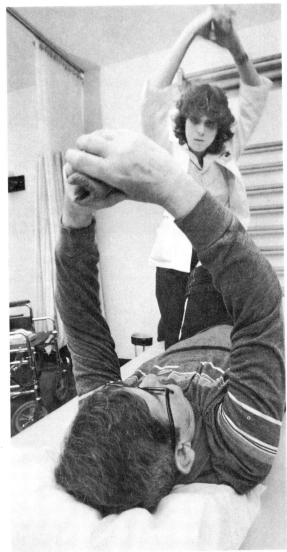

INGALLS MEMORIAL HOSPITAL

20-6 Although this man's condition is improving with therapy, he has been disabled and unable to work for two years due to injuries he received in a car accident. Social security benefits are helping keep this man and his family afloat until he can return to work again.

getting a benefit based on the disabled worker's earnings.

Survivors benefits. If a worker dies, survivors benefits can be paid to certain members of the worker's family. A single, lump-sum payment can also be made when a worker dies. This payment can only be made if there is an eligible surviving widow, widower, or entitled child. Monthly survivors benefits may be paid to a deceased worker's:

- Unmarried children under 18 (or under 19 if full-time high school students).
- Unmarried son or daughter 18 or over who was severely disabled before 22 and who continues to be disabled.
- Widow or widower 60 or older.
- Widow or widower 50 or older who becomes disabled not later than seven years after the worker's death, or within seven years after mother's or father's benefits end.
- Widow or widower, or surviving divorced mother or father if caring for worker's child under 16 (or disabled) who is getting a benefit based on the earnings of the deceased worker.
- Dependent parents 62 or older.

Social security benefits do not start automatically. When a person becomes eligible, he or she must apply for them at the nearest social security office. The *Social Security Administration* calculates the benefits and issues the monthly payments.

When you are planning to retire, contact the social security office in your area a few months before you actually retire. This will give the office plenty of time to calculate your benefits so you can get your first payment on time. It's also a good idea to check your social security record every three years to make sure that your earnings are being correctly reported to your record. You can get a free postcard form at any social security office for this purpose, 20-7.

(Please read instructions on reverse before completing)

REQUEST FOR SOCIAL SECURITY STATEMENT OF EARNINGS

Your social security number

Date of Birth

Month	Day	Year

Print Name and Address in ink or use typewriter

Please send a statement of my social security earnings to:

Name _____

Number & Street _____

City & State _____ Zip Code _____

Sign Your Name Here _____
                                (Do Not Print)

I am the individual to whom the record pertains. I understand that if I knowingly and willingly request or receive a record about an individual under false pretenses I would be guilty of a Federal crime and could be fined up to $5,000.

If you ever used a name (such as a maiden name) different from the one above, on a social security card, please print name here:

_____

FORM SSA 7004 PC (3-81)
(PRIOR EDITIONS MAY BE USED UNTIL SUPPLY IS EXHAUSTED)

20-7 Pick up a card like this at any social security office to request a free statement of earnings that have been credited to your social security record.

Medicare

Medicare is the federal government's health insurance program for people 65 or older, people of any age with permanent kidney failure, and certain disabled people, 20-8. Until Medicare became available, health insurance coverage for older and disabled people was very expensive and difficult to get because of their poor health. The Medicare program was created to provide these groups of people with affordable health insurance. The Medicare program provides two types of coverage: hospital insurance and medical insurance.

The hospital insurance helps pay for inpatient hospital care, inpatient care in a skilled nursing facility, and home health care. Medicare pays for all covered services except for the hospital insurance deductible. The deductible is the first $260 (or a similar set amount) of hospital bills. After the patient pays the deductible, Medicare pays the rest. However, if the patient stays in a hospital or nursing facility beyond a specific length of time, the patient must then pay a share of the costs.

The medical insurance of Medicare helps pay for physicians' services, outpatient health care, and outpatient physical therapy. It also helps pay for some home health care and many other health services and supplies which are not covered by the Medicare hospital insurance. There is a basic payment rule in the medical insurance plan. The patient is responsible for paying the first $75 (or similar set amount) of covered medical expenses in each calendar year. Then the medical insurance pays 80 percent of the approved charges for other services received during the rest of the year. The patient is responsible for the remaining 20 percent.

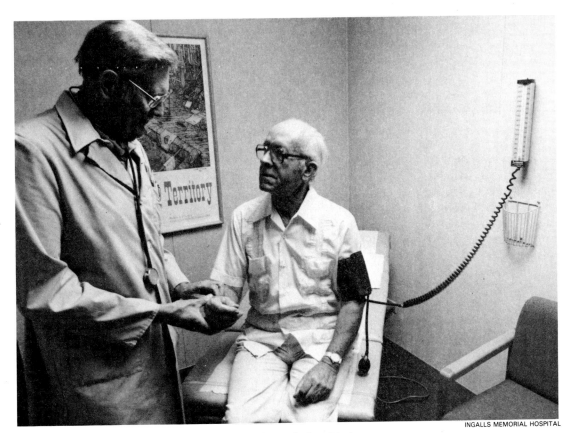

INGALLS MEMORIAL HOSPITAL

20-8 Medicare helps pay for the health services of the elderly.

to Review

1. What is the primary purpose of taxes?
2. Name the five most common taxes you probably will have to pay during your lifetime.
3. The amount of personal income tax and social security tax deducted from your paychecks depends on what two factors?
4. What is an exemption?
5. Explain the difference between direct and indirect taxes. Give an example of each.
6. Explain the difference between progressive and regressive taxes. Give an example of each.
7. What is a W-2 Form and what purpose does it serve?
8. What are the three common forms for filing federal income taxes? Which two are the simpler forms to file?
9. When should Form 1040 be used to file taxes?
10. What is the purpose of the social security program?
11. What determines the amount of social security benefits an eligible person can receive?
12. What is Medicare?

to Discuss

1. Describe at least six services or facilities funded by our tax dollars and the level or levels of government that fund these services and facilities.
2. What government services would you be willing to pay higher taxes to support? Why?
3. What do you do if too much or too little federal tax was withheld from your paycheck during the year?
4. What are deductions, adjustments to income, and tax credits? Give examples of each.
5. What financial records might you need when preparing income tax returns?
6. Describe the three types of benefits the social security program provides.
7. How does a person go about receiving social security benefits?
8. Describe the two types of coverage provided by Medicare.

to Do

1. Make an appointment to visit a local government official at your village or city hall. Find out how your village or city assesses local taxes and what services they provide. If you do not live in a village or city limits, visit the village or city hall closest to your home. Find out what services the village or city provides that you do not receive or that you have to pay extra to receive. Ask about police and fire department services, water and sewer service, garbage collection, etc.
2. Obtain copies of Form 1040EZ, Form 1040A, and instructions for filing each. Underline and discuss in class any words, phrases, or instructions on the forms that you do not understand. Then discuss the types of taxpayers who can use these forms for filing and the proper way to complete the forms.
3. Visit or write the social security office nearest you to obtain pamphlets about the social security program and Medicare. Using this information, explain in a one or two-page written report who can receive social security benefits and Medicare insurance and how a person goes about obtaining each.

Community colleges are funded with tax dollars.

Federal laws are enacted by Congress in
the U.S. Capitol located in Washington, D.C.

21

Legal matters

After studying this chapter, you will be able to:

☐ Describe the two major categories of law.
☐ Summarize the Fair Labor Standards Act and the provisions it covers.
☐ Explain how to select and deal with a lawyer.
☐ Describe the steps to take to get a consumer problem solved.

Everyone is involved with some aspect of the law at some time in his or her life. It may involve something pleasant such as obtaining a marriage license, birth certificate, or a driver's license. Or it may involve something unpleasant such as filing a death certificate or being ticketed for speeding.

Laws are written and enforced to help people live in harmony with each other. They are established to protect the safety and rights of individuals as well as society as a whole. As a citizen, you need to become aware of the many laws and legal matters which may affect you.

OUR LEGAL SYSTEM

The Constitution of the United States and the constitutions of the 50 states form the foundations upon which all laws are based. These constitutions describe how governments are to be organized. They also establish basic laws and freedoms for all citizens. Any new law enacted by local, state, or federal governments must not go against the state or U.S. Constitutions. If such a law is passed, it can be challenged in court. If declared unconstitutional, it cannot be enforced.

Within our legal system, there are two major categories of law: criminal and civil.

Criminal law

A *crime* is an offense against the public or state. The purpose of criminal law is to protect society from offenses that it considers wrong and unjust.

Crimes are generally classified according to their degree of seriousness. A *felony* is considered the most serious type of crime. It is punishable by imprisonment or even by death. Murder, rape, kidnapping, burglary, arson, narcotics sales, and other such offenses are felonies. A *misdemeanor* is a less serious crime such as disorderly conduct or speeding, 21-1. Penalities for a misdemeanor are a fine or imprisonment for less than a year.

Being convicted of a crime is serious business. In addition to having to pay a fine or serve a prison sentence, the person automatically has a criminal record. A criminal record can handicap a person's future. For example, a convicted felon would probably have a very difficult time getting hired for a job.

Civil law

Civil law involves disputes between two people or a person and a corporation. For example, a company that fails to comply with the terms of a contract could damage another person's business. According to civil law, the injured party could take legal action against the company. Suing the company for damages would help the person get what he or she expected to get out of the contract. In addition to contracts, real estate sales, divorce, and child custody also come under civil law.

A *tort* is a wrongful act committed against another person, independent of a contract. It involves injuries to another person's body, property, business, emotional well-being, and reputation. Examples of torts are personal injury in an auto accident, defamation (attack upon another person's reputation), assault (attempt to physically harm another person), and other personal and property types of hurt.

There are two classes of torts—intentional and unintentional. If someone deliberately hits your car and damages it, that's an intentional tort. If someone accidently hits your car, that's an unintentional tort.

Committing a wrongful act can be a tort and a crime at the same time. For example, if Marvin stole $100 from Carl, Marvin would be committing a tort against Carl. Marvin would also be breaking a criminal law. Therefore, Carl could bring a civil suit against Marvin to recover his $100. And the state could bring a criminal suit against Marvin because he broke a public law.

The person who files a civil suit, taking his or her case to court, is called the *plaintiff*. The person accused of wrongdoing is the *defendant*.

FAIR LABOR STANDARDS ACT

To protect employees and employers, many state and federal laws have been passed pertaining to labor. The oldest of these laws and the one that has the most influence on working standards is the Fair Labor Standards Act (FLSA). This act was passed in 1938 to protect workers from unfair treatment by their employers. Since its original passage, the act has been amended to establish minimum wage, overtime pay, equal pay, and child labor standards.

All employees who work for employers involved in interstate or foreign commerce are covered by this act. Therefore, any business producing, handling, or selling a product or service outside of its state must comply with the FLSA. Employees who work for businesses or enterprises engaged in construction, education, health care, and the laundering and cleaning of clothes are also covered. See 21-2. In fact, there are few workers who are not covered by the FLSA.

If an employee feels that any rules of the FLSA have been violated, he or she may complain to the Employment Standards Administration or the Wage and Hour Division of the U.S. Department of Labor. The complaint will be investigated by a government

21-1 If you are found guilty of speeding, you will have committed a misdemeanor.

21-2 Over 50 million full-time and part-time workers are covered by the Fair Labor Standards Act.

Legal matters 281

officer. If an employer is found in violation of the FLSA, the business may be prosecuted in court and fined.

Minimum wage

Minimum wage refers to an hourly rate of pay that covered employees are entitled to receive. Employers, of course, may pay more than minimum wage, but they cannot pay any less. The minimum hourly rate is set by the federal government. It may be changed periodically to meet the needs of inflation and recession.

Some employees are excluded from the minimum wage provision by specific employer exemptions. For example, apprentices, vocational students, and trainees may be paid less than minimum wage. Employees of certain small retail or service establishments and seasonal establishments may also not be able to collect minimum wage. An employee may want to check to see if an employer is covered by the FLSA before applying for work.

Overtime pay

Overtime must be paid at a rate of at least 1 1/2 times the employee's regular pay rate for each hour worked in excess of the maximum hours allowable. (Like minimum wage, some employees are exempt from receiving overtime pay.) When an employee is paid on a piecework basis (paid for each piece that is produced or serviced) or any plan other than an hourly basis, FLSA requires that a weekly pay rate be determined to compute the regular hourly rate and overtime pay. The following examples for computing overtime pay are based on a maximum 40-hour workweek.

Example: An employee paid $3.80 an hour works 44 hours in a workweek. The employee is entitled to at least 1 1/2 times $3.80, or $5.70, for each hour over 40. Pay for the week would be $152 for the first 40 hours, plus $22.80 for the four hours of overtime—a total of $174.80.

Example: An employee paid on a piecework basis works 45 hours in a week and earns $162. The regular pay rate for that week is $162 divided by 45, or $3.60 an hour. In addition to the straight time pay, the employee is entitled to $1.80 (half the regular rate) for each hour over 40.

Note that employers are not required to pay overtime to employees who work Saturdays, Sundays, or holidays unless they are days worked beyond the maximum work week. Weekends and holidays are treated like any other day of the week.

Equal pay

The Fair Labor Standards Act applies equally to female and male workers. The wage rate for male and female employees is to be the same for jobs that require equal skill, effort, and responsibility and which are performed under similar working conditions. Exceptions to equal pay may be taken for such differences as seniority, ability, skill, quantity of work produced, services performed, or shift work. Any violation of equal pay should be reported to the Equal Employment Opportunity Commission. More detailed information is available from their offices which are listed in most telephone directories under U.S. Government.

Child labor standards

The FLSA child labor provision are designed to do two things:
- Protect the educational opportunities of children.
- Prohibit the employment of children in jobs that may be hazardous to their health or well-being.

At 18 years of age, a person can work at any job, hazardous or not, for an unlimited number of hours. At ages 16 and 17, a young person can work at any nonhazardous job for unlimited hours. At ages 14 and 15, young people may work outside of school hours in various nonmanufacturing, nonmining, nonhazardous jobs under the following conditions. A young person may work no more than three hours on a school day, 18 hours in a school week, eight hours on a nonschool day, or 40 hours in a nonschool week. Also, work may not begin before 7 a.m. nor end after 7 p.m., except from June 1 through Labor Day when evening hours are extended to 9 p.m.

Under a special provision, 14 and 15-year-olds enrolled in an approved work experience through school may be employed for up to 23 hours in a school week and three hours on a school day (including during school hours).

Although 14 is the minimum age for most nonfarm work, young people, at any age, may deliver newspapers; perform in radio, television, movie, or theatrical productions; or work for parents in a nonfarm business.

CONSULTING A LAWYER

People tend to seek out a lawyer as a last resort or when they are in serious trouble. At this point, however, a lawyer may have a difficult time protecting a person from legal problems. Therefore, the best time to consult a lawyer is before you make an important financial or legal decision, 21-3. A good lawyer can help you make wise decisions and avoid costly legal mistakes. Here are some examples of when to contact a lawyer:

- Buying or selling real estate.
- Writing or entering into a contract.
- Getting divorced.
- Experiencing financial problems.
- Writing a will.
- Charged with a criminal action.
- Faced with a civil suit.

Choosing the best lawyer for your situation should be done carefully. Do not be in a hurry. Keep in mind that the field of law is specialized. Some lawyers specialize in divorce cases, others in business law, and others in criminal law. The more serious or

21-3 Be sure to consult a qualified lawyer before you buy or sell a home or any other type of real estate.

specialized your situation is, the more important it is for you to choose a lawyer who has handled such cases before.

How do you go about finding a good lawyer? One way is to ask a trusted teacher, friend, or family member to suggest a lawyer. Another way is to call Lawyer Referral Service (LRS) which is sponsored by local bar associations. The number for LRS can usually be found in the Yellow Pages under "Attorneys." This service can refer you to competent, reliable lawyers for the assistance you need. Under the LRS plan, a lawyer will consult with you on a legal problem for a half hour without charge or for a modest fee. Then the lawyer will render whatever services are requested for a set fee. If the lawyer cannot handle your problem, he or she will refer you to another attorney who can.

For people who cannot afford to hire a lawyer, there are places to get help. Many cities and communities have Legal Aid offices where legal problems are handled without charge or a small fee. Legal Aid Clinics are also available at many law schools. The purpose of these clinics is to help law students gain practical experience while helping those who cannot afford a lawyer. Legal Aid offices and clinics give advice in three main areas:
- Small claims for wages.
- Disputes between the client and a lender, installment seller, or landlord.
- Domestic matters (divorce, child custody, will contestation, etc.).

In criminal cases, the state will appoint a public defender if the accused cannot afford a lawyer. In our country, everyone is entitled to a defense. Therefore, in criminal cases, everyone is entitled to a lawyer whether he or she can pay for it or not.

Once you have chosen a qualified lawyer, take an active role in your case. Take your lawyer's advice, but don't hesitate to ask questions about how he or she plans to handle your case. It is a good idea to request copies of all letters and documents prepared on your behalf so you will know exactly how your case if progressing. However, don't badger your lawyer. Preparing legal cases takes time.

An important fact to remember when dealing with your lawyer is to be honest. Tell him or her all the facts related to your case. An attorney can not be expected to give you well-reasoned legal advice if you withhold information or fail to tell the truth. Also keep your lawyer informed of any new developments that might affect your case. See 21-4.

COMPLAINING ABOUT PRODUCTS AND SERVICES

What do you do when you order a product by mail and it arrives damaged? What do you do when you buy a new product and it fails to work properly one month later? What do you do if you are charged for a purchase you never made? When you have a problem with a product or service, you will need to complain to the right person in the right way.

Before you make a complaint, make sure you have your facts straight. Your new camera is broken, but did you drop it? Your new sweater shrank two sizes, but did you follow the directions on the care label correctly? The telephone company has still not repaired your telephone service, but was someone home when the repairperson said she'd be there? Don't complain about a product or service when you're the one at fault. Only complain when you have a valid reason for complaining.

As soon as you discover a problem, complain promptly. Don't let weeks or months go by before you contact the seller or manufacturer. Be sure to direct your complaint to the right person and place. Routine problems can usually be handled by salespeople or customer service employees. If an adjustment requires the approval of an authority, the department or store manager is the person to see. For billing errors and other credit problems, contact the credit or billing department.

If your problem cannot or is not settled at these levels, the next step is to complain to top management by letter. To find the names of officers of large business firms, use *Standard and Poor's Register of Corporations*. This book is available in most libraries. Or you can call the store or business and ask the receptionist for this information.

In your complaint letter, clearly identify the product or service that is not satisfactory. Then give a brief description of the problem. If possible, give the date and place of the purchase, the product name and model number, and the purchase price. At the close of the letter, suggest some type of action. Do you expect repairs, a replacement, a refund, or an apology? Let the reader know what you would like to have done about the problem.

As you write, be reasonable and calm. A sarcastic or threatening letter will not help your problem get solved.

When mailing a complaint letter, it is a good idea to use registered mail. Then you will have a record of the letter's delivery. A registered letter is hand delivered, and the receiver must sign for it. The sender is then sent a copy of the receipt showing that the letter was received. Before mailing, however, be sure to make a copy of the letter to keep in your records.

Hopefully, one letter directed to the right person will get the problem solved. However, if you don't get a response or the response you want, write a second letter. In the second complaint letter, enclose a copy of the first letter. Also include the names of consumer agencies or organizations whom you intend to contact if the situation is not settled by a certain date.

If you fail to get satisfaction from your own efforts, you will need to contact one or more of the following consumer organizations or agencies for help.

- Better Business Bureau. This is a nonprofit organization sponsored by private businesses to settle consumer complaints against local business firms. See 21-5.
- News media. Some local newspapers and radio and TV stations have action lines to help consumers settle complaints. This might be a very good source to contact if the seller has advertised through the news media.
- Regulatory agencies. Problems with mail orders, warranties, credit, billing, and deceptive advertising may be referred to the Federal Trade Association. Unsafe or hazardous products should be reported to the Consumer Product Safety Commission. The Food and Drug Administration, local health boards, housing authorities, and the state attorney general's office can also help you deal with dishonest businesses.

Your last resort for settling a complaint is to take your problem to court. Depending on the amount of money in question, you could file suit in small claims court or civil court.

Small claims court handles relatively small claims. You can explain your case directly to a judge. A lawyer does not need to be present which eliminates the costly services of a lawyer.

If you file suit in civil court, you would need a lawyer to represent you. This can be a lengthy and costly process. Use this method only when the problem is serious and all other alternatives have been tried.

21-4 When consulting a lawyer, don't hesitate to ask questions about how he or she plans to handle your case.

CUSTOMER COMPLAINT

BBB CASE NUMBER B035573

CUSTOMER'S NAME _____
ADDRESS _____
CITY _____ STATE _____ ZIP _____
PHONE _____

COMPANY'S NAME _____
ADDRESS _____
CITY _____ STATE _____ ZIP _____
PHONE _____

DATE YOU SENT YOUR ORDER _____

LIST ALL ITEMS ORDERED *(PLEASE INCLUDE SIZE, QUANTITY & CATALOG NUMBERS IF APPLICABLE)*

CATALOG NUMBER	QUANTITY	SIZE	DESCRIPTION

(ATTACH ADDITIONAL SHEET IF NECESSARY(

WHAT IS THE NATURE OF YOUR COMPLAINT *(CHECK APPROPRIATE ITEM)*

☐ NON-DELIVERY OF MERCHANDISE *(IF ONLY PART OF ORDER WAS DELAYED, LIST ITEM(S) BELOW*)*
DID COMPANY NOTIFY YOU THAT THERE WOULD BE A DELAY? ☐ NO ☐ YES IF YES, DATE _____
DID YOU RESPOND TO THE NOTICE OF DELAYED SHIPMENT? ☐ NO ☐ YES IF YES, DATE _____

☐ WRONG MERCHANDISE *(EXPLAIN BELOW*)*

☐ DAMAGED/DEFECTIVE MERCHANDISE*
HAVE YOU RETURNED THE DAMAGED ITEM(S)? ☐ NO ☐ YES IF YES, AND THE PACKAGE WAS INSURED, WHAT
IS THE POSTAL SERVICE INSURANCE RECEIPT NUMBER? _____

☐ OTHER*
FURTHER DESCRIPTION/EXPLANATION: _____
_____
_____
_____
_____

DID YOU SEND PAYMENT WITH YOUR ORDER? ☐ NO ☐ YES IF YES, AMOUNT $_____
☐ CASH ☐ CHECK ☐ MONEY ORDER

IMPORTANT! ATTACH COPY OF CANCELLED CHECK OR MONEY ORDER RECEIPT

HAVE YOU CONTACTED THE COMPANY CONCERNING THE MATTER? ☐ NO ☐ YES IF YES, GIVE
DATE(S) _____ EXPLAIN _____
_____

WHAT DO YOU WANT THE COMPANY TO DO TO RESOLVE THE MATTER?
☐ SHIP MERCHANDISE WHICH WAS ORDERED ☐ PROVIDE REPLACEMENT ☐ REFUND ☐ OTHER*
EXPLAIN _____
_____

SIGNATURE _____

DATE _____

BBB ADDRESS
**Better Business Bureau of
Metropolitan Chicago, Inc.**
35 E. Wacker Drive
Chicago, IL 60601
346-3313 — 10:00 - 2:30

21-5 You will be asked to complete a form similar to this one
whenever you contact the Better Business Bureau about a complaint.

to Review

1. Name and describe the two major categories of law within our legal system.
2. What is the difference between a misdemeanor and a felony?
3. What is a tort? Give three examples.
4. Define the words plaintiff and defendant.
5. Why was the Fair Labor Standards Act originated? What does it also cover today?
6. What is the general rule for overtime pay?
7. Who should you contact if you feel you are not receiving equal pay for the work you do?
8. When is the best time to consult a lawyer?
9. Name two ways to go about finding a good lawyer.
10. What can you do if you cannot afford to hire a lawyer?
11. What information should you include in a complaint letter?
12. If you are unable to solve a consumer problem through your own efforts, who can you contact for help?

to Discuss

1. How can a criminal record affect a person's future?
2. Explain how a wrongful act can be a tort and a crime at the same time.
3. What employers must comply with the Fair Labor Standards Act? Is your employer covered by the act?
4. What are the purposes of the child labor provisions in the FLSA?
5. In what situations would a person be wise to contact a lawyer?
6. Why would it probably be best not to hire the lawyer who handled the buying of your home to defend you in court on criminal charges?
7. How should you deal with a lawyer that you've hired to work for you?
8. How would you go about complaining about a product or service that you found unsatisfactory?
9. Why is it a good idea to use registered mail when mailing a complaint letter?

to Do

1. Invite a lawyer to class to explain how our court system works.
2. Visit or contact the nearest office of the Equal Employment Opportunity Commission. Find out how a complaint or a report concerning a violation of equal pay is handled. Report your findings to the class.
3. Imagine you are having a problem with an electric appliance you just bought and the place where you bought the appliance refuses to replace or repair it or refund your money. Write a complaint letter to the appliance manufacturer.

Leaders and followers

A good leader inspires its group members
and helps them reach their goals.

22

Leadership skills

After studying this chapter, you will be able to:

☐ Explain the different types of leadership.
☐ Describe the qualities of a good leader.
☐ Describe the vocational student organizations in which you can participate and develop good leadership skills.

Leadership! What is it? Ask ten people, and you may get ten different answers.

"Leadership means the ability to influence other people."

"It means that one person is elected to be in charge."

"It means that everybody has to do the same thing the leader does."

"Isn't that follow the leader?"

Leadership implies the ability to lead and influence others. It should inspire others and guide them to a goal. The leader tries to see that something of value is produced by the group. Through his or her leadership, the members of the group work toward a common goal or cause. That is leadership.

LEADERSHIP

People who are leaders in some situations become followers in others. The school principal is a leader during a faculty meeting but becomes a follower at a board of education meeting. The president of a bank may be the leader for the bank but becomes one of the followers in church. In church, the minister is the leader. From these examples, you can see that each of us may be leaders at some time and at other times be followers.

As followers, it is important to support the leadership. This does not mean to blindly follow the leader. Rather, it means to help the leader plan a course of action and support the course that is set. The best harmony is when leaders and followers work together for a common goal, 22-1. When everyone shares the same goals, action can be focused to achieve those goals successfully.

Chosen leader

A person elected or appointed to an office by a group or the president of a group is a chosen leader. The people chosen for leadership positions are usually those who seem capable of handling responsibility well. Chosen leaders tend to be self-confident and personable people.

A chosen leader is expected to take action of some kind. The action might be to take charge of a meeting, speak in behalf of a cause, or plan a club dance. The leader may be the committee chairperson who makes the arrangements or who gets others to help make the arrangements.

Assumed leadership

Sometimes a situation will arise when a person will be a leader for that situation only. A person may assume a leadership position if no one else is qualified or willing to take on the job. Or a person may assume leadership in an emergency situation like Susan did in the following story.

Elaine walked into the club meeting room just as the meeting started. In her hurry to find a seat, she slipped and fell, hitting her head on the floor. When Elaine failed to get up, everyone knew she was unconscious, but no one moved or seemed to know what to do. Even the chapter officers and the advisor seemed stunned. Susan, who rarely says or does anything, suddenly jumped up and took charge of the situation. She explained to the others what to do to help Elaine regain consciousness. Once medical help arrived, Susan stepped back into her previous role as a quiet, reserved person. Susan had assumed a leadership role for the time of the emergency.

The person you least expect to be a leader is likely to know exactly what to do and will take charge in an unexpected situation. There have been many stories of soldiers in battle who

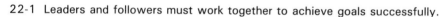

22-1 Leaders and followers must work together to achieve goals successfully.

assumed brief heroic leadership roles. Often times, people do not want the responsibility of leadership but will become leaders because they are the best ones to handle specific problems when they arise.

Leadership by domination

Leadership by domination occurs when the chosen or assumed leader's desire for personal power becomes more important than the goals and activities of the group. The leader in this situation makes decisions that will benefit himself or herself and not the group. A group that is dominated by such a leader will usually do one of two things. They will not give their full cooperation because they are left out of the decision-making process. And they will likely adopt the attitude of "I will do just what I am told and nothing more." Or the group will rebel against the dominating leader and remove him or her from the leadership position.

Opinion leaders

Those to whom others go to for advice, opinions, or information are known as opinion leaders, 22-2. They tend to give good advice when asked but do not usually volunteer information. Often, they do not hold a formal office, but their opinions influence decisions that are made. The opinion leader is usually considered the "expert" to consult on important matters.

LEADERSHIP QUALITIES

Different types of leadership are needed for different roles. The governor of a state may need different leadership qualities than a military leader or a business leader. Yet there are some common qualities which all leaders need. As you become involved with school clubs or chapters, think about the leadership qualities that club leaders should have. Then,

22-2 Club advisors are often considered opinion leaders. They are the people officers and members turn to to help them make club decisions.

when you have a chance to make officer nominations, give careful thought to the leadership abilities of your club members. A member who is a good friend or a nice person may not be a good officer. You need the best person for the job.

When you prepare to vote for a club officer, the mayor of your town, or any elected official, keep in mind a person's ability to:

- Listen to others and be responsive to their views.
- Provide stimulation when needed by challenging and encouraging others to action.
- Analyze situations clearly and take decisive action when needed.
- Assume responsibility for the duties of the office.
- Work for group success, not personal success.
- Set goals that have been expressed by the group.
- Delegate responsibility and recognize and credit others for the work they do.

You also need to keep these abilities in mind to help your own self develop good leadership qualities.

Remember that all facets of society need leaders. The working world is no different. Leaders are needed in every occupation at all job levels. Business and industry look for and reward workers with leadership skills. Learning about leadership can help you be a better worker. Having an opportunity to develop your leadership skills can help you even more. Your school organizations and vocational clubs (sometimes called chapters) can provide that opportunity for you.

STUDENT ORGANIZATIONS

Student organizations are good places to gain leadership experience, 22-3. Usually, there are many opportunities for club work in school and in the community. Student club activities and projects tend to center around five areas:

- Professional activities.
- Civic activities.

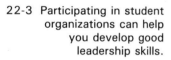

22-3 Participating in student organizations can help you develop good leadership skills.

HOMEWOOD-FLOSSMOOR HIGH SCHOOL, FLOSSMOOR, IL

- Service activities.
- Social activities.
- Fund raising activities.

Professional activities are intended to enhance the professional improvement of students. They include such activities as club meeting programs related to the occupational field, field trips, and the employer-employee banquet. Skill contests are also considered professional activities, 22-4. They help students improve and expand their career-related knowledge and skills.

Civic activities are conducted by student organizations to serve the school and community. Projects range from helping improve the school or community to participating in fairs, trade shows, and other community events.

Service activities involve projects that emphasize the need for sharing. Making a contribution to a charity, Christmas caroling at a nursing home, and making and delivering fruit baskets to shut-ins are examples of service activities.

Social activities are also an important part of student organizations. Social activities include parties, picnics, and socializing after club meetings. The employer-employee banquet is also considered a social activity as well as a professional one.

Fund raising activities are necessary to finance all the other activities of the club. Service projects and social functions are types of activities that may require fund raising.

Of course, there is no limit to the types of activities in which an organization may participate. The limit is set only by the creativity and interest of its members and officers. For a club to be successful, its members need to work willingly and enthusiastically on club activities. An active member of an organization

22-4 The Vocational Industrial Clubs of America is one of the organizations that holds skill contests each year on the state and national levels. These two students are competing in the carpentry skill test.

participates in two or more of the following ways:

- Attends meetings.
- Learns parliamentary procedure.
- Serves on a committee.
- Holds an office, if elected.
- Supports and/or participates in club activities.

If you want to be part of an active club, you and all of its members must work for the good of the club. Everyone cannot be the president, but every member can do his or her part. Assess your own abilities and decide what you can do best for your club. Taking an active role in an organization can help you develop as a person and as a leader.

Your school most likely has a student organization that is related to your vocational interests. (If there are no available vocational organizations in your career interests, one can be started with your school's approval.) Vocational student organizations help reinforce and expand what cooperative education students learn in the classroom and on the job. Students can participate in vocational organizations on the local, state, and national levels. The vocational organizations commonly found in schools are described below.

American Industrial Arts Student Association (AIASA). This is an organization for students enrolled in industrial arts courses. AIASA is designed to develop the leadership and personal abilities of students as they relate to the industrial-technical world. This is seen in the organization's motto, "Learning to live in a technical world."

Distributive Education Clubs of America (DECA). This organization is for students who are interested in marketing and distributive occupations. Any student enrolled in distributive education classes is eligible for membership in DECA. Chapter activities help students learn more about marketing, merchandising, management, and related subjects. See 22-5.

NATIONAL DECA

22-5 At National DECA conventions, DECA members have the opportunity to participate in professional and social activities.

Future Business Leaders of America (FBLA). FBLA is open to any student who has taken business education courses and is interested in business occupations. The main purposes of the organization are to assist students in choosing business occupations and to develop competent, aggressive business leaders.

Future Farmers of America (FFA). This is the organization for students studying agriculture. The foundation upon which FFA is built includes: leadership, character development, sportsmanship, cooperation, service, improved agriculture, and citizenship. Through active participation, members learn how to develop skills in agriculture, buy and sell cooperatively, and finance themselves. They also learn how to speak in public, take part in public meetings, and assume civic responsibilities.

Future Homemakers of America (FHA). This is the organization available to students who are enrolled in home economics classes. FHA places major emphasis on projects involving consumer education, homemaking, and family life education. FHA chapters also explore home economics related jobs and careers. See 22-6.

Health Occupations Student Association (HOSA). HOSA is a vocational organization for students interested in health occupations and enrolled in health and related courses. HOSA chapters help its members develop their physical, mental, and social well-being. They

FUTURE HOMEMAKERS OF AMERICA

22-6 Future Homemakers of America encourages leadership development and cooperative group action.

also help members develop into competent leaders and health care workers.

Home Economics Related Occupations (HERO). This organization is for students enrolled in occupational home economics courses such as food services, clothing services, and child care services. HERO chapters place emphasis on preparation for home economics related occupations.

Office Education Association (OEA). The OEA is for students interested in office occupations. One of the major purposes of the organization is to stimulate and promote those skills and aptitudes that are important to the development of future office workers. OEA also gives students an opportunity to develop leadership, responsibility, and an understanding of valuable group activities. See 22-7.

Vocational Industrial Clubs of America (VICA). This is an organization for all students who are enrolled in occupational education preparing for careers in the trades and in the industry. The main goal and purpose of VICA is given in its motto, "Preparing for leadership in the world of work." VICA strives to develop the whole student. This includes a student's social and leadership skills as well as his or her occupational skills.

HOMEWOOD-FLOSSMOOR HIGH SCHOOL, FLOSSMOOR, IL

22-7 These students are participating in the Illinois Office Education Association Annual Meeting. Some of these students will also take part in the National OEA Convention.

to Review

1. What is a chosen leader? Give three examples.
2. What is assumed leadership?
3. What is leadership by domination?
4. Explain how a group led by a dominating leader is likely to react.
5. What is an opinion leader?
6. List five abilities that are important for a leader to have.
7. What is the purpose of professional activities in student organizations?
8. Why do organizations have fund-raising activities?
9. What does a person need to do to be an active member of an organization?
10. What is the purpose of vocational student organizations?

to Discuss

1. What is leadership?
2. Explain how people can be both leaders and followers. Give examples.
3. Explain how a person can be a supportive follower.
4. How can developing good leadership skills help you be a better worker?
5. Give an example of a professional activity, civic activity, service activity, social activity, and a fund-raising activity that your club or another club with whom you are familiar has had or plans to have.
6. What does it take for an organization to be successful?
7. What are things you can do as an active member of a club or an organization?
8. What vocational student organizations are available at your school? Are any of these clubs at your school active at the state and national levels?
9. Are you an active member in one of the organizations you listed in the question above? Why?

to Do

1. Divide into small groups. Each group is to describe situations to illustrate various traits of good leaders and role play one or more of the situations to the class.
2. Design a bulletin board display encouraging students to take active roles in school organizations.
3. Interview the president of one of the vocational student organizations at your school. Ask him or her the purposes of the organization, how many members are active in the club, and what the organization has accomplished in the recent year and plans to accomplish in the near future. Write a one-page report summarizing what you learned from the interview.

Many organizations follow the same or
similar procedure for conducting meetings.

Participating in meetings

If you've ever been a member of a club, committee, or group, you may have noticed that many group meetings are conducted in similar ways. Most organizations base their meetings on what is known as *parliamentary procedure.* This refers to an orderly way of conducting a meeting and discussing group business. The purpose of parliamentary procedure is to help groups conduct meetings in an efficient and fair manner.

In order to understand parliamentary procedure and participate in group meetings, you need to be familiar with the terms in 23-1. When group members know the meanings of these words, meetings can proceed much more smoothly and productively.

ORDER OF BUSINESS

Many organizations follow the same or similar procedure for conducting meetings. This procedure or order of business is based on *Robert's Rules of Order,* the famous book on parliamentary procedure. The order of business, unless otherwise specified in the organization's bylaws (rules), usually goes as follows:

1. Call to order.
2. Reading and approving of minutes.

3. Reports of officers.
4. Standing committee reports.
5. Special committee reports.
6. Unfinished business.
7. New business.
8. The program.
9. Announcements.
10. Adjournment.

Call to order

The president or presiding officer of the group calls the meeting to order. He or she does this by rapping a gavel on a wooden block and then saying, "The meeting will now come to order." See 23-2.

In order to proceed with the business part of the meeting, there must be a quorum present. Quorum is a majority of members or a number of members as stated in the rules of the group.

Reading and approving of minutes

After calling the meeting to order, the president asks the secretary to read the minutes of the previous meeting. The secretary stands and reads the minutes. (The president sits during the reading of the minutes.) After the reading, the president stands and says, "You have heard the minutes of the previous meeting. Are there any corrections or additions?" At this point, any member may stand and explain corrections or additions that need to be made to the minutes. If there are no corrections, the president will say, "The minutes stand approved as read." If there are corrections and they are made, the president will then say, "The minutes stand approved as corrected."

Reports of officers

At this time, the president calls upon the vice-president, secretary, and treasurer to give any reports they may have. Often, the only officer who reports at every meeting is the treasurer. The purpose of the treasurer's report is to inform the officers and members of the group's financial status. The report should include any expenses paid since the last meeting, any income taken in, and the balance in the treasury. Balance is the amount of money that exists in the group's account.

Standing committee reports

After the reports of officers, the president calls upon each chairperson of the standing committees for a progress report. *Standing committees* are the permanent committees of the group such as the membership committee, program committee, and refreshment committee. These committees are identified in a club's bylaws.

Special committee reports

While standing committees are the regular committees, *special committees* are set up for a special purpose or for a short time. Examples of special committees are a Christmas parade float committee, spring picnic committee, and a banquet committee.

A special committee has a certain job to do. When the committee completes its job and properly reports it to the group, the committee will no longer exist. During the life of the committee, its chairperson is asked to report its progress at every group meeting.

Unfinished business

The president starts this part of the meeting by asking, "Are there any items of unfinished business that need to be discussed today?" Unfinished business might include motions that have been tabled. Suppose at the last meeting there was a motion to sell candy as a fund raising project. However, there was not enough time to discuss the motion and vote on it so the motion was tabled. Therefore, discussing and voting on the motion to sell candy as a fund raising project would be unfinished business.

New business

At this point in the meeting, the president says, "The next order of business is new business. Is there any new business?" New business includes such things as discussing future group activities, setting dates for activities, and presenting bills for payment. From this discussion, special committees may be formed to plan special activities. If decisions are not made on items of new business, they are usually discussed at the next meeting as unfinished business.

The program

At this time, the president says, "The program committee will now present the program." The president calls on the program committee chairperson who introduces the speaker or the program presentation. At the end of the program, the program committee chairperson thanks the speaker or participants. Then he or she returns the meeting to the president.

Out of consideration to program participants, some clubs have their programs first (following the call to order) and then their business meetings. This, too, is an acceptable order of business, 23-3.

Announcements

Following the program, the president should ask, "Are there any announcements?" This is the time to announce the date and time of the next meeting and to remind members of any special activities occurring before the next meeting. Any announcement can be made such as thanking a committee for doing a good job or recognizing a member for winning a contest. Sometimes refreshments are

---

TERMS USED IN PARLIAMENTARY PROCEDURE

Adjourn — To end a meeting.
Agenda — A list of things to be done and discussed at a meeting.
Amend the motion — To change the wording of a motion that has been made.
Chair — The presiding officer at a meeting, such as the president or chairperson.
Debate — To speak for or against a motion. Every member has a right to debate an issue.
Majority — At least one more than half of the members present at the meeting.
Minutes — A written record of the business covered at a meeting.
Motion — A suggestion by a member that certain action be taken by the group.
Quorum — The number of members who must be present to legally conduct business at a meeting.
Second the motion — The approval of a motion by another member.
Table the question — To delay making a decision on a motion.
The floor — The right to speak in a meeting without interruption from others.
The question — The motion upon which members are called to vote.

23-1 Learning about parliamentary procedure can help you become a more active club member.

23-2 The president or presiding officer of a group calls a meeting to order.

served after the meeting. They, too, should be announced.

Adjournment

In order for the president to end the meeting, there must be a motion from one of the members to adjourn. The president can ask for a motion to adjourn. After a motion and a second to the motion, the president declares the meeting adjourned.

MOTIONS

Members of a group are responsible for making motions and discussing them, 23-4. There are two types of motions: a main motion and a secondary motion.

A *main motion* is a suggestion for the group members to consider. It includes one item of business. The requirements for a main motion are as follows:

- It must be made at a time when no other business is before the meeting and in proper order of business. It must also be made by a member who has the floor.
- It must be seconded by another member.
- It must be stated by the chair.
- It may always be discussed.
- It must be taken care of in some manner acceptable to the group.

A *secondary motion* is one that can be made while a main motion is being considered. The purpose of a secondary motion is to change (amend) the main motion or postpone action on the motion. Secondary motions made while discussing the main motion must be voted on before voting on the main motion.

Making a motion

Here's the proper way to make a motion. Amy thinks it would be a good idea for her club to have a fund raising project to increase the amount of money available to spend on club activities. At the next meeting when the president asks if there is any new business, Amy stands up and says, "Madam President."

The presidsent recognizes Amy by calling her name, "Amy."

Amy says, "I move that we have a fund raising project to make more money available for club activities."

Kevin, another club member, agrees, "I second the motion."

Then the president says, "It has been moved by Amy and seconded that we have a fund faising project to make more money available for club activities. Is there any discussion?"

As the presenter of the motion, Amy explains why she thinks the club needs more money in its budget. Then other members comment about the motion. Individually, they stand, address the president, are recognized, and voice their opinions.

After the discussion, the president says, "Are you ready for the question?" If no speakers rise, the president says, "The question is on the motion to have a fund raising project. All in favor of the motion say 'aye' (or raise your hand)." The president counts the "yes" votes. "Those opposed say 'no' (or raise your hand)." The president counts again. "The ayes have it. The motion has passed that we have a fund raising project."

Amending a motion

Suppose Randy, a member of Amy's group, isn't exactly satisfied with Amy's motion. He is in favor of having a fund raising project, but he feels all the money earned should be used toward the club's end-of-the-year banquet. During the discussion of the main motion, Randy decides to amend the motion. He stands and says, "Madam President." After being recognized by the president, Randy continues, "I move to amend the motion by changing the words 'club activities' to 'the end-of-the-year banquet.' " Barbara, the secretary, seconds the motion.

The president handles this secondary motion just as she did the main motion. She says, "It has been moved by Randy and seconded that the pending motion be amended by changing the words 'club activities' to 'the end-of-the year banquet.' Is there any discussion?" After the discussion, the president calls for a vote on the amendment.

23-3 The program speaker or presentation may follow the call to order or new business.

23-4 Group members make motions to help the club plan activities and make decisions about club business.

If the amendment passes, the question before the group now is the motion as amended. If the amendment doesn't pass, the question before the group is the original motion.

Tabling a motion

Tabling a motion is another secondary motion that can be made. The purpose of this motion is to postpone the group from making a decision on the main motion. A member might make this motion because he or she feels the motion would have a better chance of passing at a later date. Or a member might table a motion if the business meeting is running long.

The motion to table a motion is not debatable like the motion to amend a motion. Therefore, the president states the question and goes straight to a vote. Again, the majority rules.

COMMITTEES

The work done by committees is a very important part of an organization, 23-5. In fact, most groups depend on its committees to plan and initiate all of its activities.

Committee chairpersons are either elected by the group or appointed by the president. Or in some cases, some chairpersons are elected and some are appointed. The method for determining chairpersons are described in a group's bylaws.

Once elected or appointed, each chairperson asks two or more people to serve on the committee. Once a committee is formed, the chairperson arranges a place and time for a meeting. At the first meeting the chairperson explains what the committee is expected to do and asks for suggestions from the members. Every member should feel free to participate and to discuss options for the committee. However, committee members should talk about the tasks of the committee and not get away from the subject. Part of the job of the chairperson is to guide the discussion and to keep the committee focused on the business at hand.

Before each committee meeting is over, there should be a review or summary of the items discussed. After the meeting is adjourned, the chairperson prepares a written committee report and presents and report at the next chapter meeting.

ELECTING OFFICERS

Most groups nominate and elect new officers once a year. The method of nominating officers is outlined in a group's bylaws.

23-5 These three students are the program committee for their student organization. They meet regularly to plan, discuss, and choose speakers and programs for each club meeting.

Organizations usually nominate officers by one of two methods: accepting nominations from the floor or appointing a committee to nominate a slate of officers.

Nominations from the floor are made by a member simply saying, "I nominate Gordon Brown for president." (Nominations do not have to be seconded like motions.) The chairperson waits for further nominations. After waiting a reasonable length of time, the chair asks if there are any further nominations. If there are none, he or she declares the nominations closed for the office of president and proceeds to the next office. When there is a large group participating, it is customary to have a motion to close the nominations. The motion requires a two-thirds vote.

Other clubs have a nominating committee to prepare a list of candidates to present to the group. Some clubs have the committee select only one person for each office, and others have them nominate at least two people. Then on the day of the election, the committee presents the candidates to the group. After the nominations have been presented, the president will usually ask, "Are there any further nominations from the floor?" Therefore, it is still possible for members to nominate from the floor even if a committee prepares a slate of candidates. Usually, however, no further nominations are made since the committee was assigned to do the job.

Following nominations, the president will then take a vote to determine the new slate of officers. A vote will be held for each office if there is more than one candidate. If there is only one nomination for each office, the president can take a vote for the entire slate of officers. A majority vote will make the candidates official officers, 23-6.

23-6 The officer candidates who receive the majority of votes are the candidates elected to office.

HOMEWOOD-FLOSSMOOR HIGH SCHOOL, FLOSSMOOR, IL

If you are an active member in an organization on
the local level, you probably will have the opportunity
to participate in state and national meetings.

to Review

1. What is the purpose of parliamentary procedure?
2. What does it mean to have quorum?
3. Explain the difference between standing committees and special committees. Give an example of each.
4. What is considered unfinished business and what is considered new business? Give an example of each.
5. What are the requirements for a main motion?
6. Explain the difference between a main motion and a secondary motion.
7. What is voted on first, the main motion or the secondary motion?
8. Why might a group member move to table a motion?
9. Name the two ways most organizations nominate new officers.

to Discuss

1. Why is it important for the president of an organization to be familiar with parliamentary procedure?
2. Discuss the order a business meeting should follow.
3. Who is in charge of a business meeting? How does a meeting begin?
4. Why is it important for a group's committees to report to the group every group meeting?
5. What is the purpose of making motions?
6. Explain how a group member should go about making a motion.
7. Why are active committees important to the success of an organization?
8. Explain how a group goes about accepting nominations for officers from the floor.

to Do

1. Obtain and read a copy of the constitution and bylaws of a school organization you belong to or might like to join. Then answer the following questions.
   a. What is the order of business the club should follow?
   b. What is quorum?
   c. What are the club's standing committees?
   d. How should officers be nominated and elected?
   e. How should committee chairpersons be selected?
2. Role play in class the proper way to make a motion and amend a motion. Choose someone to be the president (chair), someone to make the motion, and someone to amend the motion.

Glossary

A

abilities: physical and mental powers to perform a task or skill well which are learned through training and practice.

activities preference inventory: a test designed to help people determine if they prefer working with people, objects, or ideas.

adjustment to income: an expense that can be claimed on Form 1040 to lower a person's tax bill.

aptitudes: natural physical and mental talents for learning.

B

balanced funds: mutual fund investments in a variety of securities such as preferred stock, common stock, and bonds.

bank statement: a record of the checks, deposits, and charges on your account for a specific length of time.

basic medical insurance: health insurance coverage that pays for the costs of hospitalization which includes room, board, nursing services, and some other services such as laboratory tests, X rays, and medicine.

beneficiary: the person named by a life insurance policyholder to receive the death benefit.

Better Business Bureau: a nonprofit organization sponsored by private businesses to settle consumer complaints against local business firms.

blank endorsement: the payee's signature on the back of a check at the left end.

bond: a certificate of debt or obligation issued by a corporation or a government.

budget: a plan to help a person make the most of the money he or she has.

budget checking account: an account that does not require a minimum balance, but a fee is charged for each check written and/or a service charge is assessed.

C

canceled checks: checks a person has written and that the bank has paid.

cashier's check: a check drawn on a bank's own funds and signed by a bank officer.

certificate of deposit (CD): money deposited for a set period of time that earns a set annual rate of interest.

certified check: a personal check with a bank's guarantee that the check will be paid.

charge account: a type of credit account that allows a customer to charge merchandise. Then the customer is expected to pay in full within 25 days of the billing date.

collateral: some type of property such as a car, house, or savings account pledged to a financial institution in order to get a cash loan.

collective bargaining: the process that labor and management use to discuss what they expect from each other in the workplace.

common stock: stock that pays dividends based on company earnings and economic conditions.

cooperative education: a school program designed to help students make the adjustment from being full-time students to becoming full-time employees.

corporate bond: a bond issued by a corporation.

corporation: a business owned by many people called stockholders.

cosigner: a responsible person who signs a loan with a borrower and promises to pay the loan if the borrower fails to pay.

crime: an offense against the public or state.

D

deductible: the amount a policyholder must pay before the insurance company will pay a claim.

deduction: an expense that can be claimed on Form 1040 to lower a person's tax bill. (A percentage of charitable contributions can also be deducted on Forms 1040EZ and 1040A.)

defendant: the person accused of wrongdoing in a court suit.

direct tax: a tax charged directly to the taxpayer such as personal income taxes, property taxes, and sales taxes.

disability insurance: coverage that provides regular income payments when a person is unable to work because of injury or illness.

E

excise tax: a tax placed on certain products and services such as gasoline, cigarettes, liquor, and telephone service.

exemption: a source or an amount of income on which you do not have to pay taxes.

F

Federal Deposit Insurance Corporation (FDIC): the U.S. government agency that insures commercial bank deposits up to $100,000.

Federal Savings and Loan Insurance Corporation (FSLIC): the U.S. government agency that insures savings and loan association deposits up to $100,000.

felony: a serious type of crime punishable by imprisonment or even by death.

fixed expenses: expenses that must be paid regularly such as rent or mortgage payments, installment payments, and insurance premiums.

flexible expenses: the expenses that vary in amount such as food, clothing, utilities, home furnishings and equipment, transportation, health care, recreation, education, and savings.

follow-up letter: a brief letter written in business form to thank the interviewer for the interview.

Form 1040: the tax form that must be used by taxpayers who earn more than a certain amount of income annually and/or who have deductions, adjustments to income, and tax credits they want to claim.

Form 1040A: the tax form used by taxpayers with incomes within certain limits and who do not choose to itemize deductions.

Form 1040EZ: the tax form that can be used by certain single taxpayers with incomes within certain limits and who do not choose to itemize deductions.

franchise: the right to market a product or service owned by a large company.

fringe benefits: any financial extras in addition to the regular paycheck such as medical and life insurance coverage, paid vacations, bonuses, and retirement plans.

G

goals: the things a person wants to attain.

gross pay: the total amount of money earned for the pay period before any taxes and deductions are subtracted from a paycheck.

growth funds: mutual fund investments in common stocks with growth potential.

H

Health Maintenance Organization (HMO): a health plan that provides a variety of health care services to members for a set prepaid fee.

human resource: a resource a person has within himself or herself such as skills, knowledge, experience, and time.

I

indirect tax: a tax that is included in the price of a taxed item such as taxes included in the price of cigarettes and gasoline.

installment account: a credit account which allows the buyer to pay for merchandise according to a set schedule of payments.

interest-bearing checking account: an account that allows you to earn interest and write checks.

Internal Revenue Service (IRS): the federal government agency that enforces federal tax laws and collects taxes.

inventory control: the process of keeping up-to-date records of how many goods and supplies are in stock, how many have been ordered and received, and how many have been sold.

L

labor contract: an agreement which spells out the conditions for wages, benefits, job security, work hours, working conditions, and grievance procedures (the way a complaint is handled).

letter of application: a letter written to an employer to apply for a job.

limited partner: a person who invests money or property into a business but does not work in the business.

long-range goal: a goal a person may take several months or several years to achieve.

M

main motion: a suggestion for the group to consider.

major medical insurance: health insurance coverage that begins paying where basic coverage stops. It pays the largest share of expenses resulting from a major illness or serious injury.

Medicare: the federal government's health insurance program for people 65 or older, people of any age with permanent kidney failure, and certain disabled people.

minimum-balance checking account: an account that requires a minimum amount of money in the account at all times to avoid paying a service charge.

misdemeanor: a less serious crime punishable by fine or imprisonment for less than a year.

money market fund: a type of mutual fund that deals only in high interest, short-term investments such as U.S. Treasury Bills and certificates of deposit.

money order: an order for a specific amount of money payable to a specific payee.

monopoly: a single company that controls the entire supply of a product or service.

municipal bond: a bond issued by state, county, and city governments.

mutual fund: a company that collects money from a number of investors and invests that money in securities.

N

National Credit Union Association (NCUA): the agency that insures the deposits of many credit unions.

negotiable orders of withdrawal (NOW) account: an interest-bearing account at a savings and loan association.

net pay: the gross pay minus taxes and deductions.

nonhuman resource: any material thing a person has or can use such as money, tools, clothes, and community resources to achieve goals.

O

Occupational Safety and Health Administration (OSHA): the federal government administration that sets and enforces job safety and health standards for workers.

open shop agreement: an agreement at a workplace that allows workers to decide for themselves whether or not to join the union.

P

parliamentary procedure: an orderly way of conducting a meeting and discussing group business.

partnership: a form of business organization where two or more people go into business together.

passbook savings account: an account that allows deposits and withdrawals to be made in varying amounts at any time and pays a set rate of interest.

personal income tax: a tax on the amount of money a person earns.

plaintiff: the person who files a civil suit.

portfolio: a collection of work samples.

preferred stock: stock that pays set dividends (profits) at set rates regardless of the amount of profits the company earns.

premium: in insurance, a set amount of money paid periodically for insurance coverage.

productive resources: all the resources such as labor, land, capital, and equipment that individuals and businesses can use to produce goods and services.

profit motive: the desire to earn profits (a return on your money or other resources).

progressive tax: a tax that taxes the rich at a higher percentage than it does the poor.

property tax: a tax on the value of personal property and real estate a person owns.

proprietorship: a business that has only one owner.

R

regressive tax: a tax that taxes a lower percentage of income from the rich and a higher percentage from the poor.

resources: all the things a person has or can use to help reach his or her goals.

restrictive endorsement: a check endorsement that states what is to be done with the check, such as "For deposit only" and the payee's signature or "Pay to the order of" and the payee's signature.

resume: a brief history of a person's education, work experience, and other qualifications for employment.

revolving charge account: a type of credit card account that gives the credit cardholder a choice of paying for purchases in full each month or spreading payments over a period of time.

S

safe-deposit boxes: small metal containers that people rent at financial institutions to protect their valuables from fire and theft.

sales tax: a tax on goods and services that is charged at the time of purchase.

secondary motion: a motion that can be made while a main motion is being considered to change the main motion or postpone action on the motion.

securities: investments that represent either ownership or indebtedness such as stocks, bonds, mutual funds, and money market funds.

share draft: an interest-bearing account at a credit union.

short-range goal: a goal that a person wants to reach tomorrow, next week, or within a few months.

social security: the federal government's program for providing income when family earnings are reduced or stopped because of retirement, disability, or death.

Social Security Administration: the federal government agency that calculates benefits and issues monthly payments.

social security tax: a tax on a person's income that is used to pay for the social security program.

special committees: committees set up for a special purpose or for a short time.

specialized funds: mutual fund investments in securities of certain industries, such as all utilities, or in certain types of securities, such as all government bonds or common stock.

standards: accepted levels of achievement.

standing committees: the permanent committees of a group such as the membership committee, program committee, and refreshment committee.

stock: a share in the ownership of a corporation.

stockholder: a person who buys a share of a corporation and becomes a part owner of the business.

T

tax credit: an expense that can be claimed on Form 1040 to lower a person's tax bill.

tax evasion: an illegal means of reducing taxes by failing to declare all income and/or falsifying deductions, adjustments, and credits.

term life insurance: insurance that covers the policyholder for a set period of time—5, 10, or 20 years or for whatever term specified in the policy.

tort: a wrongful act committed against another person, independent of a contract.

training agreement: an agreement that outlines the purposes of the cooperative education program and defines the responsibilites of the student, parents or guardian, the coordinator, and the employer.

training plan: a list of skills, attitudes, and habits that a cooperative education student plans to learn during his or her work experience.

training station report: a weekly or monthly record of the duties a cooperative education student performed and the skills and attitudes he or she learned at work.

traveler's checks: checks that can be cashed most places around the world. They are often used by people who travel and don't want to carry large amounts of cash.

U

union shop agreement: an agreement at a workplace that requires all workers to join the union as a condition of employment.

U.S. Government bond: a bond issued by the federal government such as Treasury Bills, Treasury Notes, and Treasury Bonds.

U.S. Savings Bonds: a government bond issued for as little as $50 at a variable interest rate for a set length of time.

V

values: the principles and beliefs that a person considers important.

value system: a ranking of values in the order of their importance which guides a person's behavior and helps that person develop a sense of direction in his or her life.

W

W-4 Form: the Employee's Withholding Allowance Certificate which tells the employer how much tax to withhold from an employee's paychecks.

whole life insurance: insurance that covers the policyholder for a lifetime.

W-2 Form: a Wage and Tax Statement that states the amount an employee was paid in the previous year. It also gives the amounts of income tax and social security tax that were withheld during the year.

Index